Information Processing and Management

Second Edition

Information Processing and Management

Second Edition

Mark Scott
John Holland
Timothy J. O'Leary
Linda I. O'Leary

McGRAW-HILL BOOK COMPANY Sydney
New York   San Francisco   Auckland   Bogotá
Caracas   Kuala Lumpur   Lisbon   London   Madrid
Mexico City   Milan   New Delhi   San Juan
Singapore   Toronto

National Library of Australia Cataloguing-in-Publication data:

Scott, Mark.
Information processing and management. Units 3 and 4.

2nd ed.
Includes index.
ISBN 0 07 470276 9.

1. Information technology. 2. Information technology—
Problems, exercises, etc. I. Holland, John. II. O'Leary,
T. J. (Timothy J.). McGraw-Hill computing essentials. Annual
ed., 1992–1993. III. Title. IV. Title: McGraw-Hill
computing essentials. Annual ed., 1992–1993.

004

Published in Australia by
McGraw-Hill Book Company Australia Pty Limited
4 Barcoo Street, Roseville NSW 2069, Australia
Acquisitions editor: Karina Woolrich
Production editors: Marjorie Pressley, Carolyn Pike
Designer: Joan McGirr
Cover designer: Tania Edwards, Maggie Renvoize
Typeset in Century Old Style
in Australia by Midland Typesetters, Victoria
Printed in Hong Kong by South China Printing Co.

CONTENTS

CONTENTS

PREFACE

PLEASE NOTE

Visual summaries to accompany each chapter are included in this reprint (see p. 303).

THE AUDIENCE FOR THIS BOOK

This book, and the accompanying support material, have been designed for students undertaking Information Processing and Management Units 3 and 4 in the Victorian Certificate of Education. They have been designed so that no prerequisites are required.

WHY IS THIS BOOK DIFFERENT?

1. **It is designed specifically for IP&M Units 3 and 4.** The book and the accompanying support material have been designed to prepare students specifically for the Test CAT in Information Processing and Management. Case studies, which appear at the end of each chapter, provide an excellent grounding for the Test CAT.

2. **The support materials include a number of practice Test CATs on disk.** The practice Test CATs cover a range of scenarios. Complete solutions are included for each. The practice Test CATs have been included on disk to allow teachers to use them under test conditions.

3. **Students using this book will develop computer competency.** This book is intended to give students competency in computer-related knowledge and skills to support their academic pursuits. Our goal is to produce students who are:

   - **microcomputer literate**—they will be able to employ microcomputers to increase their productivity and effectiveness;

   - **familiar with commercial software**—they will know the most popular brands of applications and systems software;

   - **grounded in fundamental concepts**—they will have a basic working vocabulary and knowledge of computer and information concepts appropriate for most organisations.

TEXT FEATURES

Some special features of the text are:

- **competency objectives**—the text chapters begin with a description of the goals, 'Competencies', that the reader should hope to achieve;

- **section summaries**—sections are summarised in large type at the beginning;

- **visual summaries**—key ideas of each of the 14 chapters are summarised with words and pictures, not just words;

- **case studies**—each chapter has a case study that brings together some of the key ideas within the chapter in an organisational setting.

TEACHING MATERIALS: THE SUPPORT PACKAGE

The following teaching materials are available separately for the text:

- **Test CAT disk**—the disk provides a number of practice Test CATs with complete solutions; solutions to the case studies are also included on the disk;

- **overhead transparencies**—a set of 61 four-colour transparencies is available.

SUGGESTED COURSE OUTLINE

Term	Outline
1	Chapters 1 to 7
2	Chapters 8 to 12
3	Chapters 13 and 14
	Practice Test CATs
4	Practice Test CATs

The text has been written to be easily comprehensible: sentences are short, headings are used frequently and ideas are presented in 'bite-size' paragraphs. The text, in combination with the support materials, is flexible enough to support a range of student learning strategies. The readability of the text and its visual nature enhance a constructionist approach to learning.

What occurs in most Information Technology classes is a combination of both approaches to learning. We hope that this text will help make the teaching and learning of Information Processing and Management a more rewarding and successful venture.

ABOUT THE AUTHORS

Mark Scott
Director of Information Services
Methodist Ladies' College

- Teacher of Information Technology Units 1 and 2 1991–5
- Teacher of Information Processing and Management 1992–6

John Holland
Manager of Information Systems
Information Technology Co-ordinator
Canterbury Girls' Secondary College

- Teacher of Information Technology Units 1 and 2 1991–6
- Teacher of Computer Science 1983–91
- Teacher of Information Systems 1993–5
- Teacher of Information Processing and Management 1996

You and computer competency

CHAPTER 1

FROM THE USER'S POINT OF VIEW

The notion of computer competency may not be familiar to you, but it's easy to understand. The purpose of this book is to help you become *competent* in computer-related skills. Specifically, we want to help you walk into a job and immediately be valuable to an employer. In this chapter, we first describe why learning about the computer is important to your future. We then present an *overview* of what makes up an information system: people, procedures, software, hardware and data. In subsequent chapters, we will describe these parts in detail.

COMPETENCIES

After you have read this chapter, you should be able to:

- explain computer competency;

- distinguish four kinds of computers: microcomputer, minicomputer, mainframe, and supercomputer;

- explain the five parts of an information system: people, procedures, software, hardware, and data;

- distinguish application software from system software;

- describe hardware devices for input, processing, storage, output, and communications;

- describe document, worksheet, and database files;

- explain computer connectivity.

Fifteen years ago, most people had little to do with computers, at least directly. Of course, they filled out computerised forms, took computerised tests, and paid computerised bills. But the real work with computers was handled by specialists—programmers, data-entry clerks, and computer operators.

Then microcomputers came along and changed everything. Today it is easy for nearly everybody to use a computer. People who use microcomputers today are called 'end users' (see Figure 1.1).

- Microcomputers are common tools in all areas of life. Writers write, artists draw, engineers and scientists calculate—all on micro-computers. Businesspeople do all three.

- New forms of learning have developed. People who are homebound, who work odd hours, or who travel frequently may take courses by telephone-linked home computers. A course need not fit within the usual time of a term or a semester.

- New ways to communicate and to find people with similar interests are available. All kinds of people are using electronic mail and the Internet to meet and to share ideas.

What about you? How can microcomputers enhance *your* life?

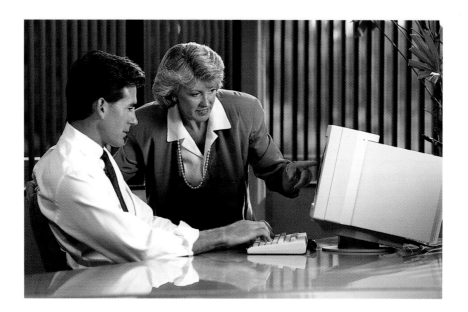

Figure 1.1 End users: people are using microcomputers to meet their information needs

END USERS AND COMPUTER COMPETENCY

By gaining computer competency, end users can use micro-computers to improve their productivity and their value in the workplace.

End users are people who use microcomputers or have access to larger computers. If you are not an end user already, you will probably become one in the near future. That is, you will learn to use packaged computer programs to meet your unique needs for information. Let us point out two things here:

- By 'packaged programs', we mean programs that you can buy rather than those you have to write yourself. Examples of packaged programs include video games on a disk and work-related programs, such as word processing for typing documents and electronic spreadsheets for analysis.

- By 'needs', we mean various organising, managing, or business needs. That is, they are *information-related* or *decision-making* needs. Becoming **computer competent**—learning how to use the computer to meet your information needs—will improve your productivity. It will also make you a more valuable employee.

How much do you have to know to be computer competent? Clearly, in today's fast-changing technological world, you cannot learn everything—but very few people need to. You don't have to be a computer scientist to make good use of a microcomputer. Indeed, that is precisely the point of this book. Our goal is not to teach you everything there is to know, but only what you *need* to know to get started. Thus, we present only what we think you will find most useful—both now and in the future.

FOUR KINDS OF COMPUTERS

Computers are of four types: microcomputers, minicomputers, mainframes and supercomputers.

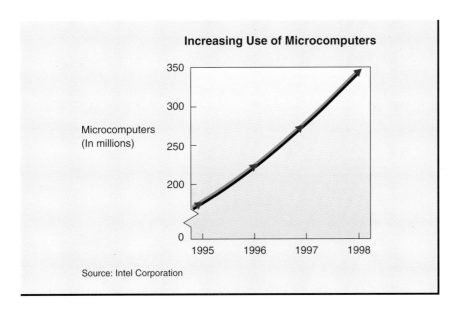

Increasing Use of Microcomputers

Source: Intel Corporation

Figure 1.2 Microcomputers in use —past, present, and future

This book focuses principally on microcomputers. However, it is almost certain that you will come in contact, at least indirectly, with other kinds of computers. Thus, we describe many features that are common to these larger machines.

Computers are electronic devices that can follow instructions to accept input, process that input, and produce information. There are four types of computers: *microcomputers, minicomputers, mainframe computers* and *supercomputers.*

Microcomputers

The most widely used and the fastest-growing type of computer is the **microcomputer** (see Figure 1.2). There are two categories of microcomputers—*desktop* and *portable.*

Desktop computers A desktop computer is small enough to fit on top or along the side of a desk and yet is too big to carry around (see Figure 1.3). **Personal computers** are one type of desktop. These machines run comparatively easy-to-use application software. They are used by a wide range of individuals from clerical people to managers.

Figure 1.3 A desktop computer (Gateway 2000)

Workstations are another type of desktop computer. Generally, these machines are more powerful. They are designed to run more advanced application software. Workstations are used by engineers, scientists and others who process lots of data. The distinction between personal computers and workstations is now blurring. The principal reason is that personal computers are now nearly as powerful as workstations and are able to run many of the same programs.

Portable computers A portable computer is small enough and light enough to move easily from one place to another. There are four categories of portable computers—*laptops*, *notebooks*, *subnotebooks* and *personal digital assistants:*

- **Laptops**, which weigh between 4.5 and 7.25 kilograms, may be either AC-powered, battery-powered or both. The AC-powered laptop weighs 5.5 to 7.25 kilograms. The battery-powered laptop weighs 4.5 to 7 kilograms, batteries included, and can be carried on a shoulder strap. The user of a laptop might be an accountant or financial person who needs to work on a computer away from the desk.

- **Notebooks** are a smaller version of the laptop (see Figure 1.4). They weigh between 2.25 and 4.5 kilograms and can fit into most briefcases. The user of a notebook PC might be a student, salesperson, or journalist, who uses the computer for note-taking. It is especially valuable in locations where electrical connections are not available. Notebook computers are the most popular portable computer today.

- **Subnotebooks** are for frequent flyers and life-on-the-road types. Subnotebook users give up a full-size display screen and keyboard in exchange for less weight. Weighing between 1 and 2.75 kilograms, these computers fit easily into a briefcase.

- **Personal digital assistants (PDA)** are much smaller than even the subnotebooks. The typical PDA combines pen input, writing recognition, personal organisational tools and communications capabilities in a very small package. A PDA user might be a worker

Figure 1.4 A notebook computer (IBM Think Pad 750)

at a warehouse who records changes in inventory or a busy executive handling daily communications (see Figure 1.5).

Minicomputers

Also known as **midrange computers, minicomputers** are desk-sized machines. They fall between microcomputers and mainframes in their processing speeds and data-storing capacities. Medium-size companies or departments of large companies typically use them for specific purposes. For example, they might use them to do research or to monitor a particular manufacturing process. Smaller-size companies typically use minicomputers for their general data processing needs, such as accounting.

Mainframe computers

Mainframes are large computers occupying specially wired, air-conditioned rooms. They are capable of great processing speeds and data storage (see Figure 1.6). They are used by large organisations—businesses, banks, universities, and government agencies—to handle millions of transactions. For example, insurance companies use mainframes to process information about millions of policyholders.

Supercomputers

The most powerful type of computer is the **supercomputer**. These machines are special, high-capacity computers used by very large organisations. For example, NASA uses supercomputers to track and control space explorations. Supercomputers are also used for oil exploration, simulations and worldwide weather forecasting (see Figure 1.7).

Figure 1.5 Personal digital assistant (Motorola Envoy Personal Communicator)

THE FIVE PARTS OF AN INFORMATION SYSTEM

An information system has five parts: people, procedures, software, hardware and data.

When you think of a microcomputer, perhaps you think of just the equipment itself. That is, you think of the monitor or the keyboard.

Figure 1.6 A mainframe computer (IBM ES/9000)

Figure 1.7 A supercomputer
(Cray Y-MP computer system)

There is more to it than that. The way to think about a microcomputer is as part of an information system. An **information system** has five parts: *people, procedures, software, hardware* and *data* (see Figure 1.8).

People It is easy to overlook people as one of the five parts of a microcomputer system. Yet that is what microcomputers are all about—making people, end users like yourself, more productive.

Procedures Procedures are rules or guidelines to follow when using software, hardware, and data. Typically, these procedures are documented in manuals written by computer specialists for particular organisations. Software and hardware manufacturers also provide manuals with their products. An example is the *Lotus 1-2-3 Reference Manual*.

Software Software is another name for a program or programs. A **program** is the step-by-step instructions that tell the computer how to do its work. The purpose of software is to convert *data* (unprocessed facts) into *information* (processed facts).

Hardware The **hardware** consists of the equipment: keyboard, mouse, monitor, system unit, and other devices. Hardware is controlled by software. It actually processes the data to create information (see Figure 1.9).

Figure 1.8 The five parts of an information system

people   procedures   software   hardware   data

Data **Data** consists of the raw, unprocessed facts. Examples of raw facts are hours you worked and your pay rate. After data is processed through the computer, it is usually called **information**. An example of such information is the total wages owed you for a week's work.

In large computer systems, there are specialists who deal with writing procedures, developing software and capturing data. In microcomputer systems, however, end users often perform these operations. To be a competent end user, you must understand the essentials of software, hardware and data.

Figure 1.9 Two well-known microcomputer hardware systems: the IBM Performance Series multimedia and the Apple Macintosh Performa 5200 CD

SOFTWARE

Software is of two kinds: application software, and system software.

Software, as we mentioned, is another name for programs. Programs are the instructions that tell the computer how to process data into the form you want. In most cases, the words *software* and *programs* are interchangeable.

There are two major kinds of software—*application software* and *system software*. You can think of application software as the kind you use. Think of system software as the kind the computer uses (see Figure 1.10).

Figure 1.10 End users interact with application software. System soft-ware interacts with the computer

Application software

Application software might be described as 'end-user' software. Application software performs useful work on general-purpose tasks such as word processing and cost estimating.

Application software may be *packaged* or *custom-made*:

- **Packaged software** is programs prewritten by professional programmers that are typically offered for sale. There are thousands of different types of application packages available for micro-computers alone.

- **Custom-made software,** or **custom programs**, is programs written for a specific purpose and for a specific organisation. Using computer languages, programmers create this software to instruct the company computer to perform whatever tasks the organisation wants. A program might compute payroll cheques, keep track of goods in the warehouse, calculate sales commissions, or perform similar business functions.

There are certain general-purpose programs that we call 'basic tools' in this book. These programs are widely used in nearly all career areas. They are the kind of programs you *have* to know to be considered computer competent. The most popular basic tools are:

- *word processing programs*, used to prepare written documents;

- *electronic spreadsheets*, used to analyse and summarise numerical data;

- *database managers*, used to organise and manage data and information;

- *graphics programs*, used to visually analyse and present data and information;

- *communications programs*, used to transmit and receive data and information;

- *integrated programs*, combining some or all of these applications in one program, and also *software suites*, with separate applications sold as a group.

There are certain programs that we call 'power tools' in this book. These programs are more specialised than the basic tools. Power tools are widely used within certain career areas. They are the kind of programs you *should* know to be truly computer competent in the future. The most popular power tools are:

- *personal information managers*, used to increase productivity through organisation;

- *groupware*, designed to co-ordinate group activities and increase team productivity;

- *project management*, used to plan projects, schedule people, and control resources;

- *desktop publishing*, combining text and graphics to create professional quality documents;

- *multimedia*, integrating all kinds of information into a single presentation;

- *artificial intelligence*, simulating human thought processes and actions.

System software

The user interacts with application software. **System software** enables the application software to interact with the computer (refer to Figure 1.10). System software is 'background' software. It includes programs that help the computer manage its own internal resources.

The most important system software program is the **operating system**, which interacts between the application software and the computer. The operating system handles such details as running ('executing') programs, storing data and programs, and processing data. System software frees users to concentrate on solving problems rather than on the complexities of operating the computer.

Microcomputer operating systems change as the machines themselves become more powerful and outgrow the older operating systems. Today's computer competency, then, requires that you have some knowledge of the following most popular microcomputer operating systems:

- *DOS*, the standard operating system for International Business Machines (IBM) and IBM-compatible microcomputers;

- *Windows*, not an operating system but an environment that extends the capability of DOS;

- *Windows 95*, a new operating system that does not require DOS;

- *Windows NT*, a powerful operating system designed for powerful microcomputers;

- *OS/2 Warp*, the operating system developed by IBM for powerful microcomputers;

- *Macintosh operating system*, the standard operating system for Apple Corporation's Macintosh computers;

- *Unix*, an operating system originally developed for minicomputers and is now important because it can run on many of the more powerful microcomputers.

HARDWARE

Microcomputer hardware consists of devices for input, processing, storage, output and communications.

Microcomputer hardware—the physical equipment—falls into five categories. They are *input devices, the system unit, secondary storage, output devices* and *communications devices*. Because we discuss hardware in detail later in the book, we will present just a quick overview here.

Input devices

Input devices translate data and programs that humans can understand into a form that the computer can process. The most common input devices for microcomputers are the keyboard and the mouse (see Figure 1.11). The **keyboard** on a computer looks like a typewriter keyboard, but it has additional specialised keys. A **mouse** is a device that typically rolls on the desktop. It directs the **insertion point,** or cursor, on the display screen. A mouse has one or more buttons for selecting commands. It is also used to draw figures.

selection buttons

Figure 1.11 A microcomputer keyboard and mouse

Figure 1.12 The system unit

Figure 1.13 The Intel Pentium microprocessor chip

The system unit

The **system unit** is electronic circuitry housed within the computer cabinet (see Figure 1.12). There are two main parts of the system:

- The **central processing unit (CPU)** controls and manipulates data to produce information. A microcomputer's CPU is contained on a single integrated circuit or microprocessor chip. These chips are called **microprocessors** (see Figure 1.13).

- **Memory**, also known as **primary storage** or **random access memory (RAM)**, holds data and program instructions for processing the data. It also holds the processed information before it is output. Memory is sometimes referred to as *temporary* storage because it will be lost if the electrical power to the computer is disrupted or cut off. Data and instructions are held in memory only as long as the electrical power to the computer is on. Memory is located in the system unit on tiny memory chips.

Secondary storage

Secondary storage also holds data and programs. However, it stores *permanently*. That is, the data and programs remain even after the electrical power is turned off. Secondary storage devices are located outside of the central processing unit, and are typically built into the system unit cabinet.

Figure 1.14 Two kinds of floppy disks: 3½-inch and 5¼-inch

For microcomputers, the most important kinds of secondary storage 'media' are as follows:

- **Floppy disks** (also called simply 'diskettes') hold data or programs in the form of magnetised spots on plastic platters. The two sizes most commonly used are 3½-inch and 5½-inch diskettes (see Figure 1.14). The smaller size is more durable, can hold more, and is more widely used.

  A floppy disk is inserted into a **disk drive** (see Figure 1.15.). This mechanism **reads** data from the disk. That is, the magnetised spots on the disk are converted to electronic signals and transmitted to primary storage inside the computer. A disk drive can also **write** data. That is, it can take the electronic information processed by the computer and record it magnetically onto the disk.

- A **hard disk** contains one or more metallic disks encased within a disk drive. Like floppy disks, hard disks hold data or programs in the form of magnetised spots. They also *read* and *write* data in much the same way as do floppy disks. However, the storage capacity of a hard-disk unit is many times that of a floppy disk and much faster.

- Unlike floppy and hard disks, **optical discs** hold data and programs by changing the reflecting surface of the disc. Some types of optical discs can read and write data. Some types can be written to only one time. The best-known type of optical disc, however, can only be read from. These are called **CD-ROM** for compact disc—read only memory.

Floppy and optical disks are inserted into and removed from their disk drives and are stored separately. The hard disk, by contrast, typically is not removable (refer to Figure 1.15).

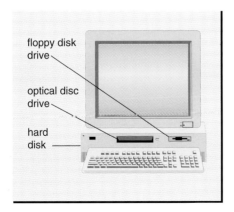

Figure 1.15 Three kinds of disk drives: floppy, optical, and hard

Figure 1.16 Newer monitors show sharp images and vibrant colours

Figure 1.17 Some printers can print colour images on paper

Output devices

Output devices are pieces of equipment that translate the processed information from the CPU into a form that humans can understand. One of the most important output devices is the **monitor**, or **video display screen**, which resembles a television screen. The quality of monitors has improved dramatically. Many monitors now offer crisp images and vivid colours (see Figure 1.16). Another important output device is the **printer**, a device that produces printed paper output. Some printers can also print in colour (see Figure 1.17).

Communications devices

Communications hardware sends and receives data and programs from one computer or secondary storage device to another. Many microcomputers use a **modem** (pronounced '*moh*-dem'). This device converts the electronic signals from the computer into electronic signals that can travel over a telephone line. A modem at the other end of the line then translates the signals for the receiving computer. A modem may be internal, or located inside a microcomputer's system cabinet. It may also be a separate unit, or external (see Figure 1.18).

THE INFORMATION PROCESSING PHASES

Data is transformed into information via a series of operations collectively known as the information processing phases.

Figure 1.18 An external modem connects a microcomputer and a telephone

Data are the basic facts concerning a particular situation, for example, an employee's hourly pay rate or the total rainfall for a day.

Information is data that has been organised and placed in a meaningful context.

The **information processing phases** are:

1. *acquisition* of data, that is, acquisition of data by the information system;

2. *input* of data into the computer system, where data is translated into a form suitable for electronic manipulation;

3. *validation* of data, that is, checking for completeness and accuracy of data;

4. *manipulation* of the data so as to produce information, usually involving at least organising the data and placing it in some meaningful context;

5. *storage* of the data and/or information;

6. *retrieval* of the data and/or information;

7. *output* of the information from the computer system, with an electronic representation of the information translated onto a form that makes it perceptible to humans, for example hard-copy print, voice, on-screen graphics;

8. *communication* or transfer of the information to those who need it;

9. *disposal* of the data and/or information when it is no longer needed.

CONNECTIVITY

Connectivity is the microcomputer's ability to communicate with other computers and information sources.

Connectivity is the capability of the microcomputer to use information from the world beyond your desk. Data and information can be sent over telephone lines or cable and through the air. Thus, your microcomputer can be *connected* to other computers. It can also be connected to many computerised data banks and other sources of information that lie well beyond your desk.

Connectivity is a very significant development, for it expands the uses of the microcomputer severalfold. Central to the concept of connectivity is the **computer network**. A network is a communications system connecting two or more computers. Networks connect people as close as the next office and as far away as halfway around the world.

The **National Information Highway (NIH)** is a term used to describe the future of communication networks and computers. The basis of today's NIH, also known as the **National Information Infrastructure (NII)** or the **information superhighway**, is the **Internet**. Internet is a huge computer network available to nearly everyone with a microcomputer and a means to connect to it. It is a resource for information about an infinite number of topics.

A LOOK AT THE FUTURE:
YOU AND COMPUTER COMPETENCY

Computer competency is understanding the rules and the power of microcomputers. Competency lets you take advantage of increasingly productive software, hardware, and the connectivity revolution that are expanding the microcomputer's capabilities.

The purpose of this book is to help you be computer competent not only in the present but also in the future. Having competency requires your having the knowledge and understanding of the rules and the power of the microcomputer. This will enable you to benefit from three important developments: more powerful software, more powerful hardware, and connectivity to outside information resources. It will also help you to remain computer competent and to continue to learn in the future.

Powerful software

The software now available can do an extraordinary number of tasks and help you in an endless number of ways. More and more employers are expecting the people they hire to be able to use it. Thus, we spend the next three chapters describing basic tools, power tools, and system software.

Powerful hardware

Microcomputers are now much more powerful than they used to be. Indeed, the newer models have the speed and power of room-size computers of only a few years ago. However, despite the rapid change of specific equipment, their essential features remain unchanged. Thus, the competent end user should focus on these features. Chapters 5 to 7 explain what you need to know about hardware: the central processing unit, input/output devices, and secondary storage. A Buyer's Guide is presented at the end of this book for those considering the purchase of a microcomputer system.

Connectivity

The principle of *connectivity* is a rapidly evolving development. No longer are microcomputers and competent end users bound by the surface of the desk. Now they can reach past the desk and link up with other computers to share data, programs, and information. Accordingly, we devote Chapters 8 and 9 to discussing connectivity: communications, files, databases, and the Internet. An Internet Guide describing how to access and use the Internet is presented at the back of this book.

Changing times

Are the times changing any faster now than they ever have? It's hard to say. People who were alive when radios, cars, and aeroplanes were being introduced certainly lived through some dramatic changes. Has technology made our own times even more dynamic? Whatever the answer, it is clear we live in a fast-paced age.

Most businesses have become aware that they must adapt to changing technology or be left behind. Many organisations are now making formal plans to keep track of technology and implement it in their competitive strategies. For example, banks have found that automated teller machines (ATMs) are vital to retail banking (see

Figure 1.19 Automated teller machines are examples of technology used in business strategy

Figure 1.19). Not only do they require fewer human tellers, but they can also be made available 24 hours a day. ATM cards can be used in many places to buy anything from petrol to groceries to movie tickets. Many banks are also trying to popularise home banking, so that customers can use microcomputers for certain financial tasks. In addition, banks are exploring the use of some very sophisticated application programs. These programs will accept and analyse cursive writing (the handwriting on cheques) directly as input.

Clearly, such changes do away with some jobs—those of many bank tellers and cashiers, for example. However, they create opportunities for other people. New technology requires people who are truly capable of working with it. These are not the people who think every piece of equipment is so simple they can just turn it on and use it. Nor are they those who think each new machine is a potential disaster. In other words, new technology needs people who are not afraid to learn it and are able to manage it. The real issue, then, is not how to make technology better. Rather, it is how to integrate the technology with people.

After reading this book, you will be in a very favourable position compared with many other people in industry today. You will learn not only the basics of hardware, software, and connectivity. You will also learn the most *current* technology. You will therefore be able to use these tools to your advantage—to be a winner.

REVIEW QUESTIONS

True/false
1. Microcomputers are also known as personal computers.

2. Hardware consists of monitor, keyboard, and software.

3. DOS is the standard operating system for Apple Corporation's Macintosh computers.

4. Memory is also known as primary storage.

5. A modem is used to send electronic signals over telephone lines.

Multiple choice

1. Computers are electronic devices that accept instructions, process input and produce:
   (a) information
   (b) prewritten programs
   (c) data
   (d) end users
   (e) system software

2. High-capacity computers used primarily for research purposes are:
   (a) microcomputers
   (b) minicomputers
   (c) mainframes
   (d) supercomputers
   (e) personal computers

3. The central processing unit (CPU) is located in the:
   (a) hard disk
   (b) system unit
   (c) memory
   (d) monitor
   (e) keyboard

4. When electrical power is disrupted or cut off, data and programs are lost in:
   (a) secondary storage
   (b) basic tools
   (c) memory
   (d) operating system
   (e) hard disk

5. Files containing highly structured and organised data are:
   (a) documents
   (b) worksheets
   (c) databases
   (d) graphics
   (e) communications

Fill in the blank

1. _____ _____ are people who use microcomputers or have access to larger computers.

2. Also known as midrange computers, _____ are frequently used by departments within larger organisations.

3. Written _____ are guidelines or rules to follow when using software, hardware, and data.

4. Secondary _____ is used to store data and programs permanently.

5. A _____ is a collection of characters organised as a single unit.

Open ended

1. What is computer competency?

2. Describe the five parts of an information system.

3. Distinguish between application software and system software.

4. Name the five categories of microcomputer hardware.

5. What is the difference between memory and secondary storage?

DISCUSSION QUESTIONS AND PROJECTS

1. *Your reasons for learning computing* How are you already using computer technology? What's happened in the computer-related world in the last six months that you might have read about or seen on television? How are companies using computers to stay on the cutting edge? These are some questions you might discuss with classmates to see why computers are an exciting part of life.

   You might also consider the reasons why you want to gain computer competency. Imagine your dream career. How do you think microcomputers, from what you already know, can help you do the work you want to do? What kind of after-hours interests do you have? Assuming you could afford it, how could a microcomputer bring new skills or value to those interests?

2. *Dealing with computer anxiety* Some newcomers to computers experience *computer anxiety,* or *technophobia*—great discomfort, even fear, about dealing with these machines. They may be afraid, for example, that they 'aren't smart enough' to work with computers or that they will 'mess up'. Or they may worry that they will accidentally break something, or that they will embarrass themselves in front of others. There are a number of ways of dealing with such anxieties and fears. If computers make you uncomfortable, discuss which of the following solutions might help.

   (a) Work with a partner. Ask another newcomer if you can sit together (whether in the classroom or laboratory) and try working things through together.

   (b) Talk back to an imaginary critic. Write out a script in which you talk to an imaginary hostile stranger who puts you down about your computer abilities. By talking back, you demolish what are really self-criticisms.

   (c) Familiarise yourself with computers gradually. Go into a computer lab by yourself and simply 'play around' with a microcomputer. Back off whenever the discomfort becomes too great. After a while, you'll find yourself less bothered by these machines.

   (d) Confront all your computer anxieties at once. Try the technique psychologists call 'flooding'. Allow yourself to experience all your fears and anxieties at once, no matter how bad they make you feel. By hanging in there, you tolerate the discomfort until the fears run their course.

3. *The general-purpose machine* The computer is a machine much like many other machines. There is, however, one fundamental difference: A computer is a general-purpose machine. Most machines are designed for one specific task. For example, a typewriter creates printed documents. A computer, on the other hand, is designed to perform and to assist in an unlimited number of tasks. It can create printed documents, analyse data, play games, and so on.

(a) Make a list of five special-purpose machines. For each machine, briefly discuss how a computer can or cannot perform the machine's task. For any tasks that a computer cannot perform by itself, consider whether a computer could assist the performance of the special-purpose machine.

(b) Make a list of five uses of a computer. Then briefly discuss any special-purpose machines that perform each task. Discuss the advantage or disadvantage of the special-purpose machine.

(c) Why is it that a computer can perform so many different tasks?

CASE STUDY

THE HARRIERS FITNESS CENTRE

The Harriers Fitness Centre is a high class fitness centre that caters for professional runners. The centre offers memberships of three, six, and twelve months duration. Fees are payable in advance on a three monthly basis. An alphabetical card index system is used to keep a record of members—their names, addresses, due dates for payment and receipt of fees.

The centre employs the following staff:

- **Julie Smith—manager**, who interviews new members and records their details onto personal record cards. Julie calculates their monthly fees and records this on the members' cards. The completed cards are given to Martin who checks the details and files them alphabetically. On a monthly basis Julie checks the card index for members whose fees are due and gives the relevant cards to Martin. Julie is also responsible for managing the finances of the centre and preparing monthly reports.

- **Martin Drake—secretary**, who does all the typing for the business and handles all correspondence. At the end of each month he sends out reminder notices to members whose fees are due. Members are asked to contact the centre if they do not wish to continue their membership. Expired membership cards are removed from the current index file.

- **Karen Smith and John Huxley—fitness advisers**, who are professional runners working in the gymnasium helping members with their individual programs.

Because of a continual increase in the number of members, Julie has decided to purchase a computer as an aid to more efficient and effective record keeping at the centre.

QUESTIONS

1. Explain how each information processing phase is undertaken using the manual information processing system at the Harriers Fitness Centre.

2. The centre is considering purchasing a new computer system.
   (a) Describe the four different kinds of computers.
   (b) Explain why each of the four types of computers is suitable (or unsuitable) for the needs of the centre.

3. (a) Briefly describe the five categories of microcomputer hardware.
   (b) Which of the five categories of hardware devices would you suggest that the centre purchase to meet their needs? Justify why you included or excluded each category of hardware.
   (c) Explain how the five hardware categories would relate to the information processing phases.

Application software: basic tools

FROM THE USER'S POINT OF VIEW

Think of the microcomputer as an *electronic tool*. People may not consider themselves as being very good at typing, calculating, drawing, or looking up information. A microcomputer, however, can help you to do all these things—and much more. All it takes is the right kind of software—the programs that go into the computer. We describe some of the most important ones in this chapter.

Not long ago, trained specialists were required to perform many of the operations you can now perform with a microcomputer. Secretaries used typewriters to create professional-looking business correspondence. Market analysts used calculators to project sales. Graphic artists drew by hand. Data processing clerks created and stored files of records on large computers. Now you can do all these tasks—and much more—with a microcomputer. And many of these tasks can be done with just *one* application program.

GENERAL-PURPOSE APPLICATION PACKAGES

Some features are common to all kinds of application packages.

Word processing, electronic spreadsheets, database managers, graphics programs, communications programs, and software that combines all five tasks are *general-purpose* application packages. That is, they may be used by many people for many different kinds of tasks. This is why we call them 'basic tools'. Some well-known software publishers are Microsoft, Lotus, and Novell.

Some features are common to most packaged programs. The following are the most important.

Version and release

Software packages are continually being improved and revised. When a package first appears, it is assigned the number 1.0. As the package changes, the number changes. The number before the full stop refers to the **version**, and the number after the full stop refers to the **release**. Changes in a version number indicate major changes; changes in releases refer to minor changes.

Insertion point

The **insertion point** or **cursor** shows you where you can enter data next. Typically, it is a blinking vertical bar on the screen. It can have other shapes depending on the software you are using. You can move the insertion point around using a mouse or the directional arrow keys.

Menus

Almost all software packages have **menus**. Typically, the menus are displayed in a menu bar at the top of the screen. When one of the menu items is selected, a pull-down menu appears. This is a list of commands associated with the selected menu (see Figure 2.1).

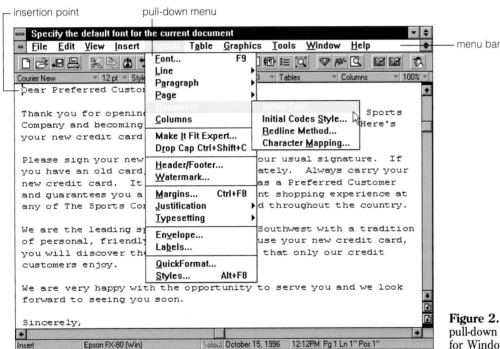

Figure 2.1 A menu bar and pull-down menu (WordPerfect for Windows, version 6.1)

Shortcut keys

Instead of using menus, many applications use **shortcut keys** for frequently used commands. They make it easier and faster to select certain commands. Many of these shortcuts use the **function keys**, F1, F2, and so on. Other shortcuts use key combinations typically consisting of the Alt, Ctrl, or Shift key used in combination with a letter, number, or function key. For example, in WordPerfect 6.0, the shortcut key F3 saves a file and the key combination Ctrl and O opens a file.

Help

For most application packages, one of the menus on the menu bar is **Help**. When selected, the help options appear. These options typically include a table of contents, a search feature to locate reference information about specific commands, and access to special learning

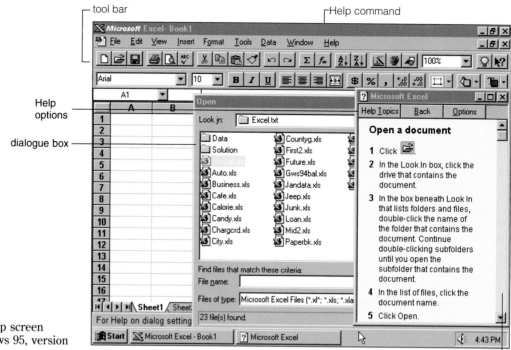

Figure 2.2 A Help screen (Excel for Windows 95, version 7.0)

features such as tutorials and step-by-step instructions. Additionally, most applications even provide what is called **context-sensitive help**. These help systems locate and display reference information directly related to the task you are performing (see Figure 2.2).

Tool bars
Tool bars, also known as **button bars**, typically are below the menu bar. They contain **icons** or graphic representations for commonly used commands. This offers the user a graphic approach to selecting commands. It is an example of a **graphical user interface (GUI)** in which graphic objects rather than menus can be used to select commands (see Figure 2.2).

Dialogue box
Dialogue boxes frequently appear after selecting a command from a pull-down menu. These boxes are used to specify additional command options (see Figure 2.2).

Scroll bars
Scroll bars are usually located on the right and/or the bottom of the screen. They enable you to display additional information not currently visible on the screen (see Figure 2.2).

WYSIWYG
Pronounced 'wizzy-wig', **WYSIWYG** stands for 'What You See Is What You Get'. This means that the image on the monitor looks the same as the final printed document. Application programs without WYSIWYG cannot always display an exact representation of the final printed document. For instance, some word processors without WYSIWYG will not display footnotes and page numbers on the screen. However, they do appear on the printed copy. The WYSIWYG feature

allows the user to preview the document's appearance before it is printed out.

Edit

Everybody makes mistakes entering data and information. The ability to change or to edit entries is a feature common to almost all applications. The **edit** feature makes revising and updating easy and is one of the most valuable features.

Cut, copy, and paste

Perhaps you have entered information that is wrong, or you decide you do not want to include the information at all. Or, perhaps you may want the same information to appear in multiple locations. You can easily make these changes using **cut, copy,** and **paste**. First, you select the information to be removed or copied by highlighting it. Then you choose the command to cut or to copy. If you select cut, the information simply disappears from your screen. If you select copy, the information remains but a copy is made. Then, by moving the insertion point to another location and selecting the paste command, the selected information appears at the new location (see Figure 2.3).

Undo

It is easy to incorrectly select a command. Frequently, these accidentally selected commands do things that make changes that are not intended—for example, deleting a paragraph or a formula. No need to panic . . . use **undo**. This feature restores your work to how it was before the last command was selected.

See Figure 2.4 for a summary of the most important common features of general-purpose application packages.

Let us now describe the categories of application software that we are calling basic software tools.

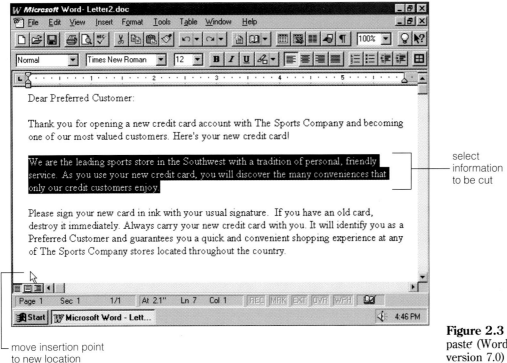

select information to be cut

move insertion point to new location

Figure 2.3 Cut, copy and paste (Word for Windows 95, version 7.0)

COMMON FEATURES

Feature	Description
Version and release	Indicates major and minor changes in software
Insertion point	Shows where data can be entered
Menu	Presents commands available for selection
Shortcut keys	Special-purpose keys for frequently used commands
Help	Presents explanations of various commands
Tool bar	Presents graphic objects for commands
Dialogue box	Used to specify additional command options
Scroll bars	Used to display additional information
WYSIWYG	'What You See Is What You Get'
Edit	Changes entered information
Cut, copy and paste	Deletes, moves, or copies information
Undo	Restores work prior to last command

Figure 2.4 Common application software features

WORD PROCESSORS

Word processing is used to create, edit, save and print documents.

Word processing software is used to create, edit, save, and print documents (see Figure 2.5). **Documents** can be any kind of *text* material. Some examples of documents are letters, memos, term papers, reports, and contracts. Once it was thought that only secretaries would use word processors. Now they are used extensively in managerial and professional life. Indeed, it has been found that, among the basic software tools, word processors produce the highest gains in productivity.

If you have used a typewriter, then you know what word processing *begins* to feel like. You type in text on the keyboard. However, with word processing, you view the words you type on a screen instead of on a piece of paper. After you are finished, you 'save' (store) your words in a file on a floppy or hard disk. Then you turn on the printer and print out the results on paper.

The beauty of this method is that you can make changes or corrections—before printing out the document. Even after your document is printed, you can easily go back and make changes. You can then print it again. Want to change a report from double spacing to single spacing? Alter the width of the margins on the left and right? Delete some paragraphs and add some others from yet another document? A word processor allows you to do all these with ease. Indeed, *deleting, inserting,* and *replacing*—the principal editing activities—can be done just by pressing keys on the keyboard.

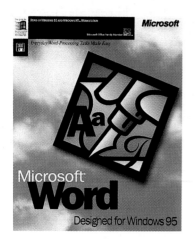

Figure 2.5 Word processing software: Microsoft Word Designed for Windows 95

Popular word processing packages include Word, WordPerfect, and Ami Pro. Some important features shared by most word processors are described in the following sections.

Word wrap and the Enter key

One basic word processing feature is **word wrap**. On a typewriter, you must decide when to finish typing a line. You indicate the end of a line by pressing a carriage return key. A word processor automatically moves the insertion point to the next line once the current line is full. As you type, the words 'wrap around' to the next line. To begin a new paragraph or leave a blank line, you press the **Enter** key.

Search and replace

A **search** or **find** command allows you to locate any character, word, or phrase in your document. When you search, the insertion point moves to the first place the item appears. If you want, the program will continue to search for all other locations where the item appears.

The **replace** command automatically replaces the word you search for with another word. For example, you could search for the word *Sydney* and replace it with the word *Melbourne*. You can do this at every place the word *Sydney* appears. Or you can do this only where you choose to. The search and replace commands are useful for finding and fixing errors. For example, suppose you misspell a person's name. You could search for the incorrect spelling and replace it with the correct spelling.

Other features

- Text can be aligned within the margins in various ways. The most common is left alignment. This means the text is displayed with an even left margin and a ragged right margin. Another common alignment is full justification. This means that the text on both the left and right margins is even.

- Text can be displayed in a variety of ways including boldfaced, underlined, and italicised.

- Tables of contents, footnotes, end notes, page numbers, tables, bulleted lists, and other features found in research papers can be easily created.

- Spelling can be checked automatically, by running your text through a **spelling checker** program. These programs identify incorrectly spelled words and suggest correct spellings. Many also include a feature to automatically correct spelling and expand abbreviations as you type.

- In a similar manner, **grammar checkers** identify poorly worded sentences, excessively long sentences, and incorrect grammar.

- **Thesaurus** programs enable you to quickly find the right word or an alternative word with a similar meaning.

- A **mail merge** or **form letter** feature allows you to merge different names and addresses. You can mail out the same form letter to different people.

- Graphics enhancements can improve the look of documents. For example, **drawing programs** let you create line art. **Clip art** allows you to include available graphic images (see Figure 2.6). And **word art** allows you to manipulate text into various shapes.

clip art ————

Figure 2.6 Clip art
(PowerPoint for Windows 95,
version 7.0)

SPREADSHEETS

A spreadsheet is an electronic worksheet used to organise and
manipulate numbers and display options for 'what-if' analysis.

The **spreadsheet** is based on the traditional accounting worksheet.
Paper worksheets have long been used by accountants and managers
to work up balance sheets, sales projections, and expense budgets.
Spreadsheets are used by financial analysts, accountants, contractors,
and others concerned with manipulating numeric data.

Spreadsheets allow you to try out various 'what-if' possibilities. This
is a powerful feature. You can manipulate numbers by using stored
formulas and calculate different outcomes. For example, a retail store
manager can estimate quarterly profits by projecting sales over a three-
month period (see Figure 2.7). The manager can then subtract
expenses from sales. Expenses might include such things as
advertising, cost of goods sold, and salaries. If expenses are too high
to produce a profit, the manager can experiment on the screen with
reducing some expenses and see the results almost instantly. For
example, the number of employees, and hence salaries, might be
reduced.

A spreadsheet has several parts (see Figure 2.7). The **worksheet
area** of the spreadsheet has letters for **column headings** across the
top. It also has numbers for **row headings** down the left side. The
intersection of a column and row is called a **cell**. The cell holds a single
unit of information. The position of a cell is called the **cell address**.
For example, 'B8' is the address for the cell located in column B and
row 8. A **cell pointer**—also known as the **cell selector**—indicates
where data is to be entered or changed in the spreadsheet. The cell
pointer can be moved around in much the same way that you move
the insertion point in a word processing program. In our illustration,
the cell pointer is located in position B8.

Popular spreadsheet packages include Excel, Lotus 1-2-3, and
Quattro Pro. Some common features of spreadsheet programs include
the following.

row headings

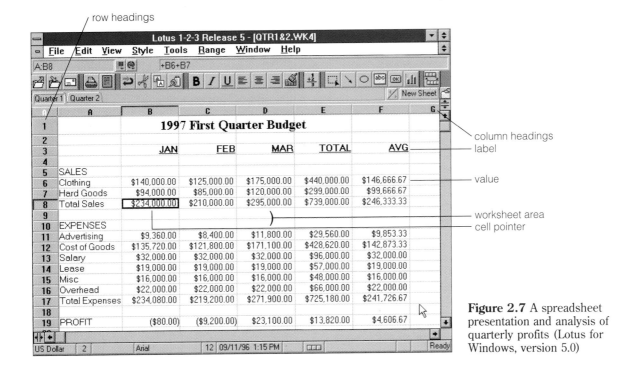

column headings
label
value
worksheet area
cell pointer

Figure 2.7 A spreadsheet presentation and analysis of quarterly profits (Lotus for Windows, version 5.0)

Format

Labels are often used to identify information in a worksheet (see Figure 2.7). Usually a label is a word or symbol, such as an asterisk (*). A number in a cell is called a **value**. Labels and values can be displayed or formatted in different ways. A label can be centred in the cell or positioned to the left or right. A value can be displayed to show decimal places, dollars, or percent (%). The number of decimal positions (if any) can be altered, and the width of columns can be changed.

Formulas

One of the benefits of spreadsheets is that you can manipulate data through the use of formulas. **Formulas** are instructions for calculations. They calculate results using the number or numbers in referenced cells. For example, in our illustration, the spreadsheet is concerned with computing total sales. The formula to calculate January's total sales is shown near the top of the screen: +B6+B7 (see Figure 2.7). This means add the value in B6 (clothing sales) to the value of B7 (hard good sales). The total is displayed in cell B8.

Functions

Functions are built-in formulas that perform calculations automatically. For example, the Lotus function @SUM(B6..E6) adds all the values in the range of cells from B6 to E6.

Recalculation

Recalculation is one of the most important features of spreadsheets. If you change one or more numbers in your spreadsheet, all related formulas will recalculate automatically. Thus, you can substitute one value for another in a cell and observe the effect on other related cells in the spreadsheet.

By manipulating the values, you can use spreadsheet formulas to explore your options. For example, consider our illustration. If the January-to-March sales are *estimates*, you can change any or all of the values in cells B6 to D7. All of the associated cells including the total in cell E8 and the average in cell F8 will change automatically (see Figure 2.7). This is called **what-if** analysis.

Analysis tools

Many programs include built-in **analysis tools** that help perform complicated what-if analysis. You can use **goal-seeking tools** and **solver tools** to find the values needed to achieve a particular end result. **Scenario tools** allow you to test the effect of different combinations of data. For example, a contractor might need to keep the cost of building a house within a budget. The contractor can run cost calculations on various grades of materials and on the going pay rates for labour.

Other features

Most spreadsheets also include additional capabilities for visually displaying and rearranging data. Among them are the following features:

Data displayed in graphic form Most spreadsheets allow users to present their data in graphic form. That is, you can display numerical information as pie charts, bar graphs, and line graphs. Some spreadsheet programs even display data in graphs and charts that have a three-dimensional look.

Graphics on worksheets This feature gives users the ability to place graphical elements such as lines, arrows, and boxes directly onto the worksheet. In addition, you can display charts and graphs directly on the worksheet. These charts and graphs automatically update when the numbers in the spreadsheet change.

3-D spreadsheets If a file contains only one spreadsheet, it has two dimensions, namely, rows and columns. If a file contains more than one spreadsheet, it has three dimensions, namely, rows, columns, and spreadsheets. For instance, an account representative may keep quarterly sales data in separate spreadsheets all stored in one file named 'SALES'.

Dynamic file links Some software offers **dynamic file links**, which allow you to link cells in one worksheet file to cells in other worksheet files. Whenever a change occurs in one file, the linked cells in the other files are automatically updated.

DATABASE MANAGERS

A database manager organises a large collection of data so that related information can be retrieved easily.

A *database* is a collection of related data that has been entered into a computer system and stored for future use. Information in the database is organised so that selected items can be retrieved easily. Database management programs are used by salespeople to keep track of clients.

They are also used by purchasing agents to keep track of orders and by inventory managers to monitor products in their warehouses. Database managers are used by many people inside and outside of business, from teachers to police officers. We describe databases in detail in Chapter 9.

A **database manager** or **database management system (DBMS)** is a software package used to set up, or *structure*, a database. It is also used to retrieve information from a database. An example of one database manager is Access (see Figure 2.8). This database contains address information about employees. The list of employee numbers, names, and addresses is a **table**. Each line of information about one employee is called a **record**. Each column of information within a record is called a **field**—for example, last name.

Another table might contain benefit information. For example, it might include information about each employee's retirement, dental, and medical plans. These two tables are linked or related by a common field called a **key field**. The information in a key field must be unique for each record in a table. In this case the key field is the employee number. This is a **relational database**. That is, the address table and the benefits table are related by a key field containing common employee numbers.

To see the value of a relational database, imagine that you are a benefits administrator. You have been asked by your boss to notify all employees using a particular dental plan that rates have changed. If the employee records were stored only on sheets of paper, it might take days or weeks to locate the appropriate names and addresses.

With a database, the names and addresses of all affected employees can be located within moments. The database software first goes to the benefits table to locate all employees who use the dental plan. Then the database software goes to the address table. There, the appropriate employee numbers are used to locate the names and addresses of all employees using that dental plan.

Figure 2.8 A database containing employee records (Access for Windows 3.1, version 2.0)

29

Popular database management programs include dBASE, Paradox, Access, and Approach. Database managers have different features, depending on their sophistication. A description of the principal features of database manager software for microcomputers follows.

Locate and display

A basic feature of all database programs is the capability to locate records in the file quickly. In our example, the program searches each record for a match in a particular field to whatever data you specify. This is called *querying* a database. The records can then be displayed on the screen for viewing, updating, or editing. For example, if an employee moves, the address field needs to be changed. The record is quickly located by searching the database to find the employee record that matches the name field you specify. Once the record is displayed, the address field can be changed.

Sort

Database managers make it easy to change the order of records in a file. Normally, records are entered into the database in the order they occur, such as the date a person is hired. This may not be the best way, however. There are a number of ways you can quickly rearrange the records in the file. For example, you might want to print out an entire alphabetical list of employees by last name. For tax purposes, you might want to list employees by tax file number.

Calculate and format

Many database programs contain built-in maths formulas. In the office, for example, you can use this feature to find the highest or lowest commissions earned. You can calculate the average of the commissions earned by the sales force in one part of the country. This information can be organised as a table and printed out in a report format.

Other features

Among other capabilities offered by some database management programs are the following:

Customised data-entry forms A person new to the database program may find some of the descriptions for fields confusing. For example, a field name may appear as 'CUSTNUM' for 'customer number'. However, the form on the screen may be customised so that the expression 'Enter the customer number' appears in place of 'CUSTNUM'. Fields may also be rearranged on the screen, and boxes and lines may be added.

Professional-looking reports A custom-report option enables you to design the elements you want in a report. Examples are the descriptions appearing above columns and the fields you wish to include. You can even add graphic elements, such as boxes or lines, so that the printed report has a professional appearance. Although the database itself may have, say, 10 fields, the report can be customised to display only the five or so important fields.

Program control languages Most people using a database management program can accomplish everything they need to do by making choices from the menus. Many database management programs include a programming control language so that advanced users can create sophisticated applications. In addition, most allow direct communication to specialised mainframe databases through languages like SQL (Structured Query Language).

GRAPHICS

Graphics programs are of three types: analytical for analysis, presentation for communication, and drawing for illustration.

Research shows that people learn better when information is presented visually. A picture is indeed worth a thousand words—or numbers. The popularity of graphics programs is expected to continue.

There are three types of graphics programs. *Analytical* graphics programs are used to analyse data. *Presentation* graphics programs are used to create attractive finished graphs for presentations and reports. *Drawing* programs are used to create illustrations.

Analytical graphics

Analytical graphics make numerical data much easier to grasp than when it is in the form of rows and columns of numbers. Most analytical graphics programs come as part of spreadsheet programs, such as Excel (see Figure 2.9). Thus, they are used by the same people who use spreadsheets. They are helpful in displaying economic trends, sales figures, and the like for easy analysis. Analytical graphics may be viewed on a monitor or printed out.

Presentation graphics

You can use **presentation graphics** to communicate a message or to persuade other people, such as supervisors or clients. Thus, presentation graphics are often used by marketing or sales people, as well as many others.

Figure 2.9 Various types of analytical graphics (Excel for Windows 3.1, version 5.0)

31

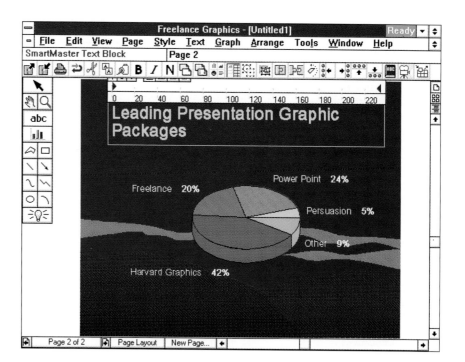

Figure 2.10 Example of presentation graphics (Freelance for Windows, version 2.0)

Presentation graphics look more sophisticated than analytical graphics, using colour, titles, and other features a graphic artist might use (see Figure 2.10). Using special equipment, you can convert graphics displays into slides, transparencies, or electronic presentations. The more powerful presentation graphics packages even include animation capabilities.

Popular presentation packages are Harvard Graphics, Persuasion, Power-Point, and Freelance.

Drawing programs

There is yet another kind of graphics program, one used by professional illustrators, such as people doing commercial art or drafting. These **drawing programs** are used to help create artwork for publications work (see Figure 2.11). They allow you to create attractive, sophisticated line art by combining lines, arcs, circles, and other shapes. Popular drawing packages are Adobe Illustrator, Aldus Freehand, and Micrografx Designer.

COMMUNICATIONS

Communications software lets you send data to and receive data from another computer.

Communications software enables microcomputer users to connect with and share resources. Communications programs are used by all kinds of people inside and outside of business. Examples are students doing research papers, consumers buying products and lawyers researching the law (see Figure 2.12). Other examples are investors getting stock quotations and economists getting government statistical data. A sales representative might use this software and a modem to retrieve an electronic file from a distant, telephone-linked information source. The file might be a list of clients. The representative could then copy the file to his or her own diskette or hard disk.

Figure 2.11 Example of a drawing program (Aldus Freehand, version 5.0)

Communications programs give microcomputers a powerful feature, as we have mentioned—namely, that of *connectivity*. Connections with microcomputers open up a world of services previously available only to users of mainframe computers. Recent developments in the National Information Highway and the Internet provide new and exciting opportunities for computer users. We devote all of Chapter 8 and a special Internet Guide to these topics. Some popular communications software includes ProComm, Smartcom, and Crosstalk. Some common features of most communications programs include the following:

Figure 2.12 Legal research (WinCin, Legal Forum)

Data banks

With a communications program, you can access enormous computerised databases: data banks of information. Some of these, such as Dialogue, resemble huge electronic encyclopaedias.

Message exchanges

Communications programs enable you to leave and receive messages on *electronic bulletin boards* or to use *electronic mail services* (see Figure 2.13). Electronic bulletin boards exist for people interested in exchanging all kinds of software or information. Such people might be job seekers, lawyers, activists, rock music fans, or students—the possibilities are almost endless. Many organisations have 'electronic mailboxes'. For instance, you can transmit a report you have created on your word processor to a faraway company executive or to a college instructor.

Financial services

With communications programs, you can look up airline reservations and stock quotations. You can order discount merchandise and even do home banking and bill paying.

Share resources

Many business people use communications software with networks to allow sharing of expensive equipment like laser printers and hard-disk drives. Users are able to share data and programs.

INTEGRATED PACKAGES AND SOFTWARE SUITES

Integrated software is an all-in-one application package. Software suites are individual windows applications that are sold together.

We have described five important kinds of application software. What happens if you want to take the data in one program and use it in

Figure 2.13 Example of an electronic mail screen (CompuServe, Information Manager)

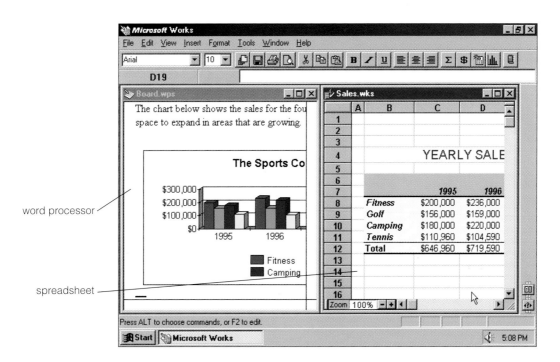

Figure 2.14 Example of an integrated package's spreadsheet and word processor (Microsoft Works for Windows 95, version 4.0)

another? Suppose you want to take information stored in the database manager and use it in a spreadsheet. This can be difficult to do with separate application packages. With an integrated package, however, it is easy to share data.

An **integrated package** is a program containing a collection of applications that work together and share information with each other. For example, to create a report on the growth of sales for a sporting goods store, you could use all parts of an integrated package. You could use the database to search and retrieve yearly sales data. The spreadsheet would be used to analyse the data and graphics to visually present the data. You could use the word processor to write the report that includes tables from the spreadsheet and visuals from the graphics program (see Figure 2.14).

Finally, you could send the report by electronic mail using the communications capability. Two well-known integrated packages are Microsoft Works and Lotus Works. Packages of this sort are easy to use. They are especially useful for microcomputers that do not have a lot of storage capacity.

An integrated package has a common structure allowing data to be exchanged easily between the applications within the package. Nevertheless, each application is generally less powerful than separate 'stand-alone' application software. The next chapter explains how programs such as Windows allow users to share data between *completely different* stand-alone programs—not just between the applications available within one integrated package.

Some software companies are selling their separate windows application programs as a group—called **software suites**. The most popular software suite is Microsoft Office. It includes up to five individual Windows application packages (see Figure 2.15). The word processor is Word, the spreadsheet is Excel, the database is Access, the presentation graphics program is PowerPoint, and the communications program is Mail. Although more expensive than most integrated packages, software suites are much less expensive than

Figure 2.15 A software suite (Microsoft Office for Windows 3.1, Professional version)

BASIC TOOLS

Application	Popular Packages
Word processors	Ami Pro, Word, WordPerfect
Spreadsheets	Excel, Lotus 1-2-3, Quattro Pro
Database managers	Access, Approach, dBASE, Paradox
Presentation graphics	Freelance, Harvard Graphics, Persuasion, PowerPoint
Drawing programs	Adobe Illustrator, Aldus Freehand, Micrografx Designer
Communications	Crosstalk, ProComm, Smartcom
Intergrated packages	Microsoft Works, Lotus Works
Software suites	Lotus SmartSuite, Microsoft Office

Figure 2.16 Basic application software tools

purchasing each of the applications separately. Another popular software suite is Lotus SmartSuites.

For a summary of the basic application software, see Figure 2.16.

A LOOK AT THE FUTURE

Tutorials, special software, and hardware add-ons help students learn complex software tasks.

Application software is one of those areas in which there are always new developments. How, then, can you keep up with newer versions?

Of course you can always take a class, which is often the easiest way. Many software manufacturers also produce *tutorials*—step-by-step directions and practice sessions. These may be available in books, on floppy disks, or on videotape cassettes. In the future, as software features multiply, the pressure will increase to make the learning process more efficient.

Already some *attempts at simplification* are being marketed. An add-on console (The Simplifier) can be plugged into a microcomputer keyboard. Its special cartridges contain instructions for students to help interpret complex commands in spreadsheet programs. Assistance is also available for learning other complex tasks. For instance, one word processing program (Wordbench) forces students to learn to write. It does this by limiting writing space, prohibiting users from going back to edit, and concealing words as they are typed.

Software manufacturers are providing more by including special capabilities right in the software. For example, Microsoft uses *wizards*, or a guided approach to performing selected tasks. PowerPoint, Microsoft's presentation software, has two such wizards. One is called the AutoContent wizard. After asking you a few questions about your presentation, the AutoContent wizard helps you to communicate and organise your ideas by suggesting an outline. The other wizard, Pick a Look, helps you create a look or style for your presentation. It provides over 100 professionally developed colour and design combinations.

REVIEW QUESTIONS

True/false

1. The insertion point or cursor indicates where you may enter data next.

2. Word wrap is a feature common to database managers.

3. Quattro Pro is a widely used word processor.

4. Spreadsheet programs are typically used to store and retrieve records quickly.

5. With communications programs, you can look up airline reservations and stock quotations.

Multiple choice

1. The feature common to most application packages that allows you to see a printed document before it is printed is:
   (a) insertion point
   (b) menu
   (c) help
   (d) WYSIWYG
   (e) dialogue box

2. When using a word processor, the command that is used to reinsert text into a document is:
   (a) cut
   (b) paste
   (c) copy
   (d) merge
   (e) align

3. In spreadsheets, the common feature that specifies instructions for calculation is:
   (a) formulas
   (b) format
   (c) recalculation
   (d) consolidation
   (e) value

4. A tool used frequently by marketing people to communicate a message or to persuade clients is:
   (a) a word processor
   (b) a spreadsheet
   (c) analytical graphics
   (d) a database manager
   (e) presentation graphics

5. A collection of separate Windows applications sold as a group is called:
   (a) combined
   (b) suite
   (c) communication
   (d) integrated
   (e) spreadsheet

Fill in the blank

1. The _____ box is a feature common to many application programs that presents additional command options.

2. The _____ is based on the traditional accounting worksheet.

3. _____ _____ programs are used to keep track of details such as inventory records or client lists.

4. _____ software lets you send data to and receive data from another computer.

5. Microsoft Works and Lotus Works are _____ packages.

Open ended

1. What is context-sensitive help?

2. How do formulas and recalculation work in a spreadsheet?

3. Explain the purpose of analytical graphics. Explain the purpose of presentation graphics. Explain the purpose of drawing programs.

4. Name three well-known spreadsheet packages.

5. What is the difference between an integrated package and a software suite?

DISCUSSION QUESTIONS AND PROJECTS

1. *Three ways to acquire application software* The following exercise can be extremely useful. Concentrate on a category of software of personal interest to you—say, word processing or spreadsheets. Go to the library and find information on the following three methods of acquiring software. Which route seems to be the best for you? Why?

   (a) *Public domain software* is software you can get free. Someone writes a program and offers to share it with everyone without charge. Generally, you find these programs by belonging to a microcomputer users group. Or you find them by accessing an electronic bulletin board using your telephone-linked computer. Be aware that the quality of the software can vary widely. Some may be excellent and some may be poor.

   (b) *Shareware* is inexpensive. It is distributed free, in the same way as public domain software. After you have used it for a while and decide you like it, you're supposed to pay the author for it. Again, the quality varies. Some shareware is excellent.

   (c) *Commercial software* consists of brand-name packages, such as those we mentioned in this chapter. Prices and features vary. Fortunately, there are several periodicals that provide ratings and guides. *PC World* polls its readers to find out the best software brands in various categories. The magazine releases the results in its October issue. Other periodicals (for example, *PC* magazine, *MacWorld, Australian Personal Computer*) also have surveys, reviews, and ratings.

2. *Interviewing users* Interview someone who uses some or all of the basic tools discussed in this chapter. Find out all you can about their use of the programs. Some questions you might ask:

   (a) What programs do they use and which one(s) do they use the most?

   (b) How did they get the programs? If they bought them, where did they buy them and how much did they cost? If they did not buy them, how did they get them?

   (c) Have they purchased any upgrades (newer versions) for any of the programs? What is their opinion of upgrades?

   (d) If they have problems with the program or need help using a program, what do they do? Do they use the program's help system? Do they use the program's manual? Do they call someone?

   (e) What features of each of the programs do they like, dislike, and use most frequently?

3. *New versions and releases* Software companies seem to be offering new versions and releases of their application packages all the time. For example, in one twelve-month period, Lotus released four variations of its 1-2-3 spreadsheet program.

   (a) Take one application package (like Lotus 1-2-3, WordPerfect, or dBASE) and find out how many variations have been released in the past two years.

   (b) If you own one variation of an application package and a new one is released, does yours become obsolete? Discuss and defend your position.

   (c) If you own one variation of a software package and a new version is released, should you upgrade to the newer version? What factors should be considered? If you decide to upgrade, how would you go about doing it?

   (d) Why do you suppose software manufacturers offer new variations of their software?

CASE STUDY

BILLBOARD EVALUATIONS

Billboard Evaluations is a small business run by a husband and wife team, Kate and Michael Wilson. It operates as a specialist outdoor advertising agency, providing a complete monitoring service to ensure that clients get what they contract for and only pay for what they get. They employ a number of inspectors both on a part-time and full-time basis. Kate is the manager of the business. She is responsible for dealing directly with clients and for the company's financial records. Michael assists her, and supervises the inspectors.

The company maintains details on a large number of outdoor advertising sites (i.e. billboards) throughout Australia. Its clients are businesses that have purchased outdoor advertising space. On behalf of its clients, Billboard Evaluations monitors the sites and ensures that they are in the right place and in the right condition. Sites are physically checked by the company's inspectors and this is done in accordance with carefully devised procedures. Sites, for which advertisers pay heavily, can be ignored or forgotten about without the advertiser being aware of it. In some instances, sites can have damaged copies, damaged panels, vision is obstructed, addresses are inaccurate or insufficient or the site may simply not be there.

The computer used by Michael consists of a Mitac 486 system with 16 Mb RAM, 540 Mb hard-disk drive and a 1.44 Mb 3.5" floppy-disk drive. The database section of the Windows package, Inform, is used to keep a record of all the site inspections.

When Michael receives a completed evaluation form on a client's site, he enters the relevant information into the database. He then hand writes a report, which includes information from the database that is required by the advertiser. He provides accurate information on the advertiser's site and the condition of the site, and also provides a report of any information the advertiser may have requested. If anything is wrong with a site, he sends a letter to a contractor, detailing the fault and requesting rectification or explanation. A copy of each letter sent is given to the manager of Billboard Evaluations, Kate Wilson. Michael also does random site visits to check on the accuracy of the inspectors' reports.

The database program provides extensive information on each billboard site. Included is an objective evaluation on each site and the following characteristics of the site: size, region, visibility, proximity to retail outlets, transport, traffic, traffic speed, environment and surroundings; whether or not the sign is illuminated, relationship to other panels, number of viewing positions, height, seasonal effects. It is Michael's responsibility to remove from the database any details of sites that are no longer in use.

The company has developed its own procedure for 'scoring' the billboard sites. Each billboard is made up of one or more panels. The procedure is designed to produce a numerical value or score for every outdoor advertising panel. Each individual element of the site is objectively assessed, and a single numerical value is produced; this measures each individual panel in the context of its unique viewing environment relative to all other panels of the same size. Further, by weighting for different sizes and types of panels, a numerical value is produced that reflects the value of each panel on each site. The sites are also assessed on the traffic volume, traffic speed, traffic control devices, bus/tram routes and pedestrian traffic. Billboard Evaluations has had a special program called OASIS written to manage this process.

QUESTIONS

1. Who are the computer users at Billboard Evaluations?

2. Which application software does Billboard Evaluations use?

3. Which of the five categories of microcomputer hardware is not used by Billboard Evaluations?

4. What are two ways that Billboard Evaluations could use the unused category of microcomputer hardware stated in your answer to Question 3?

5. The software package Inform is an intergrated package. What are two parts, other than databases or communications, that Billboard Evaluations would have an immediate use for? Describe the use to which each would be put.

6. Billboard Evaluations uses an information system to process data on billboard sites. For each phase of information processing, describe in detail how Billboard Evaluations handles the data involved and the personnel involved with that phase.

Application software: power tools

COMPETENCIES

After you have read this chapter, you should be able to:

* describe personal information managers;

* describe groupware;

* discuss project management software;

* explain what desktop publishing is;

* describe multimedia;

* explain artificial intelligence: robotics, knowledge-based and expert systems, and virtual reality.

FROM THE USER'S POINT OF VIEW

Expect surprises—exciting ones, positive ones. This is the view to take in achieving computer competency. If at first the surprises worry you, that's normal. Most people wonder how well they can handle something new. But the latest technological developments also offer you new opportunities to vastly extend your range. As we show in this chapter, software that for years was available only for mainframes has recently become available for microcomputers. Here's a chance to join the computer-competent of tomorrow.

Power tools: This is the characterisation we have given to a whole new generation of software and hardware only recently available for microcomputers. Power tools include personal information managers, groupware, project management software, desktop publishing software, multimedia, and artificial intelligence, including robotics, knowledge-based and expert systems, and virtual reality. Is there really a need to know anything about these new developments? There is if you want to be like those professionals in every area who are at the forefront of their disciplines. They are there because they have found more efficient ways to use their time and talents. You owe it to yourself, therefore, to be aware of what this software and hardware can do.

PERSONAL INFORMATION MANAGERS

A personal information manager is a program that helps you get organised and keeps you organised.

Stop and think for a minute about what you do in a typical day, week, month, and year. Professionals in all kinds of jobs do similar things. They schedule meetings, make to-do lists, and record important names, addresses, and telephone numbers. They jot down notes, make future plans, and record important dates like anniversaries and birthdays.

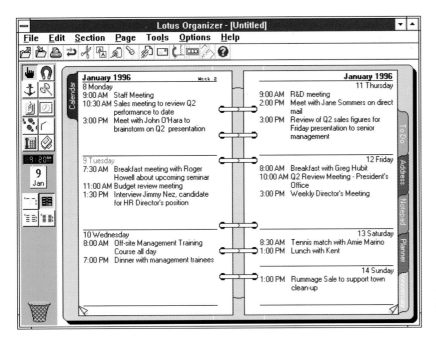

Figure 3.1 Personal information manager (Lotus Organiser)

You may use some of the same tools that many professionals use to keep track of all these things. Such tools include calendars, Rolodex files, address books, index cards, wall charts, notepads, binders, and Post-it notes. That's what **personal information managers (PIMs)** do and more (see Figure 3.1).

PIMs are designed to get you organised and keep you organised. Most importantly, they are designed to help maximise your personal productivity. Typically, they include electronic calendars, to-do lists, address books, and notepads. Some have automatic reminders that produce a sound when important meetings are to begin. Others alert users whenever electronic mail has been received. Examples of PIM software are Lotus Organiser, Computer Associates International Inc.'s UpToDate, and Franklin Quest Co.'s Ascend.

PIMs are quite handy. You could join the thousands of managers who review their electronic calendars each morning to see what appointments they have. Later, while you're working on a spreadsheet, say, someone calls to schedule an important business meeting. You just type a command that 'pops up' the PIM on the screen and type in the meeting time on your calendar. You then save the information. With another command, you make the PIM disappear from the screen and return to your spreadsheet.

PIMs are called **memory-resident programs**. Also known as **TSRs** (for terminate and stay resident), these programs stay in the computer's memory (primary storage) all the time, until the computer is turned off. The value of a PIM is that it enables you to keep your desk free of notepads, phone directories, and calculators.

PIMs are good for scheduling your own time. However, one of the most difficult tasks is to schedule group meetings with busy people. A recent version of Organiser can help people who are connected by a network. It graphically shows the time slots when each person is available and can identify a time when everyone is free (see Figure 3.2). Applications that extend beyond personal productivity to group productivity are called *groupware*—the topic of our next section.

Figure 3.2 Group scheduling
(Lotus Organiser for Windows)

GROUPWARE

Groupware supports group activities over networks to increase team productivity.

Most application software is designed for individuals working alone. These programs focus on personal or individual productivity. However, in many organisations today, the focus is more on teams and team productivity.

As more and more networks become established, a new kind of software is becoming popular. Known as **groupware** or *collaborative technology*, this software provides services to support group activities. These include scheduling and holding meetings, communicating, collaborating on ideas, and sharing documents, knowledge, and information. With groupware, two or more people can work on the same information at the same time. This type of software is one of the fast-growing network applications. Businesses are investing heavily in groupware to improve group productivity (see Figure 3.3).

The most widely used groupware software is Lotus Notes with nearly a million users. Basically, Lotus Notes is a way to share a database over a network so that many users can create and share information. The database is made up of *documents* containing many different kinds of information. They include text, graphics, sounds, images, and even videos. Users can create these documents using so-called *forms*. Users can *view* summaries of the database, share information, collaborate with others, and do many other group activities (see Figure 3.4).

There are hundreds of commercially available Lotus Notes applications, ranging from work flow management to sales order processing. Additionally, Lotus Notes can link or connect users with many kinds of application software such as Lotus 1-2-3, Freelance, Organiser, and Ami Pro. Another popular groupware program is Microsoft's Windows for Workgroups.

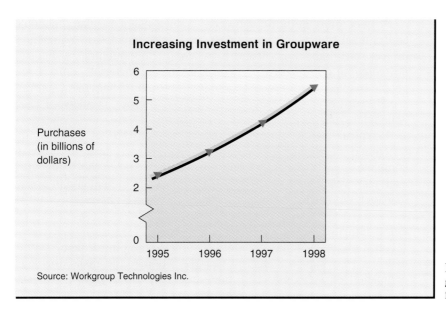

Figure 3.3 Investment in groupware—past, present and future

Figure 3.4 Groupware (Lotus Notes)

PROJECT MANAGEMENT

Project management software allows you to plan projects, schedule people, and control resources.

There are many occasions in business where projects need to be watched to avoid delays and cost overruns. A **project** may be defined as a one-time operation composed of several tasks that must be completed during a stated period of time. Examples of large projects are found in construction, aerospace, or political campaigns. Examples of smaller jobs might occur in advertising agencies, corporate marketing departments, or management information systems departments. You may have projects like term papers and lab experiments.

Project management software enables users to plan, schedule, and control the people, resources, and costs needed to complete a project on time. For instance, a contractor building a housing development might use it to keep track of the materials, dollars, and people required for success. Examples of project management software are Harvard Project Manager, Microsoft Project for Windows, Project Scheduler 4, SuperProject, and Time Line.

A typical use of project management software is to show the scheduled beginning and ending dates for each task in order to complete a particular project on time. It then shows the dates when each task was actually completed. Two important tools found in project management software are Gantt charts and PERT charts.

Gantt charts

A **Gantt chart** uses bars and lines to indicate the time scale of a series of tasks (see Figure 3.5). You can see whether the tasks are being completed on schedule. The time scale may range from minutes to years.

Figure 3.5 A Gantt chart
(Microsoft Project)

Figure 3.6 A PERT chart
(Microsoft Project)

PERT charts

A **PERT (Program Evaluation Review Technique) chart** shows not only the timing of a project but also the relationships among its tasks (see Figure 3.6). The chart identifies which tasks must be completed before others can begin. The relationships are represented by lines that connect boxes stating the tasks, completion times, and dates. The critical path, the sequence of tasks that takes the longest to complete, is also identified. With project management software, tasks and their completion times can be easily changed to see the effect on the overall schedule.

DESKTOP PUBLISHING

A desktop publishing program allows you to mix text and graphics to create publications of professional quality.

How would you like to generate a report that combined text and graphics and *really* impressed people with its looks? Suppose you wanted to create a report that looked like an article in a newsmagazine? When you present a report prepared on a word processing program, you are basically concerned with content; the appearance is secondary. When you do that same report with a desktop publishing program, the looks can be outstanding. An example of a page spread prepared by desktop publishing is shown in Figure 3.7.

Figure 3.7 A page produced by desktop publishing software

47

Many publications—most books and magazines, for instance—are created by professionals trained in graphic arts and typesetting. They use equipment that often costs several thousand dollars. However, there are many publications where such experience and expenses are not necessary. Examples are newsletters, forms, catalogues, brochures, posters, menus, and advertisements. These are all candidates for desktop publishing. Real estate agents may use desktop publishing for sales sheets. Travel agents may use it for advertisements, architects for proposals, and government officials for presentations.

Desktop publishing is the process of using a microcomputer, a laser printer, and the necessary software to mix text and graphics. Some word processing programs are being developed with this capability. However, here we are concerned with specialised software that allows you to create publications that are of professional quality. The software enables you to select a variety of typestyles, just like those that commercial printers use. It also allows you to create and select graphic images. The laser printer produces a higher-quality printed result than is possible with other microcomputer printers. A typical display screen from a desktop publishing program is shown in Figure 3.8. Popular programs are Quark Express, PageMaker, Ventura Publisher, and First Publisher.

Desktop publishing lets you place various kinds of text and graphics together in a publication designed almost any way you want. For instance, imagine you are helping a marketing manager for an aeroplane manufacturer to prepare a presentation on a new aircraft. You could use a word processing program to type the text. You could then use other software to create graphics. Or you might use graphics that have already been created from a graphics program. You can even use images that have been scanned from photographs. The desktop publishing program lets you integrate all these and look at your work on the monitor as one page. You can also look at two facing pages in reduced size or an enlarged view of a partial page. You can rearrange

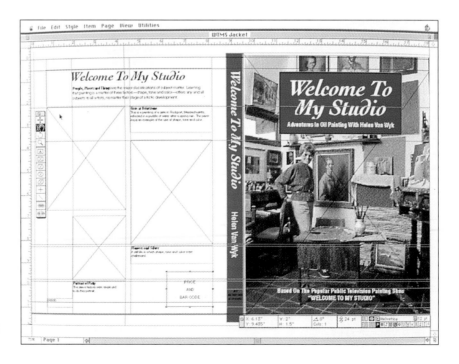

Figure 3.8 Desktop publishing (Quark Express)

text and columns. You can enlarge or reduce any element and choose from all kinds of typestyles and sizes.

Desktop publishing programs let you decide how many columns of text will be placed on a page. **Style sheets** automate the selection of size and style of text for headings, captions, and so on. Their use promotes consistency throughout a document. You can select with a single mouse click the size, width, and shading of the lines and boxes that separate and emphasise text. You can place a graphic image anywhere on a page. Text will automatically realign around an image or overwrite the image.

If you are not trained as a graphic designer, desktop publishing programs will not make you into one. However, they can help. Ventura, for example, offers 25 sample style sheets. These can be used for brochures, newsletters, books, and so on. As you become more experienced, you can modify these style sheets or even create your own.

Once a document is composed on the screen, it must be transmitted to an output device that can print it out. This task is accomplished by what are known as **page description languages**. A page description language describes the shape and position of letters and graphics to the printer. An example is Adobe's PostScript, which is used in the PageMaker product. Other examples are Interpress from Xerox and Document Description Language (DDL) from Imagen.

MULTIMEDIA

Multimedia integrates all kinds of information. Multimedia PCs are specially equipped microcomputers. Hypermedia databases store multimedia data.

Multimedia is one of the fastest-growing computer applications. More than 1 in 4 microcomputer systems sold today are equipped for multimedia. The trend is expected to continue (see Figure 3.9).

Multimedia, also called **hypermedia**, is the integration of all sorts of media into one form of presentation. These media may include text, graphics, animation, video, music, and voice.

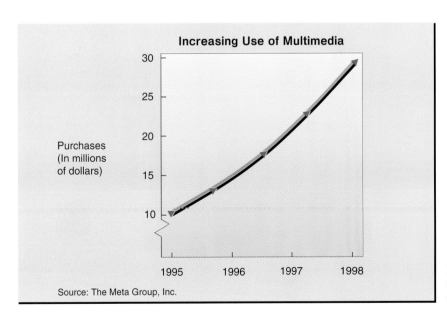

Figure 3.9 Multimedia systems in use—past, present, and future

Figure 3.10 Multimedia presentation: the leopard

Consider how a zoology professor might use multimedia for a lecture on felines. For hardware, he attaches a microcomputer and a CD-ROM drive to a speaker system and a large monitor. For software, he uses a readily available application, *The San Diego Zoo Presents . . . The Animals!*, written by The Software Toolworks. After a brief introduction, the professor begins the multimedia lesson by showing photos of leopards in their natural surroundings (see Figure 3.10). Then he shows a video clip of leopards hunting on an African plain. He then presents a narrated story explaining the animal and its environment, followed by a few pages of detailed information. All of this is stored on the CD-ROM. Even better, if students want more information about leopards or other animals, the instructor can quickly present information on 225 animals. The CD-ROM also contains 1500 photos, 150 video clips, 12 narrated stories, and 100 pages of information.

Multimedia PC

The typical **multimedia PC** is similar to many other powerful microcomputer systems. It has a fast microprocessor and a large hard-disk drive. Additionally, multimedia systems have a soundboard, speakers, and CD-ROM drive (see Figure 3.11). The soundboard and speakers capture and play back sound. The CD-ROM drive is needed to store the massive data requirements for multimedia. For instance, just 1 minute of video with stereo sound requires 25 Mb of disk space. The most common use for multimedia systems is to run previously created applications stored on CD-ROM. There are thousands of commercially available multimedia applications (see Figure 3.12).

Most multimedia PCs are used to run multimedia applications. Of course, someone must create these applications. Creating multimedia applications requires additional hardware and software. Microphones, video cameras, and scanners may be used to capture inputs. Additional hardware is required to save these inputs. While CD-ROMs are excellent for running multimedia applications, they are 'read-only' and cannot be used to save data. Special optical discs with large storage capacities are typically used to save and create multimedia applications. Special software called *authoring software* is used to create presentations by linking various types of input (see Figure 3.13).

Figure 3.11 Multimedia PC: the IBM Aptiva system

TOP-SELLING CD-ROMS		
Rank	Title	Publisher
1	Myst	Broderbund
2	Dark Forces	Lucas Arts
3	Doom II: Hell on Earth	ID/GT
4	Nascar Racing	Virgin
5	NSA Live '95	Electronic Arts

Figure 3.12 The five top-selling CD-ROMs

Figure 3.13 Authoring software: IconAuthor, version 5.1

Hypermedia databases

Typical database management systems are not able to handle multimedia data. They are designed to store numeric-only data. **Hypermedia databases** store and link a wide range of data including graphics, animation, video, music, and voice. They are based on the concept of card files, just like note cards, only these are electronic. Information is recorded on basic filing units called *cards*. A card is a computer screen filled with data comprising a single record. Cards in turn are organised into related files (bodies of information) called *stacks*. Cards and stacks are easily created and edited by the user through the use of typing and drawing tools.

You can create various connections between cards and stacks, and by fields of information on the cards, by means of *buttons*. A button is an area of the screen that is sensitive to the 'click' of a mouse. Using your mouse to guide the cursor, you move to one of these buttons on the screen. You then click the mouse, and you are connected to another card or stack.

By clicking buttons, you can 'navigate' through the cards and stacks to locate information or to discover connections between ideas contained in the stacks. For example, suppose an electronic 'encyclopaedia' or 'textbook' has been developed containing information about Native Americans. Figure 3.14 shows how you might do research on this subject. Each stack contains pertinent data: numbers, maps, text, charts, sounds, or pictures. You can define buttons to link the information. The links may be sequential, going from one card to the next in a stack. Or the links may be non-sequential so that you can jump from one topic to another. Once the links have been created you can sort through and access related information in a way that's convenient to you.

ARTIFICIAL INTELLIGENCE

AI attempts to simulate human thought processes and actions. Three areas are robotics, knowledge-based and expert systems, and virtual reality.

Does human intelligence really need the presence of 'artificial intelligence', whatever that is? Indeed, you might worry, do we need the competition? Actually, the goal of artificial intelligence is not to

Figure 3.14 How hypermedia databases work

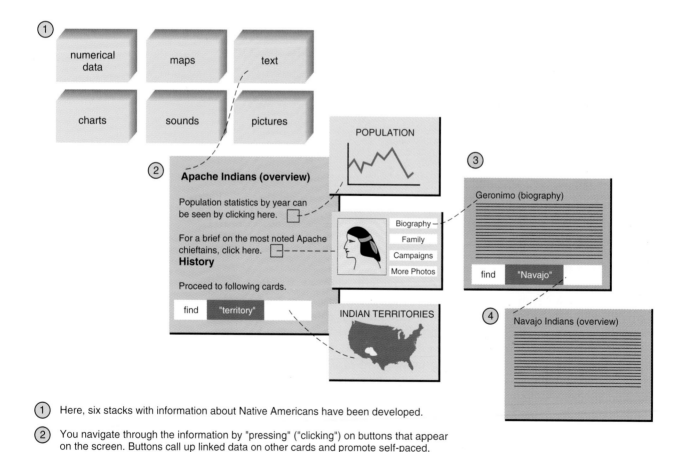

(1) Here, six stacks with information about Native Americans have been developed.

(2) You navigate through the information by "pressing" ("clicking") on buttons that appear on the screen. Buttons call up linked data on other cards and promote self-paced, self-guided study. Information can also be accessed using the "find" feature.

(3) Linking data is not a one-way street. From any card, you can access other cards to probe deeper into a line of thought.

(4) Or you can embark on an entirely new course of investigation.

replace human intelligence, which is probably not replaceable. Rather, it is to help people be more productive. Let us describe how this might work.

In the past, computers used calculating power to solve *structured* problems, the kinds of tasks described throughout this book. People—using intuition, reasoning, and memory—were better at solving *unstructured* problems, whether building a product or approving a loan. Most organisations have been able to computerise the tasks once performed by clerks. However, knowledge-intensive work, such as that performed by many managers, is only beginning to be automated.

Now the field of computer science known as **artificial intelligence (AI)** is moving into the mainstream. AI attempts to develop computer systems that can mimic or simulate human thought processes and actions. These include reasoning, learning from past actions, and simulation of human senses such as vision and touch. True artificial intelligence that corresponds to human intelligence is still a long way off. However, several tools that emulate human problem solving and information processing have been developed. Many of these tools have practical applications for business, medicine, law, and many other fields.

Let us now consider three areas in which human talents and abilities have been enhanced with 'computerised intelligence':

- robotics

- knowledge-based systems

- virtual reality

Robotics

Robotics is the field of study concerned with developing and using robots. **Robots** are computer-controlled machines that mimic the motor activities of humans. Some toy-like household robots (such as the Androbots) have been made for entertainment purposes. Most, however, are used in factories and elsewhere. They differ from other assembly-line machines in that they can be reprogrammed to do more than one task. Robots are often used to handle dangerous, repetitive tasks. There are three types of robots:

Industrial robots Industrial robots are used in factories to perform certain assembly-line tasks. Examples are machines used in automobile plants to do welding, painting, and loading (see Figure 3.15). In the garment industry, robot pattern cutters create pieces of fabric for clothing. Some types of robots have claws for picking up objects.

Perception systems Some robots imitate some of the human senses. For example, robots with television-camera vision systems are particularly useful. They can be used for guiding machine tools, for inspecting products, for identifying and sorting parts, and for welding (see Figure 3.16). Other kinds of perception systems rely on a sense of touch, such as those used on microcomputer assembly lines to put parts into place.

Mobile robots Some robots act as transporters, such as 'mailmobiles'. They carry mail through an office, following a preprogrammed route. Others act as computerised carts to deliver supplies and equipment at medical centres.

Figure 3.15 Industrial robot: spraying and polishing on car plant production line

Figure 3.16 Perception system: vision-system robot, used for welding

Knowledge-based (expert) systems

People who are expert in a particular area—certain kinds of law, medicine, accounting, engineering, and so on—are generally well paid for their specialised knowledge. Unfortunately for their clients and customers, they are expensive, not always available, and hard to replace when they move on.

What if you were to somehow *capture* the knowledge of a human expert? What if you then made it accessible to everyone through a computer program? This knowledge could be reasonably priced and always available. Indeed, if you were an expert yourself, you could use such a program to double-check your own judgments. Moreover, as an expert, you could create your own computer program containing much of what you know. All this is exactly what is being done with so-called *knowledge-based* or *expert systems*. **Expert systems** are computer programs that provide advice to decision makers who would otherwise rely on human experts. These programs are unlike conventional programs in several ways:

- Conventional programs typically are used to perform routine tasks on data and to process sequentially from top to bottom. These programs use very highly structured logic. For example, a payroll program performs routine calculations using an employee database following a standard and precise sequence of operations.

- Expert system programs are used to provide advice on very specialised tasks that typically require a human expert.

Rather than use a database, expert systems use knowledge bases. These contain specific facts, rules to relate these facts, and user input to formulate recommendations and decisions. These rules are used only when needed. The sequence of processing is determined by the interaction of the user and the knowledge base. Many expert systems use so-called *fuzzy logic*, which allows users to respond to questions in a very human-like way. For example, if an expert system asked how your classes were going, you could respond, 'great', 'OK', 'terrible', and so on.

Over the past decade, expert systems have been developed in areas such as medicine, geology, chemistry, military science, and photography (see Figure 3.17). There are expert systems with such names as Oil Spill Advisor, Bird Species Identification, and even Midwives Assistant. A system called Grain Marketing Advisor helps farmers select the best way to market their grain. Another, called Senex, shows how to treat breast cancer based on advanced treatment techniques.

Expert systems are created using a programming language or a shell. Expert system **shells** are special kinds of software that allow a person to custom-build a particular kind of expert system. For instance, the shell called VP-Expert has a database and can work with Lotus 1-2-3 and dBASE. This shell can then be used to build different kinds of expert systems. For example, VP-Expert has helped gardeners to assemble information about the most effective natural pest controls to use for specific purposes. Texas Instruments has developed an entire line of microcomputer-based shells called the Personal Consultant

Figure 3.17 Expert system: diagnosing problems with cameras

Series. These shells have been used to build Senex and Grain Marketing Advisor, among others we mentioned.

Virtual reality

Suppose you could create and virtually experience any new form of reality you wish. You could see the world through the eyes of a child, a robot—or even a lobster. You could explore faraway resorts, the moon, or inside a nuclear waste dump, without leaving your chair. This simulated experience is rapidly becoming possible with a form of AI known as *virtual reality*.

Virtual reality is also known as **artificial reality** or **virtual environments**. Virtual reality hardware includes headgear and gloves. The headgear (one type is called Eyephones) has earphones and three-dimensional stereoscopic screens. The gloves (DataGlove) have sensors that collect data about your hand movements. Coupled with software (such as a program called Body Electric), this interactive sensory equipment lets you immerse yourself into a computer-generated world.

An example of virtual reality is shown in Figure 3.18. In the photo is a person wearing an interactive sensory headset and glove. The rest of the photo shows what the person is actually seeing—in this instance a molecular view of a human cell. When the person moves their head, the stereoscopic views change.

There are any number of possible applications for virtual reality. The ultimate recreational use might be something resembling a giant virtual amusement park. More seriously, we can simulate important experiences or training environments such as flying, surgical operations, spaceship repair, or nuclear disaster clean up.

A LOOK AT THE FUTURE

The downsizing of computer applications will continue. So will the broadening of the scope of applications, as in current research into artificial life.

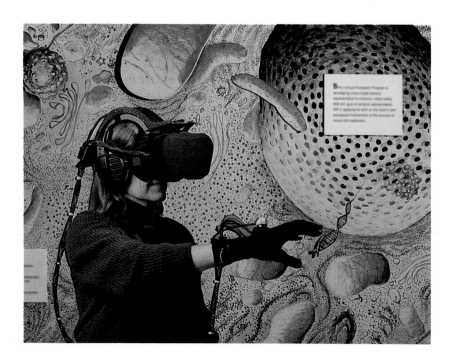

Figure 3.18 Virtual reality: looking inside a molecule

We can expect the trend of *downsizing of applications* to continue. That is, tasks that could once be performed only by mainframes will increasingly be done with microcomputers. Computer networks will link mainframes, microcomputers, workstations, and servers of all kinds—file servers, database servers, and communications servers. These developments will have an effect on the kinds of resources available to you in your career.

Just as important, we will probably also see a *broadening of the scope of applications*. Already well along in development, for instance, are *pen-based computers*. These are portable computers with handwriting-recognition capabilities that can identify printed letters, digits, and punctuation. They can even be modified to accept particular handwriting styles. Also presently being marketed are compact disc players that display audio and video programs on a TV set. These enable viewers to navigate by sight and sound through encyclopaedias and atlases. These and similar devices may be forerunners to so-called *information appliances*. Such appliances would bundle a computer, telephone, fax machine, photocopier, colour printer, and laser discs or CDs into one intelligent machine.

In the 21st century, the concepts applied in artificial intelligence, such as robotics, will be applied to all sorts of things. Even now, for instance, an experimental house in Japan, the 'TRON House', has microprocessors and sensors built into everything. Windows open and close to maintain optimum ventilation. Background music reduces in volume when the telephone rings. Kitchen computers take the guesswork out of cooking. Bathroom computers monitor one's health. No doubt we will see a similar extension of computer technology to the workplace.

Most spectacularly, there are already attempts to go beyond artificial intelligence to something called *artificial life*. In this field, researchers are trying to develop programs that learn and develop on their own. Computers are used to simulate living systems and make computerised environments in which simulations of organisms eat, reproduce, and die. The outcome of these investigations may produce defences against the computer viruses that have damaged networks and databases. They may also further our understanding of how human urban communities work.

REVIEW QUESTIONS

True/false
1. PIMs typically include electronic calendars, to-do lists, address books, and notepads.

2. Groupware is also known as collaborative technology.

3. Desktop publishing software helps you to plan, schedule, and control the people, resources, and costs of a project.

4. Multimedia sales are expected to remain constant for the next few years.

5. Expert systems are programs that give advice to individuals who would otherwise rely on human experts.

Multiple choice

1. A one-time operation composed of several tasks that must be completed during a stated period is called a:
   (a) plan
   (b) organiser
   (c) manager
   (d) schedule
   (e) project

2. The application software that allows you to mix text and graphics to create documents of professional quality is:
   (a) AI
   (b) PIM
   (c) groupware
   (d) desktop publishing
   (e) project management

3. The application that can link all sorts of media into one form of presentation is:
   (a) organiser
   (b) word processor
   (c) multimedia
   (d) spreadsheet
   (e) PIM

4. _____ supports group activities over networks.
   (a) hypermedia
   (b) groupware
   (c) AI
   (d) PIM
   (e) a knowledge-based system

5. An area of artificial intelligence that simulates certain experiences using special headgear, gloves, and software that translates data into images is:
   (a) virtual reality
   (b) expert system
   (c) collaborative technology
   (d) hypermedia
   (e) shell

Fill in the blank

1. Lotus Organiser is an example of a _____ .

2. In desktop publishing, a _____ _____ helps you to create the basic appearance of single or multiple pages.

3. Linking text, graphics, animation, video, music, and voice into one presentation can be done using _____ .

4. Unlike most assembly-line machines, _____ can be reprogrammed to do more than one task.

5. Expert system _____ are special programs that allow a person to custom-build an expert system.

Open ended

1. What are personal information managers? What are they used for?

2. Explain what project management software does. Give an example of how one might be used.

3. What does a desktop publishing program let you do? What does a page description language do?

4. Explain how multimedia works.

5. What are the three areas of artificial intelligence?

DISCUSSION QUESTIONS AND PROJECTS

1. *New areas for expert systems* There are numerous expert systems designed to pick winning stocks in the stock market. However, not everyone using these systems has become rich. Why? List and discuss three other areas in which you think it would be difficult to devise an expert system.

2. *A picture of things to come* Over the next 10 to 15 years, say some experts, electronic miniaturisation will produce small, portable devices that you can wear like clothing. These devices will do all kinds of wonderful things. For example, they will incorporate display screens, keyboards, CD memories, faxes, telephones, scanners, cameras, and satellite transmitters and will recognise handwriting and voice. What kind of wearable, lightweight 'information and entertainment machine' would you design for yourself? What would it do?

CASE STUDY

TECHNOLOGY EDUCATION AND TRAINING

Technology Education and Training ('TET') is a business education centre providing training courses to business and government organisations. TET provides computer training on most of the popular software products, at introductory, intermediate and advanced levels. The organisation has training centres in Melbourne, Sydney, Canberra, Adelaide, Brisbane and Perth. Participants in the courses run by TET receive practical training at TET centres, and are provided with detailed printed course manuals to go with their hands-on practice.

Each TET training centre is equipped with a network of Pentium computers, set up in several classrooms of 15 to 20 computers each. The centres also have administrative computer facilities to manage their financial and enrolment information. The administrative computers of all TET sites are linked via modem, to allow enrolment information to be transferred between centres quickly and easily.

The TET courses are presented by professional trainers who work for TET on a contract basis; that is, each trainer contracts to deliver a particular course for TET. The contract trainers are not employees of TET. TET only employs four staff directly at each of its centres: a manager, two receptionist/enrolment clerks, and an accounts clerk. Course enrolments are entered directly into the administrative computer system as they are received. This system automatically prints a confirmation notice and an invoice for the client, and provides a participant list for each course.

TET is constantly monitoring its course enrolment patterns, to see which courses are most in demand, and monitors software developments, to be prepared with courses on new software releases as soon as possible. In addition to the courses run at its centres, TET provides individually designed courses for particular organisations if required, and can provide training at the organisation's premises rather than at the TET training centre.

QUESTIONS

1. TET has to prepare student manuals, advertising materials, and course brochures.

   (a) What sort of software would TET use to prepare these publications?

   (b) Briefly (in two or three sentences) describe the features of this software.

2. At present, the TET trainers do all of their training by talking to the class from the front of the room, using a whiteboard if necessary, and making occasional use of the printed notes. One of their trainers has suggested that multimedia software may enable more effective training. Briefly describe the features of multimedia software, and how it might be used for training.

3. TET has been approached by a small manufacturing company seeking to increase its use of computer technology with the aim of making their operations more efficient. They want TET to advise them on the sorts of software they might find useful, and to provide appropriate training. TET has recommended Project Management software as an area that might be useful.

   Briefly describe the features of 'Project Management' software.

System software

FROM THE USER'S POINT OF VIEW

Becoming a microcomputer end user is like becoming the driver of a car. You can learn just enough to start up the car, take it out on the street, and pass a driver's licence test. Or you can learn more about how cars work. That way you can drive any number of vehicles, know their limitations, and compare performance. Indeed, you could go so far as to learn to be a mechanic. Similarly, by expanding your knowledge about microcomputers, you extend what you can do with them. You don't have to be the equivalent of a mechanic—a computer technician. But the more you know, the more you expand your computer competency and productivity.

All cars do the same thing—take you somewhere. But there was a time when you could choose between different automotive power systems: steam, electricity, diesel, or petrol. Some systems were better for some purposes than others. You could have a car that was quiet or cheap to run, for instance. However, that same car perhaps took too long to start, wouldn't take you very far, or didn't have enough power on the hills.

Microcomputers are in a comparable phase of evolution. Some computers do some things better than others—are easier to learn, for instance, or run more kinds of application software. Why is this? One important reason is the *system software*, the 'background' software that acts as an interface between the microcomputer and the user. System software also acts as an interface between the application program and the input, output, and processing devices (see Figure 4.1). The most important types of microcomputer system software are *DOS, Microsoft Windows, OS/2 Warp, Macintosh*, and *Unix*. Which of these you can use depends in part on what kind of computer you have.

WHY LEARN ABOUT SYSTEM SOFTWARE?

Because standards are changing, users need to know more about system software than was previously required.

COMPETENCIES

After you have read this chapter, you should be able to:

- understand the importance of learning about system software;

- distinguish among five kinds of operating systems;

- explain the advantages and disadvantages of DOS;

- discuss the differences among the three Microsoft Windows programs;

- discuss the benefits and drawbacks of OS/2 Warp;

- describe what's good and bad about Macintosh system software;

- explain the advantages and disadvantages of Unix for microcomputers.

Figure 4.1 End users interact with application software. System software interacts with the computer

Are you buying a pricey racing machine that you don't really need? Or are you buying an inexpensive, practical vehicle that may nonetheless soon become obsolete? These are the kinds of things many people think about when buying cars. Similar considerations apply in buying microcomputers and software. It's important to know what each type of operating system can and can't do (see Figure 4.2). Moreover, you hope the buying decision you make will be good for the next several years.

If the study of system software seems to be remote from your concerns, it shouldn't be. Here's why:

Competing system software In earlier editions of this book there might not have been a need for this chapter. The kind of microcomputer system software that predominated was the one for IBM and IBM-compatibles known as DOS. These IBM and IBM-compatibles are often referred to as *DOS-based* microcomputers. The other popular system software was the one designed for the Apple Macintosh. Without specialised hardware and software, Macintosh programs wouldn't run on DOS-based microcomputers, and DOS programs wouldn't run on Macintosh computers. Today's very powerful microcomputers are demanding more and more from last year's system software. Now there are several competing forms of system software.

Figure 4.2 The IBM Value Point (left) and Apple Macintosh Power PC (right) use different system software. Although similar in many ways, these systems also have significant differences

DOS limitations If DOS was so popular, why didn't the microcomputer industry just stay with it? The answer is that it has some practical limitations, as we shall discuss. Because it is so widespread, DOS will probably continue to be used for the next several years. Thus, it is well worth learning. However, as more powerful microcomputers become commonplace, other system software will likely replace DOS. In sum, DOS is popular today but will likely fade in the years to come.

One computer, many kinds of system software Now there are microcomputers that run more than one kind of system software. Employers may require that you know more than one kind. For instance, many office workers may need to know how to work with DOS, Microsoft Windows, and OS/2. These systems can run on the same computer.

More networking More and more computers are being connected together to share information and resources. Not all operating systems can efficiently support network operations. And some of the ones that do can support only certain types of networks.

More sophisticated users Previously, microcomputer users were satisfied with the performance offered by DOS. However, users are becoming more sophisticated. Now they want to be able to fully exploit the power of these newer microcomputers. They are beginning to demand that microcomputers run programs that previously could run only on minicomputers and mainframes. To do this, more sophisticated system software is required.

Even if you use only *one* type of system software, such as Windows, it's important to realise that such software is frequently revised. Revisions are made in order to handle new technology such as newly developed input and output devices. As system software changes, you need to know what the effects are on your old application software.

FOUR KINDS OF PROGRAMS

System software consists of the bootstrap loader, diagnostic routines, basic input-output system, and operating system.

System software deals with the physical complexities of how the hardware works. System software consists of four kinds of programs: bootstrap loader, diagnostic routines, basic input-output system, and operating system. The last one, the operating system, is the one we are most concerned with in this chapter. However, we will briefly mention the others, which operate automatically:

- The **bootstrap loader** is a program that is stored permanently in the computer's electronic circuitry. When you turn on your computer, the bootstrap loader obtains the operating system from your hard disk (or floppy disk) and loads it into memory. This is commonly called **booting** the system.

- The **diagnostic routines** are also programs stored in the computer's electronic circuitry. They start up when you turn on the machine. They test the primary storage, the central processing unit (CPU), and other parts of the system. Their purpose is to make sure the computer is running properly. On some computers, the screen may say 'Testing RAM' (a form of computer memory) while these routines are running.

- The **basic input-output system** consists of service programs stored in primary storage. These programs enable the computer to interpret keyboard characters and transmit characters to the monitor or to a floppy disk.

- The **operating system**, the collection of programs of greatest interest to us, helps the computer manage its resources. The operating system takes care of a lot of internal matters so that you, the user, don't have to. For instance, it interprets the commands you give to run programs. It also enables you to interact with the programs while they are running. It manages memory, data, and files.

One set of programs within the operating system is called **utility programs**. These programs perform common repetitious tasks or 'housekeeping tasks'. One important utility program is used for **formatting** (or **initialising**) blank floppy disks. This program is very important. Although you can purchase disks already formatted, many are not and must be formatted before you can use them. Formatting prepares the disk so that it will accept data or programs. With a formatted disk, you can use a utility program to **copy** or duplicate files and programs from another disk. You can **erase** or remove old files from a disk. You can make a **backup** or duplicate copy of a disk. You can **rename** the files on a disk—that is, give them new file names.

Every computer has an operating system. Larger computer systems like mainframes and minicomputers have very sophisticated ones. A popular operating system for IBM's mainframes, for example, is MVS. Digital Equipment Corporation (DEC) uses VAX/VMS as the operating system for its minicomputers. These operating systems have very powerful capabilities, including virtual memory, multiprogramming, and multiprocessing.

An operating system with **virtual memory** increases the amount of memory available to run programs. Without virtual memory, an entire program must be read into the computer system's memory before it can run. Therefore, the size of memory determines the largest program that can be run. With virtual memory, the operating system divides large programs into parts and stores these parts on a secondary storage device, usually a disk. Each part is then read into the computer system's memory only when needed. This allows a computer system to run very large programs.

Multiprogramming and multiprocessing allow more than one person to use a computer system. For **multiprogramming**, the operating system interrupts and switches rapidly back and forth between several programs while they are running. This allows several different users to run different programs seemingly at the same time. For **multiprocessing**, the operating system controls two or more central-processing units. This allows several different users to independently run different programs at the same time.

There are several similarities between larger computer and microcomputer operating systems. One difference, however, is that the larger systems tend to focus on multiple users of a computer system. Microcomputer operating systems, on the other hand, tend to focus on single users.

For end users, the most important operating systems are those for microcomputers. To achieve computer competency, it is important for

SYSTEM SOFTWARE PROGRAMS

Program	Function
Bookstrap loader	Reads operating system from disk and loads into memory
Diagnostic routines	Tests parts of system to ensure computer is running properly
Basic input–output	Transmits characters from the keyboard to a monitor or disk
Operating system	Helps manage computer resources Most important types are DOS, Microsoft Windows, OS/2, Macintosh, and Unix

Figure 4.3 Types of system programs

you to know something about the principal types of operating systems on the market for microcomputers today. These are *DOS, Microsoft Windows, OS/2 Warp, Macintosh*, and *Unix*.

For a summary of system software programs, see Figure 4.3.

DOS

DOS is the standard. It is widely used, runs thousands of applications, and requires inexpensive hardware.

DOS stands for *D*isk *O*perating *S*ystem. Its original developer, Microsoft Corporation, sells it under the name *MS-DOS*. (The 'MS', of course, stands for Microsoft.) It is the standard operating system for all microcomputers advertising themselves as 'IBM-compatible' or 'DOS-based', such as Compaq. Whatever machine it is used with, it is usually referred to simply as *DOS*.

There have been several upgrades since MS-DOS was introduced. The 1981 original was labelled version 1.0 (see Figure 4.4). Since then there have been numerous new versions, including 6.0, 6.1, and 6.2. An important characteristic of the more recent or newer versions is that they are 'backward compatible'. That is, you can still run application programs with them that you could run on the older versions. The newest versions feature pull-down menus (see Figure 4.5). With pull-down menus, you use your mouse-directed insertion point or cursor to unfold ('pull down') a menu from the top of your display screen.

Advantages

There is no question that DOS has many advantages. The reasons for learning it are very compelling:

Widely used DOS is the most popular microcomputer operating system ever sold. It is installed on 85 percent of all the microcomputers (personal computers) in the world.

DIFFERENT VERSIONS OF MS-DOS

Version	Features
1.0	Original operating system for IBM PC and compatibles. Supported only floppy-disk drives
2.0	Developed for IBM XT microcomputer. First version to support hard-disk drives
3.0	Appeared about the same time as IBM AT microcomputer. Starting with 3.2 release, supported networking and 3½-inch disk drives
4.0	Included pull-down menus and other sophisticated modifications
5.0	Allowed access to more memory and task switching
6.0	Included disk compression, advanced memory and file management, and virus protection

Figure 4.4 Different versions of MS-DOS

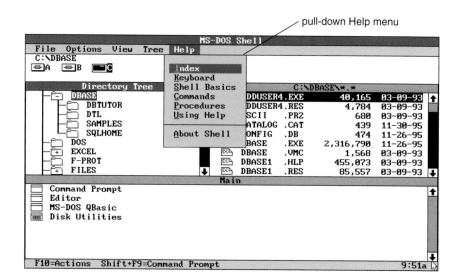

Figure 4.5 Example of pull-down menu from MS-DOS 6.0

Number of applications An enormous number of application programs have been written for DOS. Indeed, more specialised software is available for DOS than for any other operating system. This software includes not just the basic tools and power tools mentioned in Chapters 2 and 3 but many others as well.

Runs on inexpensive hardware DOS runs on many computers—old and new—that are reasonably priced. In addition, DOS is available for all kinds of domestic- and foreign-made IBM-compatible machines. The IBM Personal Computer set the standard for the business market. However, the appearance of similarly designed competitors has driven prices down, making microcomputers available to more people.

Disadvantages

DOS is software, but software can perform only as well as the hardware for which it was designed. The first version of DOS was introduced in 1981 for microcomputers with floppy-disk drives. This first version did not support hard-disk drives. Since that time, hardware has evolved significantly, and new versions have also evolved. Fortunately, these newer versions of DOS were written so that older application programs could still work with them. Unfortunately, DOS' ability to fully use all the power of today's microcomputers has been constrained. This is because DOS must support these older application packages.

Limited primary storage Before an application program can be used, it must be stored in the computer's primary storage. An application program running with DOS has direct access to only 640 kilobytes (about 640 000 characters) of primary storage. With the newer versions of DOS, several additional kilobytes can be accessed. However, most of the new spreadsheet, database management, and graphics programs require more primary storage. New microcomputers have much more primary storage. Still, DOS by itself as the operating system cannot access all of this available primary storage. This restriction is an inherent limitation of DOS.

'Single tasking' only **Multitasking** is the term given to operating systems that allow a single user to run several application programs at the same time. We discuss multitasking further in the next section. Unfortunately, MS-DOS by itself can only do *single tasking*: it can support only one user and one application program at the same time. The newer versions of MS-DOS, however, do support *task switching*. That is, they can switch or interrupt one application to do another application. But they cannot run both applications at the same time.

Character-based interface In DOS, users issue commands by typing or by selecting items from a menu. This approach is called a **character-based interface** or **command line interface**. Many users find another arrangement for issuing commands, the graphical user interface, much easier.

The widespread use and success of Microsoft's MS-DOS has encouraged other software companies to introduce similar competing products. The two best known are PC-DOS by IBM and Novell DOS by Novell Incorporated. Although the most recent versions of MS-DOS, PC-DOS, and Novell DOS are very similar, Microsoft's MS-DOS is by far the most widely used.

The long-term future of DOS is clear. It will likely continue to be updated, with newer versions designed to minimise its current disadvantages. However, DOS will eventually be replaced by newer operating systems that take advantage of new technologies.

MICROSOFT WINDOWS

Windows is an operating environment, while Windows 95 and Windows NT are powerful new operating systems.

There are three basic variations of Microsoft Corporation's windowing programs. The first is simply called Windows. The other two are Windows 95 and Windows NT.

Windows

Unlike Windows 95 and Windows NT, **Windows** is not an operating system. It is a program that runs with DOS (see Figure 4.6). Windows extends the capabilities of DOS by creating an easy-to-use **operating environment**. Other companies make similar programs: Desqview by Quarterdeck Office Systems and NewWave by Hewlett-Packard Company.

Windows is designed to run on IBM and compatible micro-computers with particular kinds of microprocessors. They are the Intel 80486 ('486') chip, and Pentium chip.

Advantages

Windows extends the capabilities of DOS to include the following:

Multitasking When DOS is combined with Windows, a number of applications ('multiple tasks') can share the same microprocessor. With multitasking you could be running a word processing program and a database management program at the same time. While printing a report using the word processing program, the other program could search a database for more information. Windows does this by switching back and forth between the two applications.

Graphical user interface Windows (and other windowing programs available for DOS) offers a graphical user interface (GUI). A graphical user interface allows the user to move a mouse (or use keyboard commands) to move a pointer or cursor on the screen. The user positions the pointer on graphic symbols called **icons** or on pull-down menus and then clicks (presses a button on) the mouse. For example, to specify printer commands using Windows, the user can simply click on the printer icon.

Number of applications Although more programs have been written for DOS, there are thousands of programs written for Windows.

Figure 4.6 Windows 3.1 running with DOS

More memory As mentioned before, DOS by itself has limited access to memory, thereby severely limiting software and hardware capabilities. Windows, however, has a **memory manager** that allows access well beyond 640 kilobytes. Windows can access billions of characters of memory.

Sharing data between applications Windows can share data from one application with other applications. For example, you may have created a cost report using a word processing program. The report contains a table based on a spreadsheet analysis of various items. If the two applications were linked, a change in the spreadsheet's values would automatically be reflected in the word processing document.

Disadvantages
Windows has dramatically improved upon DOS. Of course, Windows has some limitations:

Minimum system configuration Windows requires a more powerful microcomputer to run. To effectively use Windows, the system should have at least a 486 microcomputer. It also requires at least four times as much memory as DOS and a hard disk.

Unrecoverable errors When running the earlier versions of Windows, users sometimes encountered the message 'Unrecoverable application error' on their screen. This means that the application program cannot proceed and the user must restart the program to begin again. Fortunately, these unrecoverable errors are rare with the newer versions of Windows.

Windows 95
Unlike Windows, **Windows 95** does not require DOS to run (see Figure 4.7). It is a new, powerful operating system. Introduced by Microsoft in 1995, Windows 95 is considered by many to be the future

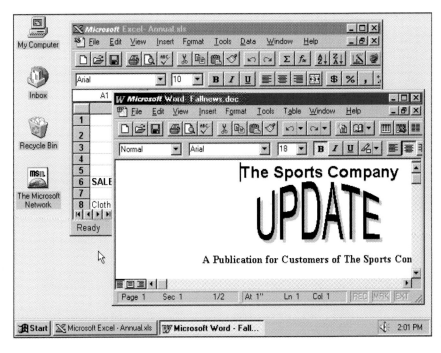

Figure 4.7 Windows 95

replacement for Windows and for DOS. It is an advanced operating system designed for today's very powerful microcomputers.

Advantages

Windows 95 has some major advantages compared with Windows. These include the following:

Multiprocessing Multiprocessing is similar to multitasking except that the applications are run independently and at the same time. For instance, you could be printing a word processing document and using a database management program at the same time. With multitasking, the speed at which the document is printed is affected by the demands of the database management program. With multiprocessing, the demands of the database management program do not affect the printing of the document.

Flexibility Windows 95 does not require DOS and is able to run with a much wider variety of powerful computers and microprocessors.

Internet access As we will discuss in the Internet Guide, to connect to the Internet through an online service, your microcomputer must have TCP/IP and Internet utilities. Both are built into Windows 95. To gain access using Windows 95, all you have to do is click the appropriate icon (see Figure 4.7).

Easy upgrades Installation of new hardware such as a modem can be very complex and difficult. A new standard called Plug and Play (to be discussed in detail in Chapter 5) promises to greatly simplify the installation process. Windows 95 is the first operating system for DOS-based computers to fully support Plug and Play.

Disadvantages

Compared with Windows, Windows 95 has one major disadvantage:

Minimum system configuration Like Windows, Windows 95 requires at least a 486 microprocessor and a hard-disk drive to operate effectively. Windows 95, however, requires more hard disk space—nearly five times as much. Additionally, Windows 95 requires much more memory—three to four times as much.

Fewer applications Compared with DOS and Windows, fewer applications have been written specifically for Windows 95. It can, however, run most DOS and Windows applications.

Windows NT

Windows NT is a very sophisticated and powerful operating system (see Figure 4.8). It is not considered a replacement for either Windows or Windows 95. Rather, it is an advanced alternative designed for very powerful microcomputers and networks.

Advantages

Windows NT has some major advantages when compared with Windows 95. These advantages include:

Figure 4.8 Windows NT

Multiuser Windows NT allows more than one person, or multiusers, to use the same computer at the same time. At one time, multiuser systems were considered to have a very significant cost advantage. Now, as hardware costs have come down, this advantage for microcomputers is not nearly as significant.

Networking In many business environments, workers often use computers to communicate with one another and to share software using a network. This is made possible and controlled by special system software. Windows NT has network capabilities and security checks built into the operating system. This makes network installation and use relatively easy.

Flexibility Windows NT does not require DOS and is able to run with a much wider variety of powerful computers and microprocessors.

Disadvantages
Windows NT has some disadvantages when it is compared with Windows 95.

Minimum system configuration Like Windows 95, the system should have at least the power of a 486 microprocessor. However, Windows NT requires more memory and more than twice the hard disk space as Windows 95.

Fewer applications Like Windows 95, fewer applications have been written specifically for it than for either DOS or Windows.

Upgrade support Windows NT does not provide the same level of support for Plug and Play as Windows 95. Therefore, upgrading or installation of new hardware under Windows NT can be much more difficult.

OS/2

OS/2 was originally developed jointly by IBM and Microsoft.

OS/2 stands for Operating System/2 (see Figure 4.9). It was originally developed jointly by IBM and Microsoft (who have since gone their separate ways). The most recent version is OS/2 Warp.

Advantages
Like Windows 95 and Windows NT, OS/2 Warp is designed for very powerful microcomputers and has several advanced features. Some of its advantages include these:

Minimum system configuration OS/2 Warp requires nearly the same system configuration as Windows 95. Compared with Windows NT, however, OS/2 requires only one-third the memory and about nearly half the hard disk space.

Multiprocessing Like Windows NT, OS/2 Warp supports multi-processing. Windows 95 does not support multiprocessing.

Disadvantages
OS/2 Warp has some disadvantages compared with Windows 95 and Windows NT:

Networking Compared with Windows NT, neither OS/2 Warp nor Windows 95 have the same level of network and security capabilities.

Upgrade support Like Windows NT, OS/2 Warp does not provide the same level of support for Plug and Play as does Windows 95. Therefore, upgrading or installation of new hardware can be much more difficult.

Figure 4.9 OS/2 Warp

MACINTOSH OPERATING SYSTEM

Macintosh operating system, which runs only on Macintosh computers, offers a high-quality graphical user interface and is very easy to use.

What can you do with OS/2 Warp or Microsoft Windows that you can't already do with an Apple Macintosh computer? That's what many people are asking. If it's a graphical user interface or Plug and Play capabilities you want, that's been available for some time with the Mac. In the opinion of many industry observers, OS/2 Warp and Microsoft Windows look very similar to the Macintosh operating system. To appreciate the differences, let us look at how the Macintosh works.

The **Macintosh operating system** is contained in two primary files—the System file and the Finder. These two files work together to perform the standard operating system procedures. These procedures include tasks such as formatting disks, copying files, erasing files, and running application programs. These files also manage the user interface, displaying menus and activating tasks that are chosen from the menus by the user.

Remember that the advantages and disadvantages of microcomputer operating systems are associated with the microprocessors for which they were originally designed. DOS, Microsoft Windows, and OS/2 were designed for microprocessor chips built by Intel, most recently the 486 and Pentium chips. Macintoshes, on the other hand, are built around Motorola's 68040 and PowerPC microprocessors. These Motorola chips cannot run DOS application programs, and the Intel chips cannot run Macintosh application programs. In the beginning, Apple found its Macintoshes hard to sell to corporations because nearly all business application programs—such as Lotus 1-2-3—were written to run on DOS-based machines.

Apple has introduced numerous versions of its operating system. A recent version is the Macintosh **System 7.5** designed for Apple computers using Motorola's PowerPC microprocessor. This operating system is a significant milestone for Apple. It is a very powerful operating system like Windows NT and OS/2. System 7.5 has network capabilities and can read DOS, Windows, and OS/2 files.

Advantages
The Apple Macintosh popularised the graphical user interface, including the use of windows, pull-down menus, and the mouse (see Figure 4.10). The graphical user interface has several advantages:

Ease of use The graphical user interface has made the Macintosh popular with many newcomers to computing. This is because it is easy to learn. In fact, studies show that user training costs are *half* as much for Macintoshes as for DOS-based computers.

Quality graphics Macintosh has established a high standard for graphics processing. This is a principal reason why the Macintosh is popular for desktop publishing. Users are easily able to merge pictorial and text materials to produce professional-looking newsletters, advertisements, and the like.

Consistent interfaces Macintosh applications have a consistent graphics interface. Across all applications, the user is provided with similar screen displays, menus, and operations.

Figure 4.10 The Macintosh
graphical user interface

Multitasking Like the Microsoft Windows programs and OS/2, the
Macintosh System 7.5 enables you to do multitasking. That is, several
programs can run at the same time.

Easy upgrades Like Windows 95, the Macintosh System 7.5 supports
Plug and Play. As mentioned earlier, Macintosh was the first operating
system to support this concept.

Disadvantages
Many characteristics that were previously considered disadvantages
may no longer prove to be so. Nevertheless, let us consider what these
disadvantages are:

A 'business' machine? Apple has had to struggle against the corporate
perception that its products are not for 'serious business users'.
Corporate buyers have had a history of purchasing from IBM and other
vendors of large computers. Many have viewed Apple from the
beginning as a producer of microcomputers for students, game players,
and hobbyists. This is changing fast.

Multiprocessing Unlike Windows NT and OS/2 Warp, Macintosh
System 7.5 does not support multiprocessing.

Compatibility difficulties The incompatibility of DOS with Macintosh
microprocessors made Macintoshes less attractive to corporate users
interested in compatibility and connectivity. However, hardware and
software are now available for the Mac to allow it to run DOS,
Windows, and OS/2 applications. In addition, communications
networks connect Macintoshes to other computers that use DOS.
Apple has co-operated with Digital Equipment Corporation (DEC) and
others to produce communications links between Macintoshes, IBM
PCs, and mainframe computers.

UNIX

Unix can run on many different computers (is 'portable'), can perform multitasking, can be shared by several users at once, and can network reliably.

Unix has been around for some time. It was originally developed by AT&T for minicomputers and is very good for multitasking. It is also good for networking between computers. It has been, and continues to be, popular on very powerful microcomputers called workstations (see Figure 4.11).

Unix initially became popular in industry because for many years AT&T licensed the system to universities for a nominal fee. This led to Unix being carried by recent computer science and engineering graduates to their new places of employment.

One important consequence of its scientific and technical orientation is that Unix has remained popular with engineers and technical people. It is less well known among businesspeople. All that, however, is changing. The reason: with the arrival of very powerful microcomputers, Unix is becoming a larger player in the microcomputer world.

Let us consider the advantages and disadvantages of Unix.

Advantages

Unix has the advantage of being a portable operating system. That means that it is used with ('is portable to') different types of computer systems. It is used with microcomputers, minicomputers, mainframes, and supercomputers. The other operating systems are designed for microcomputers and are not nearly as portable. Having said this, however, we must hastily state that there are *different versions* of Unix, as we will describe. Let us first consider the advantages:

Multitasking Unix enables you to do multitasking. It allows you to run several programs at the same time, each one sharing the CPU.

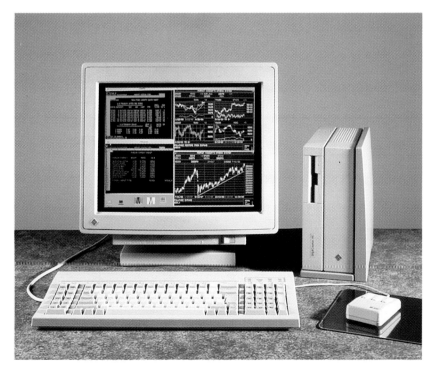

Figure 4.11 Unix workstation: Sun IPX

Multiprocessing Unix, like Windows NT and OS/2 Warp, is able to run several programs independently and at the same time.

Networking Unix is able to share files over electronic networks with several different kinds of equipment. Although the other operating systems can also do this, Unix systems have been successfully and reliably sharing across networks for years.

Disadvantages

Unix was a minicomputer operating system used by programmers and computer science professionals some time before the rise of the microcomputer. This means it has certain qualities that make it useful to programmers—lots of supporting utility programs and documentation, for instance. However, some of its features make it difficult for end users. Let us consider the disadvantages:

Limited business application software This is a great barrier at the moment. There are many engineering application programs. Unfortunately, there are fewer business application programs. Businesses that are dependent on off-the-shelf programs for microcomputers will find offerings very limited.

No Unix standard This may be *the* biggest stumbling block. There is no Unix standard. This means that an application written for one version of Unix may not run on other versions. The principal microcomputer versions are AT&T's Unix System V, IBM's AIX, Novell's UnixWare 2, and the University of California/Berkeley's 4.2 Unix. An organisation called the X/Open Co. is trying to create a standard. This organisation is a consortium of major computer suppliers led by DEC, Hewlett-Packard, Novell, and SunSoft.

More difficult to learn Unix is a very powerful and complex operating system. Its commands are frequently long and complex. Because of this, many microcomputer users find Unix difficult to learn and use.

Unix is a popular operating system for researchers and educators. Some observers think it could yet become a leader among microcomputer operating systems.

The principal advantages and disadvantages of the present microcomputer operating systems are summarised in Figure 4.12.

A LOOK AT THE FUTURE

The popularity of DOS is declining while Windows is increasing in popularity. Many new operating systems will use object-oriented programming.

We continually read that this or that operating system is going to overturn DOS as the most widely used microcomputer operating system. However, DOS remains strong and, when coupled with Windows, it will likely remain strong through the next few years. Although opinions vary, most expect DOS used alone to decline in the next few years and Windows to increase. Following that, most expect DOS and Windows to give way to other operating systems.

COMPARISONS OF OPERATING SYSTEMS

Operating System	Advantages	Disadvantages
DOS	Many existing users, applications, and microcomputers; easy to use:	Limited primary storage; single tasking only; character-based interface
Windows	Multitasking; graphical user interface; many applications; more memory; share data between applications	System requirements; occasional unrecoverable errors
Windows 95	Multitasking; graphical user interface; more memory; share data between applications; flexibility; Internet access; easy upgrades	System requirements; few applications
Windows NT	Multitasking; graphical user interface; more memory; share data between applications; multiprocessing; multiuser; networking capabilities; flexibility	System requirements, few applications; upgrade support
OS/2 Warp	Multitasking; graphical user interface; more memory; share data between applications; system requirements; flexibility; multiprocessing;	Few applications; networking capabilities, upgrade support
Macintosh	Ease of use; quality graphics; graphical user interface; multitasking; communication among programs	Market perception; compatibility
Unix	Multitasking; multiprocessing; multiuser; networking capabilities	Limited business applications; no standard version; difficult to learn

Figure 4.12 Advantages and disadvantages of present microcomputer operating systems

In the near future, DOS, Windows, and Macintosh will probably continue to serve many people. These include students, people with microcomputers at home, and owners of small businesses. Windows, Windows 95, and OS/2 Warp will first be used in larger businesses, higher education, and local government. Eventually, they will replace DOS and Windows.

One thing is certain for the future of operating systems. Newer, more powerful, and easier-to-use versions will keep evolving. These new systems will be created with *object-oriented programming*. It involves creating the operating system with a series of interchangeable software objects or modules. This differs from the way DOS and other popular operating systems are constructed. They use layer after layer of lines of computer code instead. Using object-oriented programming, new operating systems can be developed faster and more efficiently.

Microsoft Corporation is developing a major new version of Windows, code-named 'Chicago'. This operating system is expected to have a user interface to match Windows 95, an advanced Internet connection, and powerful network security capabilities. Apple, IBM, and Hewlett-Packard are working on a joint project called Taligent.

This project is expected to provide the foundation for IBM's next major revision of OS/2, called Workplace. Taligent is also the foundation for Apple's next generation of operating systems, code-named 'Copland' (likely to be called System 8) and 'Gershwin'. These operating systems may already have been released by the time you read this. Another Microsoft Corporation project, code-named 'Cairo', is under development to upgrade the high-end Windows NT operating system.

REVIEW QUESTIONS

True/false

1. One computer can only run one kind of system software.

2. Virtual memory increases the amount of memory available to run application programs.

3. Mainframe and minicomputer systems tend to focus on multiple users of a single computer system.

4. Macintosh computers are designed to use the 486 microprocessor.

5. One of Unix's primary strengths is the large number of applications written for it.

Multiple choice

1. The collection of programs that helps the computer manage its resources is called:
   (a) bootstrap loader
   (b) applications
   (c) operating system
   (d) diagnostic routines
   (e) backup

2. An operating environment:
   (a) Windows
   (b) Windows NT
   (c) OS/2
   (d) Macintosh
   (e) Unix

3. The ability to have a number of applications running at the same time is called:
   (a) GUI
   (b) integrated
   (c) windowing software
   (d) multitasking
   (e) networking

4. An operating system developed jointly by IBM and Microsoft Corporation is:
   (a) Unix
   (b) OS/2
   (c) Windows NT
   (d) Desqview
   (e) Macintosh

5. Designed to run the System 7.5 operating system:
   (a) Unix
   (b) OS/2
   (c) Windows
   (d) Desqview
   (e) Macintosh

Fill in the blank

1. _____ the system means that the computer has been turned on and the operating system has been loaded into memory.

2. Of all the microcomputer operating systems, _____ is able to run on the least expensive hardware.

3. Windows NT is an operating _____ .

4. The System file and the Finder are the two primary files in the _____ operating system.

5. The lack of a standard version for _____ is likely its most significant disadvantage.

Open ended

1. What, in a phrase, is the difference between application software and system software?

2. What are utility programs?

3. What is meant by multitasking?

4. What is a graphical user interface?

5. What is meant by the term multiuser?

DISCUSSION QUESTIONS

1. *Apple versus IBM—you be the judge* Suppose you're working for a small, family-run company that is in need of 10 new microcomputers. The computers must all be the same. They will all be hooked together in an electronic network so that information and programs can be shared. No more computers will be purchased for another three to four years. The head of the business has put you in charge of researching this project. You need to buy either Apple Macintoshes, which run the Macintosh operating system, or IBM-compatibles, which run DOS, Windows, Windows NT, or OS/2. Which operating system would you choose, and why?

2. *An operating system for everybody?* Readers always have the advantage over writers because the words they read exist in the present, not in the uncertain future. As we write this, we don't know how Microsoft's 'Cairo', the IBM–Apple Corporation Taligent experiment, Apple's 'Copland' (likely to be called System 8), or 'Gershwin' will turn out. To find out more about them, go to the library and do some research in various computer magazines, business magazines, and newspapers.

CASE STUDY

THE TYPING POOL

A medium-sized business has a typing pool that consists of seven staff: a manager and six typists.

The typists are responsible for generating all typed material necessary for the operation of the business. This consists of producing memoranda, letters, reports, etc. Each typist has an electric typewriter with 2K of memory. The memory has two functions: it allows the typewriter to erase any errors that have occurred within the last twenty keystrokes and it permits the typist to store a short letter or memo.

The manager is responsible for:

• ensuring that each typist has appropriate and sufficient work;

• ensuring that each typewriter is in good working order and arranging for repair when necessary;

• remaining aware of current typewriter models and authorising purchase of these when it is deemed that the new models would help the typing pool to increase its productivity;

• arranging for training in the use of the typewriters for any new staff or for all staff when the typewriters are upgraded to a new model.

The manager of the typing pool has never used a computer and hence has been hesitant to upgrade to word processors. Pressure from his staff, combined with advice from higher management, has forced him to consider purchasing computers equipped with word processing software in the immediate future. By reading some current computer magazines and visiting several local shops, he has narrowed his decision down to either:

• Macintosh systems together with System 7.5 and Microsoft Word word processing software; or

• IBM-compatible systems together with the Microsoft Windows operating environment and Microsoft Word for Windows word processing software.

Although the manager believes either of these systems would satisfy his requirements, he feels inadequately qualified to make the final decision. He has therefore allocated part of his budget to employing a computer consultant to provide further advice, and to assist with the preparation of detailed specifications of the final purchase, for the managing director's approval.

QUESTIONS

1. What advantages does a computer equipped with word processing software have over a memory typewriter?

2. With particular reference to the manager's four main responsibilities, explain how his job would change once his typists began using word processors.

3. For the IBM-compatible computers, why do you think the manager:

   (a) selected the Windows environment rather than choosing a purely DOS-based word processing system;

   (b) chose Windows in preference to OS/2;

   (c) didn't consider the Unix operating system?

4. Imagine you are the computer consultant advising the manager of the typing pool regarding the type of hardware he should recommend for purchase. Compare and contrast the Macintosh and IBM-compatible systems (both hardware and software), commenting on the relative advantages and disadvantages of each.

5. As the computer consultant, what would be your final recommendation to the manager of the typing pool? Support your answer with valid reasons.

6. The manager used magazines, shops and a consultant to help him with his decision. What other sources of information could he have used?

The processing unit

CHAPTER 5

COMPETENCIES

After you have read this chapter, you should be able to:

- explain the two main parts of the central processing unit—the control unit and the arithmetic-logic unit;

- understand the workings and the functions of memory;

- describe how a computer uses binary codes to represent data in electrical form;

- describe the components of the system unit in a microcomputer.

FROM THE USER'S POINT OF VIEW

How is the data in 'data processing' actually *processed*? That is the subject of this chapter. Why do you need to know anything about it? The answer lies in three words: *speed, capacity* and *flexibility*. After reading this chapter, you will be able to judge how fast, powerful, and versatile a particular microcomputer is. As you might expect, this knowledge is valuable if you are planning to buy a new microcomputer system. (The Buyer's Guide at the end of this book provides additional buying information.) It will also help you to evaluate whether or not an existing microcomputer system is powerful enough for today's new and exciting applications.

Some time you may get the chance to watch when a technician opens up a microcomputer to fix it. You will see that it is basically a collection of electronic circuitry. There is no need for you to understand how all these components work. However, it is important to understand the principles. Once you do, you will then be able to determine how powerful a particular microcomputer is. This will help you judge whether it can run particular kinds of programs and can meet your needs as a user.

THE CPU

The central processing unit has two components—the control unit and the arithmetic-logic unit.

The part of the computer that runs the program (executes program instructions) is known as the **processor** or *central processing unit (CPU)*. In a microcomputer, the CPU is on a single electronic component, the **microprocessor chip**, within the *system unit* or *system cabinet*. The system unit also includes circuit boards, memory chips, ports, and other components. A microcomputer's system cabinet may also house disk drives, but these are considered separate from the CPU (see Figure 5.1).

Figure 5.1 Inside a microcomputer system unit

In Chapter 1 we said the system unit consists of electronic circuitry with two main parts, the processor (the CPU) and memory. Let us refine this further by stating that the CPU itself has two parts: the control unit and the arithmetic-logic unit. In a microcomputer, these are both on the microprocessor chip.

The control unit

The **control unit** tells the rest of the computer system how to carry out a program's instructions. It directs the movement of electronic signals between memory—which temporarily holds data, instructions, and processed information—and the arithmetic-logic unit. It also directs these control signals between the CPU and input and output devices.

The arithmetic-logic unit

The **arithmetic-logic unit**, usually called the **ALU**, performs two types of operations—arithmetic and logical. *Arithmetic* operations are, as you might expect, the fundamental maths operations: addition, subtraction, multiplication, and division. *Logical* operations consist of comparisons. That is, two pieces of data are compared to see whether one is equal to (=), less than (<), or greater than (>) the other.

MEMORY

Memory temporarily holds data, program instructions and information.

Memory—also known as **RAM, primary storage, internal storage** or **main memory**—is the part of the microcomputer that holds:

• data for processing;

- instructions for processing the data—that is, the *program*;

- information—that is, processed data—waiting to be output or sent to secondary storage such as a floppy disk in a disk drive.

One of the most important facts to know about memory is that part of its content is held only temporarily. In other words, it is stored only as long as the microcomputer is turned on. When you turn the machine off, the contents immediately vanish. We have said this before, but it bears repeating: the stored contents in memory are volatile and can vanish very quickly, as during a power failure, for example. It is therefore a good practice to repeatedly save your work in progress to a secondary storage medium such as a floppy disk or hard disk. For instance, if you are writing a report on a word processor, every 5 to 10 minutes you should stop and save your work. Some word processors and other application software have the ability to automatically save every few minutes.

The next important fact to know about memory is that its capacity varies in different computers. The original IBM Personal Computer, for example, could hold up to approximately 640 000 characters of data or instructions. By contrast, the IBM ValuePoint can hold 128 *million* characters, or over 24 times as much. If you are using an older computer with small memory, it may not be able to run such powerful programs as Excel. Thus, you need to look at the software package before you buy and see how much memory it requires.

Registers

Computers also have several additional storage locations called **registers.** These appear in the control unit and ALU and make processing more efficient. Registers are special high-speed staging areas that hold data and instructions temporarily during processing. They are parts of the control unit and ALU rather than memory. Their contents can therefore be handled much faster than the contents of memory can.

The processing cycle

To locate the characters of data or instructions in main memory, the computer stores them at locations known as **addresses**. Each address is designated by a unique number. Addresses may be compared to post office mailboxes. Their numbers stay the same, but the contents continually change.

Our illustration gives an example of how memory and the CPU work to process information (see Figure 5.2). Note that the various components of the CPU are linked by special electrical connections. In this example, the program will multiply two numbers—20 $\times$ 30— yielding 600. Let us assume the program to multiply these two numbers has been loaded into memory. The program asks the user to enter two values (20 and 30). It then multiplies the two values together (20 $\times$ 30). Finally, it prints out the result (600) on a printer. Our illustration describes the process just after the program has been loaded into memory. Follow the steps in the figure to walk yourself through the diagram.

Note: This figure simplifies the actual processing activity in order to demonstrate the essential operations of the CPU. For instance, there are actually many more memory addresses—thousands or millions—

① The control unit recognises that the entire program has been loaded into memory. It begins to execute the first step in the program.

② The program tells the user, ENTER FIRST NUMBER.

③ The user types the number *20* on the keyboard. An electronic signal is sent to the CPU.

④ The control unit recognises this signal and routes the signal to an address in memory—address 7.

⑤ After completing the above program instruction, the next program instruction tells the user, ENTER SECOND NUMBER.

⑥ The user types the number *30* on the keyboard. An electronic signal is sent to the CPU.

⑦ The control unit recognises this signal and routes it to memory address 8.

⑧ The next program instruction is executed: MULTIPLY FIRST AND SECOND NUMBERS.

⑨ To execute this instruction, the control unit informs the arithmetic-logic unit (ALU) that two numbers are coming and that the ALU is to multiply them. The control unit next sends the ALU a copy of the contents of address 7 (*20*) and then sends a copy of the contents of address 8 (*30*).

⑩ The ALU performs the multiplication: *20 x 30 = 600*.

⑪ The control unit sends a copy of the multiplied results (*600*) back to memory, to address 9.

⑫ The next program instruction is executed: PRINT THE RESULT.

⑬ To execute this instruction, the control unit sends the contents of address 9 (*600*) to the printer.

⑭ The printer prints the value *600*.

⑮ The final instruction is executed: END. The program is complete.

than are shown here. Moreover, the addresses are in a form the computer can interpret—electronic signals rather than the numbers and letters shown here.

Figure 5.2 How the CPU and memory work

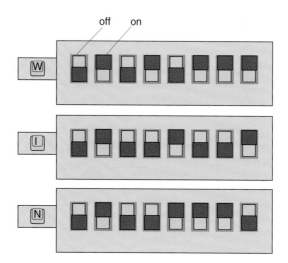

Figure 5.3 How the letters W-I-N are represented in on/ off, 0/1 binary code (ASCII)

THE BINARY SYSTEM

Data and instructions are represented electronically with a binary, or two-state, numbering system. The three principal binary coding schemes are ASCII, EBCDIC, and Unicode.

We have described the storage and processing of data in terms of *characters*. How, in fact, are these characters represented inside the computer?

We said that when you open up the system cabinet of a microcomputer, you see mainly electronic circuitry. And what is the most fundamental statement you can make about electricity? It is simply this: it can be either *on* or *off*.

Indeed, there are many forms of technology that can make use of this two-state on/off, yes/no, present/absent arrangement. For instance, a light switch may be on or off, or an electric circuit open or closed. A magnetised spot on a tape or disk may have a positive charge or a negative charge. This is the reason, then, that the binary system is used to represent data and instructions.

The decimal system that we are all familiar with has 10 digits (0, 1, 2, 3, 4, 5, 6, 7, 8, 9). The **binary system**, however, consists of only two digits—0 and 1. In the computer, the 0 can be represented by electricity being off, and the 1 by electricity being on. Everything that goes into a computer is converted into these binary numbers (see Figure 5.3). For example, the letter *W* corresponds to the electronic signal 0 1 0 1 0 1 1 1.

Units of measure for capacity

Each 0 or 1 in the binary system is called a **bit**—short for *bi*nary digi*t*. In order to represent numbers, letters, and special characters, bits are combined into groups of eight bits called **bytes**. Each byte typically represents one character—in many computers, one addressable storage location. The capacity of main memory, then, is expressed in numbers of bytes. There are four commonly used units of measurement to describe memory capacity (see Figure 5.4).

MEMORY CAPACITY	
Unit	**Capacity**
Kilobyte	one thousand bytes
Megabyte	one million bytes
Gigabyte	one billion bytes
Terabyte	one trillion bytes

Figure 5.4 Memory capacity

- One **kilobyte**—abbreviated **K, Kb,** or **K-byte**—is equivalent to approximately 1000 bytes. (More precisely, 1 kilobyte is equal to 1024 bytes. However, the figure is commonly rounded to 1000 bytes.) This is a common unit of measure for memory or storage capacity of microcomputers. The older IBM PCs, for example, had a top capacity of 640 K, or about 640 000 characters of data.

- One **megabyte**—**Mb** or **M-byte**—represents 1 million bytes. Thus, a microcomputer system listed with a '16 Mb main memory' has primary storage capacity of about 16 million bytes.

- One **gigabyte**—**Gb** or **G-byte**—represents about 1 thousand million bytes. This is a measure that until recently was used only with larger computers. Now it is also used to describe very powerful microcomputers.

- One **terabyte**—**Tb** or **T-byte**—represents about 1 trillion bytes. This is a measure used with large computers.

Binary coding schemes

Now let us consider an important question. How are characters represented as 0s and 1s ('off' and 'on' electrical states) in the computer? The answer is in the use of *binary coding schemes.*

Two of the most popular binary coding schemes use eight bits to form each byte. These two codes are *ASCII* and *EBCDIC* (see Figure 5.5). A recently developed code, *Unicode,* uses sixteen bits.

ASCII, pronounced '*as*-key', stands for *A*merican *S*tandard *C*ode for *I*nformation *I*nterchange. This is the most widely used binary code for microcomputers.

EBCDIC, pronounced '*eb*-see-dick', stands for *E*xtended *B*inary *C*oded *D*ecimal *I*nterchange *C*ode. It was developed by IBM and is used on many IBM and other kinds of computers. As a result, EBCDIC is almost an industry standard for large computers.

Unicode is a sixteen-bit code designed to support international languages like Chinese and Japanese. These languages have too many characters to be represented by the eight-bit ASCII and EBCDIC codes. It was developed by Unicode, Inc. with support from Apple, IBM, and Microsoft.

When you press a key on the keyboard, a character is automatically converted into a series of electronic pulses. The CPU can recognise these pulses. For example, pressing the letter *W* on a keyboard causes an electronic signal to be sent to the CPU. The CPU then converts it to the ASCII value of 0 1 0 1 0 1 1 1.

Why are coding schemes important? Whenever files are used or shared by different computers or applications, the same coding scheme must be used. Generally, this is not a problem if both computers are microcomputers since both would most likely use ASCII code. And most microcomputer applications store files using this code. However, problems occur when files are shared between microcomputers and larger computers that use EBCDIC code. The files must be translated from one coding scheme to the other before processing can begin. Fortunately, special conversion programs are available to help with this translation.

BINARY CODES

Character	ASCII	EBCDIC
A	0100 0001	1100 0001
B	0100 0010	1100 0010
C	0100 0011	1100 0011
D	0100 0100	1100 0100
E	0100 0101	1100 0101
F	0100 0110	1100 0110
G	0100 0111	1100 0111
H	0100 1000	1100 1000
I	0100 1001	1100 1001
J	0100 1010	1101 0001
K	0100 1011	1101 0010
L	0100 1100	1101 0011
M	0100 1101	1101 0100
N	0100 1110	1101 0101
O	0100 1111	1101 0110
P	0101 0000	1101 0111
Q	0101 0001	1101 1000
R	0101 0010	1101 1001
S	0101 0011	1110 0010
T	0101 0100	1110 0011
U	0101 0101	1110 0100
V	0101 0110	1110 0101
W	0101 0111	1110 0110
X	0101 1000	1110 0111
Y	0101 1001	1110 1000
Z	0101 1010	1110 1001
0	0011 0000	1111 0000
1	0011 0001	1111 0001
2	0011 0010	1111 0010
3	0011 0011	1111 0011
4	0011 0100	1111 0100
5	0011 0101	1111 0101
6	0011 0110	1111 0110
7	0011 0111	1111 0111
8	0011 1000	1111 1000
9	0011 1001	1111 1001

Figure 5.5 ASCII and EBCDIC binary coding schemes for representing data

The parity bit

As you know, there is often static on the radio. Similarly, there can be 'static', or electronic interference, in a circuit or communications line transmitting a byte. When you are typing the letter *W*, for example, the *W* should be represented in the CPU (in ASCII) as

$$0\ 1\ 0\ 1\ 0\ 1\ 1\ 1$$

However, if the last 1 is garbled and becomes a 0, the byte will be read as 0 1 0 1 0 1 1 0—*V* instead of *W*. Is there a way, then, for the CPU to detect whether it is receiving erroneous data?

Indeed there is. Detection is accomplished by using a **parity bit**—an extra bit automatically added to a byte for purposes of testing accuracy. There are even-parity systems and odd-parity systems. In a computer using an even-parity system, the parity bit is set to either 0 or 1 so that the number of 1s is even (see Figure 5.6). For instance, when the letter *W* is pressed on the keyboard, the signal 0 1 0 1 0 1 1 1 is emitted. Before the signal is sent to the CPU, the number of 1s is counted—in this case, 5. A parity bit is added to the front and set to 1, thereby making the number of 1s even. The signal 1 0 1 0 1 0 1 1 1 is sent. When the signal is received by the CPU, the number of 1s is checked again. If it is odd, it means an error has occurred. This is called a *parity error*. When a parity error occurs, the CPU requests that the signal be sent again. If the parity error occurs again, the message 'parity error' might appear on your display. (Odd-parity systems act just the reverse of even-parity systems.)

Of course, the system does not guarantee accuracy. For example, if *two* erroneous 0s were introduced in the byte for *W*, the computer would accept the byte as correct. This is because the two erroneous 0s would add up to an even 4 bits.

We have explained the principles by which a computer stores and processes data. We can now open up the system unit and take a look at some of the parts.

THE SYSTEM UNIT

It's important to understand what's inside the system unit, so that you can talk intelligently to computer specialists.

Figure 5.6 How parity bits check for transmission errors

As mentioned, the part of the microcomputer that contains the CPU is called the *system unit*. The system unit is housed within the system cabinet. If you take off the cabinet, you will find that many parts can be easily removed for replacement. Almost all computers are modular. That is, entire sections can be replaced, as one would the parts of a car. In addition, microcomputers are *expandable*. That is, more memory may be added, as well as certain other devices.

Let us consider the following components of the system unit:

- system board
- microprocessor chips
- memory chips—RAM and ROM
- system clock
- expansion slots and boards
- bus lines
- ports

System board

The **system board** is also called the **motherboard** (see Figure 5.7). It consists of a flat board that usually contains the CPU and some memory *chips*. A **chip** consists of a tiny circuit board etched on a small square of sandlike material called silicon. A chip is also called a **silicon chip, semiconductor**, or **integrated circuit**. Chips are mounted on carrier packages, which then plug into sockets on the system board. In addition, system boards usually contain expansion slots, as we describe in another few paragraphs.

Microprocessor chips

In a microcomputer, the CPU is contained on a single silicon chip called the *microprocessor*—'microscopic processor'. Different microprocessors have different capabilities (see Figure 5.8).

Some chips or 'families' of chips have become famous as the basis for several important lines of microcomputers. However, they are

Figure 5.7 A microcomputer system board

port

bus line

expansion slot

memory chips

microprocessor chip

system board

MICROPROCESSORS

Microprocessor	Typical Applications	Users
Intel 80486	DOS, Windows, basic tools, personal information management	Single user, office staff, home user, home office user
Pentium	Windows 95, OS/2 Warp, groupware, desktop publishing, project management	All of the above, networked users, workgroups
P6	Windows NT, Unix, multimedia, artificial intelligence, network communications, large database applications	All of the above, specialists
Motorola 68040	Macintosh operating system, basic tools, personal information management, desktop publishing	Single user, home user, home office user
PowerPC	Unix, groupware, project management, artificial intelligence, network communications, large database applications	All of the above, networked users, workgroups, specialists

Figure 5.8 Typical microprocessor applications and users

known by distinctly undramatic names: their names are just their product numbers.

Chip capacities are often expressed in word sizes. A **word** is the number of bits (such as 16, 32, or 64) that can be accessed at one time by the CPU. The more bits in a word, the more powerful—and the faster—the computer. A 32-bit-word computer can access 4 bytes at a time. A 64-bit-word computer can access 8 bytes at a time. Therefore, the 64-bit computer is faster.

Microcomputers process data and instructions in millionths of a second, or **microseconds**. Supercomputers by contrast, operate at speeds measured in nanoseconds and even picoseconds—1 thousand to 1 million times as fast as microcomputers (see Figure 5.9).

As we mentioned, the growing power of microprocessor chips is what is changing everything about microcomputers. Motorola's Power PC chip, for example, is the basis for Apple's Power PCMacintosh 710 (see Figure 5.10). This machine can scroll through documents the length of *War and Peace* up to four times faster than Apple's previously most powerful machine, the Quadra 800. Intel's P6 chip is twice as powerful as its predecessor, the Pentium chip.

There are two types of microprocessors:

CISC chips The most common type of microprocessor is CISC ('complex instruction set computer'). This design was popularised by Intel and is the basis for their line of microprocessors. It is the most widely used chip design and has thousands of programs written specifically for it. Intel's Pentium is a recent CISC chip.

RISC chips RISC ('reduced instruction set computer') chips use fewer instructions. The design is becoming more widely used. This design is simpler, faster, and less costly than CISC chips. A recent Motorola chip developed with IBM and Apple is the Power PC chip. Two other

PROCESSING SPEEDS

Unit	Speed
Millisecond	thousandth of a second
Microsecond	millionth of a second
Nanosecond	billionth of a second
Picosecond	trillionth of a second

Figure 5.9 Processing speeds

Figure 5.10 The Power Macintosh 710, which uses a Power PC microprocessor

recent RISC chips are Digital Equipment Corporation's (DEC) Alpha chip and MIPS' R4400 chip. These chips are used in many of today's most powerful microcomputers (see Figure 5.11).

The major advantage of the CISC chip is that it can run a large number of existing application programs. However, this advantage is offset somewhat by special programs called emulation programs. Emulation programs allow RISC chips to run CISC application programs. Unfortunately, the RISC advantage in speed is lost when the emulation programs are used. Another approach taken by two competitors to Intel's Pentium chip is to produce 'RISC-like' chips. These chips are based on the CISC design but incorporate some of the techniques used in RISC chips. They can run applications designed

Figure 5.11 This IBM RISC System/6000 is one of several IBM workstations using the fast RISC chip

for CISC chips with speeds comparable to RISC chips. Two such chips are AMD's K5 and Cyrix's M1 chips.

Some specialised processor chips are available. One example is the tiny built-in microprocessor used in **smart cards**. Smart cards are about the size of a credit card. They can be used to hold health insurance information, frequent flier records, or driver licence information, to name a few. While this technology has been around for some time, it has received more attention lately. In the United States, President Clinton has suggested a National Health Security smart card for all individuals. This card would be used for a number of applications, including monitoring federal financial assistance programs.

Memory chips

There are two well-known types of memory chips. One type is called *RAM*. The other type is *ROM*. **RAM (random-access memory)** chips hold the program and data that the CPU is presently processing. That is, it is *temporary* or volatile storage. (Secondary storage, which we shall describe in Chapter 7, is permanent storage, such as the data stored on diskettes. Data from this kind of storage must be loaded into RAM before it can be used.)

RAM is called temporary because as soon as the microcomputer is turned off, everything in RAM is lost. It is also lost if there is a power failure that disrupts the electric current going to the microcomputer. For this reason, as we mentioned earlier, it is a good idea to save your work in progress. That is, if you are working on a document or a spreadsheet, every few minutes you should save, or store, the material.

In addition, when programs or data are written, or encoded, to RAM, the previous contents of RAM are lost. This is called the *destructive write process*. However, when programs and data are read, or retrieved, from RAM, their contents are not destroyed. Rather, the read process simply makes a copy of those contents. Consequently, this activity is called the *non-destructive read process*.

RAM storage is frequently expressed in megabytes. Thus, a microcomputer with 16 Mb RAM has memory that will hold about 16 million characters of data and programs.

Knowing the amount of RAM is important! Some software programs may require more memory capacity than a particular microcomputer offers. For instance, Lotus 1-2-3 for Windows requires 2 Mb of RAM. Additional RAM is needed to hold any data. However, many microcomputers—particularly older ones—may not have enough memory to hold the program, much less work with it.

Microcomputer memory in RAM is of four types (see Figure 5.12). These types are mentioned in the instruction manuals you use to install system software like DOS or application software like Lotus 1-2-3.

Conventional memory **Conventional memory** consists of the first 640 K of RAM. It is the area used by DOS and application programs.

Upper memory **Upper memory** is located between 640 K and 1 Mb of RAM. DOS uses this area to store information about the microcomputer's hardware. However, it is frequently underused and can be used by application programs.

Extended memory **Extended memory** is available on most microprocessors. It includes directly accessible memory above 1 Mb. Some

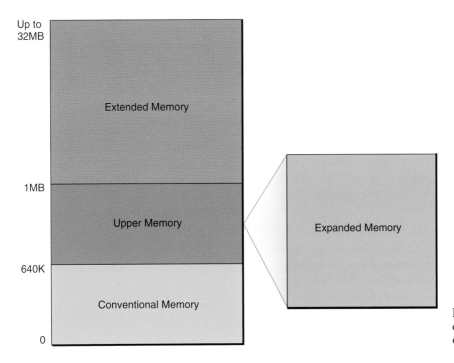

Up to
32MB

Extended Memory

1MB

Upper Memory

640K

Conventional Memory

0

Expanded Memory

Figure 5.12 Types of RAM:
conventional, upper, extended,
expanded

programs can use extended memory (for example, Windows), and
some cannot.

Expanded memory **Expanded memory** is intended to help older
microprocessors that cannot directly access memory over 1 Mb.
Expanded memory is a special 'island' of memory of up to 32 Mb that
exists outside of the DOS 640 K limit. That is, it temporarily uses a
portion of the reserved memory area between 640 K and 1 Mb and
switches it with information from the island.

Another term you are apt to hear about in conjunction with RAM is
cache memory. Cache (pronounced 'cash') memory is an area of
RAM set aside to store the most frequently accessed information
stored in RAM. The cache acts as a temporary high-speed holding area
between the memory and the CPU. In a computer with a cache (not
all machines have one), the computer detects which information in
RAM is most frequently used. It then copies that information into the
cache, so that the CPU can access that information more quickly than
usual.

ROM (read-only memory) chips have programs built into them at
the factory. Unlike RAM chips, the contents of ROM chips cannot be
changed by the user. 'Read only' means that the CPU can read, or
retrieve, the programs written on the ROM chip. However, the
computer cannot write—encode or change—the information or
instructions in ROM.

ROM chips typically contain special instructions for detailed
computer operations. For example, ROM instructions may start the
computer, give keyboard keys their special control capabilities, and put
characters on the screen. ROMs are also called **firmware**.

Two important variations on the ROM chip are the following:

PROM (programmable read-only memory) This means that a software
manufacturer can write instructions onto the chip using special
equipment. However, once it is written, it cannot be changed.

EPROM (erasable programmable read-only memory) This is a PROM chip that can be erased with a special ultraviolet light. New instructions can then be written on it. (There are also some electrically erasable chips—EEPROM.)

System clock

The **system clock** controls the speed of operations within a computer. This speed is expressed in **megahertz** (abbreviated **MHz**). One megahertz equals 1 million cycles (beats) per second. The faster the clock speed, the faster the computer can process information. In computer ads, you may see that microcomputers built with Intel's Pentium chip typically have a 90 MHz or 100 MHz speed.

Expansion slots and boards

Computers are known for having different kinds of 'architectures'. Machines that have **closed architecture** are manufactured in such a way that users cannot easily add new devices. Most microcomputers have **open architecture**. They allow users to expand their systems by inserting optional devices known as **expansion boards**. Expansion boards are also called **plug-in boards, controller cards, adapter cards**, or **interface cards**.

The expansion boards plug into slots inside the system unit. Ports on the boards allow cables to be connected from the expansion boards to devices outside the system unit. Among the kinds of expansion boards available are the following:

Memory expansion boards These circuit boards consist of several additional RAM chips, which increase the capacity of the computer's memory. Early microcomputer users found that additional memory was their first requirement for handling newer, more sophisticated programs, such as integrated software. Memory can be added by using plug-in boards, which gives you expanded memory. Memory can also be added by inserting RAM chips directly onto the system board, which gives you extended memory (see Figure 5.13).

Network adapter cards These cards are used to connect a computer to one or more other computers. This forms a communication network whereby users can share data, programs, and hardware. The network

Figure 5.13 A microcomputer expansion board

adapter card plugs into a slot inside the system unit. The adapter card typically connects the system unit to a cable that connects to the other devices on the network.

Small computer system interface (SCSI—pronounced 'scuzzy') card Most computers have only a limited number of expansion slots. A **SCSI card** uses only one slot and can connect as many as seven devices to the system unit. These cards are used to connect such devices as printers, hard-disk drives, and CD-ROM drives to the system unit.

Figure 5.14 A PCMCIA card

PC cards To meet the size and constraints of portable computers, credit card-sized expansion boards have been developed. These cards can be easily inserted and replaced from the outside of a portable computer. They are called **PC cards** or **PCMCIA (Personal Computer Memory Card International Association) cards** (see Figure 5.14). These cards can be used for a variety of purposes, including increasing memory and connecting to other computers.

A wide variety of other expansion boards exist. Some of the most widely used are the following. Video adapter cards are used to adapt a variety of colour video display monitors to a computer. CD-ROM cards connect optical disc drives (which we discuss in Chapter 7), and sound boards can record and play back digital sound.

To access the capabilities of an expansion board, the board must be inserted into a slot in the system unit and the system reconfigured to recognise the new board. This reconfiguration can require setting special switches on the expansion board and creating special configuration files. This can be a complex and difficult task. A recent development known as **Plug and Play** promises to eliminate this task.

Plug and Play is a set of hardware and software standards recently developed by Intel, Microsoft, and others. It is an effort by hardware and software vendors to create operating systems, processing units, and expansion boards, as well as other devices, that are able to configure themselves. All you have to do is insert the board and turn on the computer. As the computer starts up, it will search for these Plug and Play devices and automatically configure the devices and the computer system.

Plug and Play is an evolving capability. Only a few completely Plug and Play-ready systems exist today. However, observers predict that within the next few years this will become a widely adopted standard, and adding expansion boards will be a simple task.

Bus lines
A **bus line**—or simply **bus**—connects the parts of the CPU to each other. It also links the CPU with other important hardware. Examples are RAM and ROM chips and ports connecting with outside devices. A bus is a data roadway along which bits travel. Such data pathways resemble a multilane highway. The more lanes there are, the faster traffic can go through. Similarly, the greater the capacity of a bus, the more powerful and faster the operation. A 64-bit bus has greater capacity than a 32-bit bus, for example.

Why should you even have to care about what a bus line is? The answer is that, as microprocessor chips have changed, so have bus lines. Many devices, such as expansion boards, will only work with one type of bus line.

The four principal bus lines (or 'architectures') are the following:

Industry Standard Architecture (ISA) This bus was developed for the IBM Personal Computer. First it was an 8-bit-wide data path, then (when the IBM AT was introduced) it was 16 bits wide. The older microprocessors and add-on expansion boards were able to satisfactorily move data along this 16-bit roadway. But then along came the 386 chip—which requires data paths that are 32 bits wide. And suddenly there was a competition between two 32-bit standards.

Micro Channel Architecture (MCA) IBM decided to support the 386 chip with a 32-bit bus line that was entirely new. You cannot simply remove your expansion boards from an older computer and put them into a new IBM computer with Micro Channel. It simply won't work. If you are not concerned about transferring boards, IBM's new standard is not a problem. You can take full advantage of the faster processor. Recently, a 64-bit MCA bus was introduced.

Extended Industry Standard Architecture (EISA) This 32-bit bus standard was proposed in September 1988 by nine manufacturers of IBM-compatibles, led by Compaq Computer Corporation. The purpose of EISA is to extend and amend the old ISA standard, so that all existing expansion boards can work with the new architecture. Like MCA, EISA has introduced a 64-bit bus.

Peripheral Component Interconnect (PCI) The most recently developed category of buses is called **local buses**. These buses were originally developed to meet the tremendous video demands of today's graphical user interfaces. PCI is the most widely used local bus. (**VESA local bus [VL-bus]** is another widely used local bus.) PCI is a high speed 64-bit bus that is nearly ten times faster than either MCA or EISA buses. Now, PCI buses are widely used to connect the CPU, memory, and expansion boards. Many observers predict that PCI will replace MCA and EISA buses in the future.

Ports

A **port** is a connecting socket on the outside of the system unit. This allows you to plug in a variety of devices, such as keyboards, mouse devices, video displays, modems, and printers. Ports may be parallel or serial (see Figure 5.15):

- Parallel ports are used to connect external devices that need to send or receive a lot of data over a short distance. These ports typically send eight bits of data simultaneously across eight parallel wires. Parallel ports are mostly used to connect printers to the system unit.

- Serial ports are used for a wide variety of purposes. They are used to connect a mouse, keyboard, modem, and many other devices to the system unit. Serial ports send data one bit at a time and are very good for sending information over a long distance.

Ports are used to connect input and output devices to the system unit. We usually refer to all hardware outside the system unit—but not necessarily outside the system *cabinet*—as **peripheral devices**. In

Figure 5.15 The ports in the back of a microcomputer

many microcomputers, disk drives are built into the system cabinet. In some laptop computers, the keyboard and monitor are also an integral part of the system cabinet.

For a summary of system unit components, see Figure 5.16.

A LOOK AT THE FUTURE

Four new technologies could make computing faster: RISC, superconducting, optical computing, and neural networking. The result will be 'downsizing applications'.

We have already mentioned RISC (reduced instruction set computer) microprocessors. Some observers think the RISC chip will triple performance every one and a half to two years. Memory chips are also increasing in capacity. A new technology developed by Rambus Inc. promises RAM chips with ten times the speed of today's chips.

Another technological improvement may come in the form of the materials used for microprocessors. At present, microprocessor chips are made out of silicon. Such chips are called *semiconductors* because electricity flows through the material with some resistance. *Superconducting* material, in contrast, conducts electricity without resistance. Until recently, superconduction was considered impractical because the materials had to be at extremely low, subzero temperatures. However, research is now being done on 'warm' superconductors. These offer the promise of faster on-and-off processing to give us lightning-quick computers.

A third area being explored is that known as *optical computing*. This technology features a machine consisting of lasers, lenses, and mirrors. An optical computing machine uses pulses of light rather than currents of electricity to represent the on-and-off codes of data. Light is much faster than electricity.

A fourth area, *neural networks*, is not a different kind of technology so much as a new arrangement using existing technology. Present computers—even supercomputers—are relatively slow because of a built-in structural limitation: the processor and the memory are physically separated. Although joined by a communications link, the processor spends a long time waiting for data coming from or going to memory. (The arrangement is known as the *von Neumann architecture*, after its originator, John von Neumann.) A neural network, however, consists of layers of processors interconnected somewhat like the neurons of biological nervous systems. One such computer developed by TRW has 250 000 processors and 5.5 million connections. As a result, data is transmitted to and from a processor at many times the speed of the old arrangements.

With these kinds of developments, it's clear that we are on the road to 'downsizing applications'. That is, computers will get not only smaller, as we are seeing with the newer portables, but also more powerful. Indeed, it's easy to believe—as some industry observers suggest—that by the year 2000 desktop computers will be as powerful as the first supercomputer.

SYSTEM UNIT	
Component	**Function**
System board	Holds the various other system components
Microprocessor	Contains the CPU on a single chip
Memory	Holds programs and instructions
System clock	Controls the speed of computer operations
Expansion slots and boards	Increases memory and other system capabilities
Bus lines	Connects various internal system components
Ports	Connects outside devices to system unit

Figure 5.16 Components of the system unit

REVIEW QUESTIONS

True/false

1. In a microcomputer, the CPU is located on a single clip called the microprocessor.

2. A grouping of eight bytes is called a bit.

3. Another name for the system board is the processor board.

4. CISC chips use fewer instructions than RISC chips.

5. A SCSI card can be used to connect several different devices to the system unit.

Multiple choice

1. The ALU performs arithmetic operations and:
   (a) stores data
   (b) logical operations
   (c) binary calculations
   (d) reduced instruction calculations
   (e) parity checks

2. The binary code that is widely used with microcomputers is:
   (a) ASCII
   (b) EBCDIC
   (c) BCD
   (d) DEC/MVS
   (e) Unicode

3. The number of bits that can be processed at one time is a:
   (a) register
   (b) cycle
   (c) byte
   (d) word
   (e) PROM

4. Two types of memory chips are RAM and:
   (a) RISC
   (b) main
   (c) MCA
   (d) CD-ROM
   (e) ROM

5. The local bus that is predicted to replace the other types in the future is called:
   (a) EISA
   (b) ISA
   (c) PCI
   (d) MCA
   (e) PCMCIA

Fill in the blank

1. Data and instructions are stored in memory at locations known as _____ .

2. A _____ bit is an extra bit that is added to a byte to help detect errors.

3. _____ memory is directly accessible above 1 Mb.

4. The system clock controls the _____ of operations within a computer.

5. _____ and _____ is a set of standards designed to assist in the reconfiguration of computer systems.

DISCUSSION QUESTIONS AND PROJECTS

1. *An inexpensive microcomputer system* The prices of microcomputer systems have been decreasing for some time. You can buy them from computer stores, mail-order companies, and oftentimes from your school bookstore. Look through your local newspaper or through a computer magazine to locate three low-priced systems. Read each advertisement, make a list of all the computer terms used, and write down their definitions. Prepare a table comparing the three systems. Some factors to include in your table are: price, memory capacity, storage capacity, processor type, display type, expansion capability, and software included. If you were to purchase one of these systems, which one would you select, and why?

2. *Buying from mail-order companies* A lot of microcomputer users purchase hardware (and software) from mail-order companies, such as those advertising in computer magazines. The primary reason is cost. Prices may be considerably discounted from those found at a local computer store. However, you can always do some bargaining with the store by asking how close it can come to matching the mail-order company's price. Yet mail-order houses may be almost as convenient as a local store. Most offer a technical-support telephone line (often a toll-free number) to help with installation problems.

   An important caution, however: nearly anyone can start a mail-order company. The ones offering the lowest prices are precisely those that may be the most recent entrants to the field and therefore the most unstable. Thus, a company may take your order and accept your cheque or bill your credit card. And they may promise you'll receive the product within a week. And then they may go out of business without delivering, making it hard for you to get your money back. Discuss how you might try to check whether the company you are considering purchasing from is reliable.

3. *The mobile office* The mobile office does not have a fixed location, but like the traditional office has support facilities such as computers, printers, and fax and copy machines. The central piece of equipment is the notebook computer. Many jobs require being on the road away from home one week every month. For those road warriors, the mobile office is essential.

   Many hotels now offer specially equipped hotel rooms and business centres. For example, many Hyatt Hotels have the Hyatt Business Plan that provides guest rooms with microcomputers, modems, and fax machines. Additionally, a 24-hour business centre provides printer, photocopy, and office-supply support.

Suppose you have a job that requires a mobile office. Before making any hotel reservations, you should ensure that essential support facilities are available. Contact a major hotel chain to determine their support for mobile computing. Specifically, find out the following:

(a) Are in-room microcomputers and fax machines available? What are the charges?

(b) Is there a business centre on site? What support is provided? What are the hours? What are the charges?

(c) If a business centre is not available, will the front desk provide basic services such as faxing, copying, and printing? What are the charges?

CASE STUDY

PETER'S COMPUTER   PART 1

Peter has been using computers at his work for several years. Now he is interested in acquiring one for home use. Since electronics has been his hobby for some time, he has decided to build his own computer. He believes the benefits of this approach are:

• he will learn how computers work and be able to repair same if faults occur; and

• purchasing individual components and assembling them himself would be cheaper than buying a complete pre-assembled system.

After reading some current magazines and speaking to several people, Peter has decided that the open architecture of an IBM-compatible computer is the best choice for his purposes.

Peter compared prices from a number of vendors and has purchased the following components:

• 100 MHz 486DX4 motherboard with 8 Mb RAM (expandable to 64 Mb) and 16-bit ISA expansion slots and three VL-bus expansion slots;

• 16-bit I/O card, which contains two serial ports and one parallel port;

• 200 W power supply;

• 101 key keyboard;

• Super VGA colour monitor and VL-bus controller;

• Two-button mouse;

• 540 Mb hard-disk drive and VL-bus controller.

QUESTIONS

1. Peter chose an IBM-compatible system because of its open architecture. Explain the term open architecture and hence his reasons for this decision.

2. With reference to the motherboard, explain the meaning of each of the following:

(a) 100 MHz
(b) 486DX4
(c) 8 Mb RAM
(d) expandable to 64 Mb
(e) expansion slot
(f) ISA
(g) VL-bus

Input
and
output

COMPETENCIES

After you have read this chapter, you should be able to:

- explain the difference between keyboard and direct-entry input devices and the POS terminal;

- describe the features of keyboards and the three types of terminals: dumb, smart, and intelligent terminals;

- describe direct-entry devices used with microcomputers, which include the mouse, touch screen, light pen, digitiser, pen-based computer, image scanner, fax, bar-code reader, MICR, OCR, OMR, and voice-input devices;

- describe monitors (desktop and portable) and monitor standards (CGA, EGA, VGA, Super VGA, and XGA);

- describe printers (dot-matrix, laser, ink-jet, thermal) and plotters (pen, ink-jet, electrostatic, and direct image);

- describe voice-output devices.

FROM THE USER'S POINT OF VIEW

How do you get data to the CPU? How do you get information out? Here we describe the two most important places where the computer interfaces with people. The first half of the chapter covers input devices; the second half covers output devices.

People understand language, which is constructed of letters, numbers, and punctuation marks. However, computers can understand only the binary machine language of 0s and 1s. Input and output devices are essentially *translators*. Input devices translate symbols that people understand into symbols that computers can process. Output devices do the reverse: they translate machine output to output people can comprehend. Let us, then, look at the devices that perform these translations.

INPUT: KEYBOARD VERSUS DIRECT ENTRY

Input devices convert people-readable data into machine-readable form. Input may be keyboard or direct entry.

Input devices take data and programs people can read or understand and convert them to a form the computer can process. This is the machine-readable electronic signals of 0s and 1s that we described in the last chapter. Input devices are of two kinds: keyboard entry and direct entry.

Keyboard entry Data is input to the computer through a *keyboard* that looks like a typewriter keyboard but has additional keys. In this method, the user typically reads from an original document called the **source document**. The user enters that document by typing on the keyboard.

Direct entry Data is made into machine-readable form as it is entered into the computer; no keyboard is used.

Figure 6.1 A point-of-sale terminal

An example of an input device that uses both is a **point-of-sale (POS) terminal**. This is the sort of 'electronic cash register' you see in department stores (see Figure 6.1). When salespeople sell a sweater, for example, they can type in the information (product code, purchase amount, tax) on the keyboard. Or they can use a hand-held **wand reader** or **platform scanner** to read special characters on price tags as direct entry. The wand reflects light on the characters. The reflection is then changed by photoelectric cells to machine-readable code. Whether by keyboard entry or direct entry, the results will appear on the POS terminal's digital display (see Figure 6.1).

KEYBOARD ENTRY

In keyboard entry, people type input. The input usually appears on a monitor.

Probably the most common way in which you will input data, at least at the beginning, is through a keyboard.

Figure 6.2 Traditional keyboard

Figure 6.3 Microsoft's Natural Keyboard (800) 426-9400

Keyboards

Keyboards have different kinds of keys (see Figure 6.2).

Typewriter keys The keys that resemble the regular letters, numbers, and punctuation marks on a typewriter keyboard are called **typewriter keys**. Note the position of the **Enter** key, which is used to enter commands into the computer.

Function keys The keys labelled *F1, F2*, and so on are the **function keys**. These keys are used for tasks that occur frequently (such as underlining in word processing). They save you keystrokes.

Numeric keys The keys 0 to 9, called the **numeric keys** or **numeric keypad**, are used for tasks principally involving numbers. These may be useful when you are working with spreadsheets.

Special-purpose and cursor control keys Examples of **special-purpose keys** are *Esc* (for 'Escape'), *Ctrl* (for 'Control'), *Del* (for 'Delete'), and *Ins* (for 'Insert'). These are used to help enter and edit data and execute commands. The **cursor control keys** or **directional arrow keys** are used to move the cursor.

As we mentioned in Chapter 5, these keys convert letters, numbers, and other characters into electrical signals that are machine readable. These signals are sent to the computer's CPU.

There are two basic keyboard designs. The traditional design or straight design is shown in Figure 6.2. The contour design splits and slopes the keyboard (see Figure 6.3). Many people prefer the contour design because it is more natural and comfortable.

Terminals

A **terminal** is a form of input (and output) device that consists of a keyboard, a monitor, and a communications link. There are three types of terminals:

- A **dumb terminal** can be used to input and receive data, but it cannot process data independently. It is used only to gain access to information from a computer. Such a terminal may be used by an airline reservations clerk to access a mainframe computer for flight information.

- A **smart terminal** has some memory. It allows users to perform some editing or verification of data before it is sent to a large computer. A bank loan officer might do some calculations associated with making a loan on the smart terminal. The loan officer would do this before the information is stored in the bank's mainframe.

- An **intelligent terminal** includes processing unit, memory, and secondary storage such as a magnetic disk. Essentially, an intelligent terminal is a microcomputer with some communications software and a telephone hookup (modem) or other communications link. These connect the terminal to the larger computer.

Nearly all large organisations have terminals connected to their minicomputers and mainframe computers. At one time, all terminals were dedicated input devices. Now, microcomputers with the appropriate software and communications links can operate exactly like any of the dedicated terminals. With microcomputers dropping in price and increasing in power and flexibility, companies have tended to buy these instead of dedicated terminals.

DIRECT ENTRY

Direct entry creates machine-readable data that can go directly to the CPU. Direct entry includes pointing, scanning, and voice-input devices.

Direct entry is a form of input that does not require data to be keyed by someone sitting at a keyboard. Direct-entry devices create machine-readable data on paper or magnetic media, or feed it directly into the computer's CPU. This reduces the possibility of human error being introduced (as often happens when data is being entered through a keyboard). It is also an economical means of data entry.

Direct-entry devices may be categorised into three areas:

- pointing devices
- scanning devices
- voice-input devices

Pointing devices

Pointing, of course, is one of the most natural of all human gestures. There are a number of devices that use this method as a form of direct-entry input, as follows.

Mouse There are three basic **mouse** types. For one type the mouse has a ball on the bottom and is attached with a cord to the system unit (see Figure 6.4). When rolled on the tabletop, the mouse controls the cursor or pointer. The second type does not require a flat surface. The cursor is controlled by rotating a ball with your thumb. This type of mouse is often called a trackball or rollerball (see Figure 6.5). The newest type is a touch-surface. The cursor is controlled by moving and tapping your finger on the surface of a pad (see Figure 6.6). The trackball and touch-surface are common on portable computers and are often built into keyboards.

At one time, the mouse was identified only with Apple micro-computers. However, it is now standard for almost all microcomputers. Many people like the mouse because it reduces the need to input commands through a keyboard.

Touch screen A **touch screen** is a particular kind of monitor screen covered with a plastic layer. Behind this layer are crisscrossed invisible beams of infrared light. This arrangement enables someone to select

Figure 6.4 Microsoft mouse

Figure 6.5 Trackball: Macintosh Notebook

Figure 6.6 Touch-surface: Epson Action Note 880

Figure 6.7 A touch screen: an industrial application

Figure 6.8 A light pen: a hospital application

Figure 6.9 A digitiser: an industrial design application

actions or commands by touching the screen with a finger (see Figure 6.7). Touch screens are easy to use, especially when people need information quickly. You may see touch screens at bank automatic teller machines (ATMs) and at visitor information centres in airports and hotels. However, they also have military and industrial applications. More recently, they are being used with microcomputers in applications that formerly used a mouse.

Light pen A **light pen** is a light-sensitive penlike device (see Figure 6.8). The light pen is placed against the monitor. This closes a photoelectric circuit and identifies the spot for entering or modifying data. Light pens are used by engineers, for example, in designing anything from microprocessor chips to aeroplane parts.

Digitiser A **digitiser** is a device that can be used to trace or copy a drawing or photograph. The shape is converted to digital data. A computer can then represent the data on the screen or print it out on paper. A **digitising tablet** enables you to create your own images using a special stylus (see Figure 6.9). The images are then converted to digital data that can be processed by the computer. Digitisers are often used by designers and architects.

Pen-based computing A **pen-based computer** is a small (about 1¾–2 kilograms) computer. It lets you write directly on the display screen with a stylus (see Figure 6.10). The system is less a triumph of hardware than of software. What is revolutionary is that these devices contain software that can recognise a person's handwriting. The handwriting can be stored as it was scrawled—not too difficult a task. More difficult is the task of converting a person's distinctive cursive writing—is that a 'c' or an 'e' or an 'o'?—into typescript. Some pen-based computers do this.

Scanning devices
Direct-entry scanning devices record images of text, drawings, or special symbols. The images are converted to digital data that can be processed by a computer or displayed on a monitor. Scanning devices include the following:

Image scanner An **image scanner** identifies images on a page (see Figure 6.11). It automatically converts them to electronic signals that can be stored in a computer. The process identifies pictures or different typefaces by scanning each image with light and breaking it into dots. The dots are then converted into digital code for storage. Image scanners are becoming widely used input devices. They are commonly used in desktop publishing to scan graphic images that can then be placed in a page of text.

Fax machines **Facsimile transmission machines**, commonly called **fax machines**, have become popular office machines because they can transfer documents at electronic speeds (see Figure 6.12). Fax machines scan the image of a document to be sent. The light and dark areas of the image are converted into a format that can be sent electronically over telephone lines. The receiving fax machine converts the signals back to an image and recreates it on paper. The machine uses a process much like those used by office photocopiers. Fax machines are useful to anyone who needs to send images rather than text. Examples are engineering drawings, legal documents with signatures, and sales promotional materials.

Many people use **dedicated fax machines**. These are specialised devices that do nothing else except send and receive documents from one place to another. Indeed, these are found not only in offices and print shops but even alongside phone booths in hotel lobbies and airports.

Figure 6.10 A pen-based computer: recording inventory

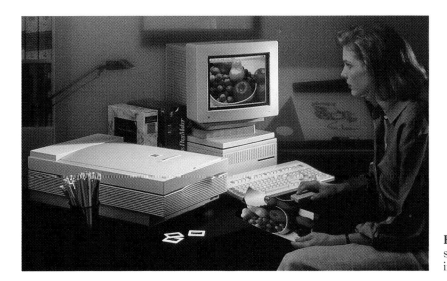

Figure 6.11 An image scanner: reproducing colour images

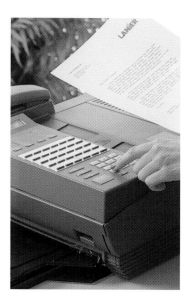

Figure 6.12 A fax machine: sending documents electronically

Many people use their microcomputers to send and receive fax. One way is to install a **fax board** into their system unit. Most users, however, install a **fax/modem board** that provides the independent capabilities of a fax and a modem.

Bar-code readers You are probably familiar with **bar-code readers** from grocery stores (see Figure 6.13). Bar-code readers are photoelectric scanners that read the **bar codes**, or vertical zebra-striped marks, printed on product containers. Supermarkets use a bar-code system called the Universal Product Code (UPC). The bar code identifies the product to the supermarket's computer, which has a description and the latest price for the product. The computer automatically tells the POS terminal what the price is. And it prints the price and the product name on the customer's receipt.

Character and mark recognition devices There are three kinds of scanning devices—formerly used only with mainframes—now found in connection with the more powerful microcomputers:

- **Magnetic-ink character recognition (MICR)** is a direct-entry method used in banks. This technology is used to automatically read those futuristic-looking numbers on the bottom of cheques. A special-purpose machine known as a **reader/sorter** reads characters made of ink containing magnetised particles.

- **Optical-character recognition (OCR)** uses special preprinted characters, such as those printed on utility and telephone bills. They can be read by a light source and changed into machine-readable code. A common OCR device is the hand-held *wand reader* (see Figure 6.14). These are used in department stores to read retail price tags by reflecting light on the printed characters.

- **Optical-mark recognition (OMR)** is also called **mark sensing**. An OMR device senses the presence or absence of a mark, such as a pencil mark. OMR is often used to score multiple-choice tests such as the General Achievement Test.

Voice-input devices
Voice-input devices convert a person's speech into a digital code (see Figure 6.15). These input devices, when combined with the appropriate software, form **voice recognition systems**. These systems enable users to operate microcomputers and to create documents using voice commands.

Some of these systems must be 'trained' to the particular user's voice. This is done by matching his or her spoken words to patterns previously stored in the computer. More advanced systems that can recognise the same word spoken by many different people have been developed. However, until recently the list of words has been limited. A newly developed voice recognition system, the Dragon Dictate, identifies over 30 000 words and adapts to individual voices. There are even systems that will translate from one language to another, such as from English to Japanese.

There are two types of voice recognition systems:

Continuous speech A **continuous speech recognition system** is used to control a microcomputer's operations and to issue commands to

Figure 6.13 A bar-code reader: recording product codes

special application programs. For example, rather than using the keyboard to save a spreadsheet file, the user could simply say 'save the file'. Two popular systems are Apple Computer's PlainTalk and IBM's Continuous Speech Series.

Discrete-word A common activity in business is preparing memos and other written documents. **Discrete-word recognition systems** allow users to dictate directly into a microcomputer using a microphone. The microcomputer stores the memo in a word processing file where it can be revised later or directly printed out. Two such systems are available from Kurzweil Applied Intelligence Inc. and IBM's Voice Type Dictation.

Figure 6.14 A wand reader: recording product codes

OUTPUT: MONITORS, PRINTERS, PLOTTERS, VOICE

Output devices convert machine-readable information into people-readable form.

Data input to and then processed by the computer remains in machine-readable form until output devices make it people-readable.

The output devices we shall describe for microcomputers are monitors, printers, plotters, and voice-output.

MONITORS

Monitor standards indicate screen quality. Some monitors are used on the desktop, others are portable.

The most frequently used output device is the monitor, also known as the **display screen, video display, video display terminal** and **VDT**. Two important characteristics of monitors are the number of colours that can be displayed and the clarity of images produced. Images are represented on monitors by individual dots or 'picture elements' called **pixels**. A pixel is the smallest unit on the screen that can be turned on and off or made different shades. The *density* of the dots—that is, the number of rows and columns of dots—determines the images' clarity, the resolution.

Figure 6.15 A voice-input device: dictating a letter

COLOUR MONITORS

Monitor Type	Pixels	Colours
CGA	320 × 200	4
EGA	640 × 350	16
VGA	640 × 480	16
	320 × 200	256
Super VGA	800 × 600	256
	1024 × 768	256
XGA	1024 × 768	65 536

Figure 6.16 Monitor standards

Standards

To indicate a monitor's colour and resolution capabilities, several standards have been created. The three most common are VGA, Super VGA and XGA (see Figure 6.16):

- **VGA** stands for *V*ideo *G*raphics *A*rray. You can display 16 colours at a resolution of 640 by 480. Or, you can display 16 times as many colours—256 colours—with a resolution of 320 by 200. VGA has been a widely used monitor standard for general use.

- **Super VGA** or **SVGA** stands for *S*uper *V*ideo *G*raphics *A*rray. SVGA has a higher resolution capability. It has a minimum of 800 by 600 resolution. Some higher-priced models have a 1600 by 1200 resolution. It is the most common standard today. SVGA is widely used in many applications, including industrial design, which requires precise measurements taken directly from the screen.

- **XGA** stands for *E*xtended *G*raphic *A*rray and has a resolution of up to 1024 by 768 pixels. It can display more than 18 million colours. XGA may become the next widely accepted standard. It is used primarily by experts in engineering design and in graphic arts.

Desktop monitors

The most common type of monitor for the office and the home is the **desktop monitor** (see Figure 6.17). These monitors are typically placed directly on the system unit or on the top of the desk. Also called **cathode-ray tubes** or **CRTs**, these monitors are similar in size to technology televisions.

An important characteristic of desktop monitors is how the cathode-ray tube creates images on the screen. **Interlaced monitors** create images by scanning down the screen skipping every other line. This technology can cause flickering and may lead to eye strain. **Non-interlaced monitors** avoid these problems by scanning each line.

Portable monitors

Because CRTs are too bulky to be transported, portable monitors were developed (see Figure 6.18). This type of monitor is also known as a

Figure 6.17 A desktop monitor: SVGA display

flat-panel monitor or **liquid crystal display (LCD)**. Unlike the technology used in CRTs, portable monitors use liquid crystals.

There are two basic types of portable monitors: *passive-matrix* and *active-matrix*. **Passive-matrix monitors** create images by scanning the entire screen. This type requires very little power, but the clarity of the images is not as sharp. **Active-matrix monitors** do not scan down the screen; instead, each pixel is independently activated. More colours with better clarity can be displayed. Active-matrix monitors are more expensive and require more power.

An exciting new development is the merger of microcomputers and television called **PC/TV**. This is becoming possible through the establishment of all-digital **high-definition television (HDTV)**. HDTV delivers a much clearer and more detailed wide-screen picture. Additionally, because the output is digital, it enables users to readily freeze video sequences to create still images. These images can then be digitised and output as artwork or stored on laser disks. This technology will likely be very useful to graphic artists, publishers, and educators.

Figure 6.18 A portable monitor: active matrix panel

In the United States, cable operators like Time Warner Cable have recently introduced **ITV**, also known as **interactive TV**, to select markets. ITV provides viewers with videos on demand, video games, interactive shopping, and a dazzling array of entertainment and informational services. ITV uses normal telephone lines to transmit information, a terminal or microcomputer connected to the television to interpret information, and a supercomputer at a centralised site to co-ordinate the entire system. ITV promises to revolutionise the TV world.

PRINTERS

Four kinds of printers used with microcomputer systems are dot-matrix, ink-jet, laser, and thermal.

The images output on a monitor are often referred to as **soft copy**. Information output on paper—whether by a printer or by a plotter—is called **hard copy**.

Four popular kinds of printers used with microcomputers are dot-matrix, ink-jet, laser, and thermal (see Figure 6.19).

Dot-matrix printer

Dot-matrix printers can produce a page of text in less than 10 seconds and are highly reliable. These inexpensive printers were once the most widely used microcomputer printers. In general, they are used for tasks where a high-quality image is not essential. Thus, they are often used for documents that are circulated within an organisation rather than shown to clients and the public. However, some dot-matrix printers print colour and *are* used for advertising and promotional purposes.

The dot-matrix printer forms characters or images using a series of small pins on a print head (see Figure 6.20). The pins strike an inked ribbon and create dots that form an image on paper. Printers are available with print heads of 9, 18, or 24 pins. The pins print a character in a manner resembling the way individual lights spell out a number on a basketball scoreboard. One disadvantage of this type of printer is noise.

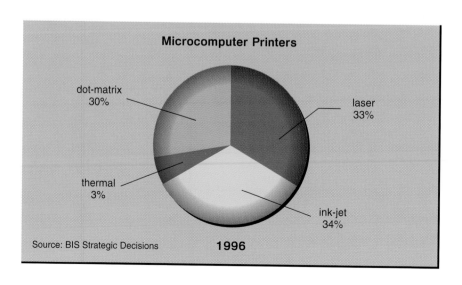

Figure 6.19 Microcomputer printers in 1996

Ink-jet printer

An **ink-jet printer** sprays small droplets of ink at high speed onto the surface of the paper. This process not only produces a letter-quality image but also permits printing to be done in a variety of colours (see Figure 6.21). Ink-jet printers have recently become the most widely used printer. They are reliable, quiet, and inexpensive. Ink-jet printers are used wherever colour and appearance are important, as in advertising and public relations.

Laser printer

The **laser printer** creates dot-like images (like a dot-matrix printer) on a drum, using a laser beam light source (see Figure 6.22). The characters are treated with a magnetically charged ink-like toner and

Figure 6.20 A dot-matrix printer: Epson ActionPrinter 5000+

Figure 6.21 An ink-jet printer: Hewlett-Packard PaintJet XL300

Figure 6.22 A laser printer: Hewlett-Packard LaserJet

then are transferred from drum to paper. A heat process is used to make the characters adhere. This technology is similar to that of a photocopying machine.

The laser printer produces images with excellent letter and graphics quality. It is widely used in applications requiring high-quality output. This has made possible the whole new industry of desktop publishing. As we've mentioned earlier, desktop publishing software enables people to merge text and graphics. The publications produced have a polish that rivals the work of some professional typesetters and graphic artists.

There are two categories of laser printers. **Personal laser printers** are inexpensive and widely used by single users to produce black-and-white documents. They typically can print 4 to 6 pages a minute. **Shared laser printers** are more expensive and are used (shared) by a group of users to produce black-and-white documents. Some can produce colour output. Shared laser printers typically print over 30 pages a minute.

Thermal printer

A **thermal printer** uses heat elements to produce images on heat-sensitive paper. Originally these printers were used in scientific labs to record data. More recently, colour thermal printers have been widely used to produce very high-quality colour artwork and text (see Figure 6.23).

Colour thermal printers are not as popular because of their cost and the requirement of specifically treated paper. They are a more special

Figure 6.23 A thermal printer: Tektronix's Phaser 200i

use printer that produces near-photographic output. They are widely used in professional art and design work where very high quality colour is essential.

Some of the important characteristics of the four most widely used microcomputer printers are summarised in the table in Figure 6.24.

Other printers

There are several other types of printers. Two are the daisy-wheel printer and the chain printer. Daisy-wheel printers produce very high quality, professional-looking correspondence. However, they are slower and less reliable than dot-matrix, ink-jet, and laser printers. Their sales have declined dramatically in the past few years.

You probably won't find a chain printer standing alone on a desk next to a microcomputer. This is because a chain printer is an expensive, high-speed machine originally designed to serve minicomputers and mainframes. However, you may see one in organisations that link several microcomputers together by a communications network.

PRINTERS

Printer	Characteristics	Typical use
Dot-matrix	Reliable, inexpensive; forms text and graphics by dots; some colour printing	In-house communications
Ink-jet	High colour quality; sprays drops of ink on paper	Internal and external communications advertising pieces
Laser	Very high quality; forms text and graphics by dots, using photocopying process	Desktop publishing, external documents
Thermal	Very high quality; uses heat elements on special paper	Art and design work

Figure 6.24 Four types of printers

Printer features

Some general qualities to note about microcomputer printers are as follows:

Friction and tractor feed In a typewriter the paper is gripped by the roller (platen). Some printers use this method. It is called friction feed. In other microcomputer printers the paper is held in place by a **tractor feed** mechanism. This reduces the chance of the paper getting out of alignment. The tractor feed has sprockets that advance the paper, using holes on the edges of continuous-form paper.

Type styles Some printers allow you to change type styles by changing the printing element. Others require you to do something with the software. Still others do not allow a change in type style.

Shared use Ink-jet, laser, and chain printers can be quite expensive. Thus, in organisations they are often found linked to several microcomputers through a communications network. Dot-matrix printers are quite often used to serve individual microcomputers.

Portability Some people (travellers, for instance) require not only a portable computer but also a portable printer. Rugged printers are available that are battery-powered and weigh less than 3 kilograms. These printers typically are either dot-matrix or ink-jet. Such printers are recharged using a special connection that can be plugged into an AC outlet. Some can even be recharged through a car's cigarette lighter.

PLOTTERS

Plotters are special-purpose drawing devices.

Plotters are special-purpose output devices for producing bar charts, maps, architectural drawings, and even three-dimensional illustrations. Plotters can produce high-quality multicolour documents and also documents that are larger in size than most printers can handle.

Plotters are of four types: pen, ink-jet, electrostatic, and direct imaging.

Pen plotter

Pen plotters (see Figure 6.25) create plots by moving a pen or pencil over drafting paper. (For some pen plotters, the paper moves and the pen remains stationary.) These plotters are the least expensive and easiest to maintain. Their major limitations are speed and inability to produce solid fills and shading. They have been the most popular type of plotter.

Ink-jet plotter

Ink-jet plotters create line drawings and solid-colour output by spraying droplets of ink onto paper. Their best features are their speed, high-quality output, and quiet operation. The major disadvantage of ink-jet plotters is that the spray jets can become clogged and require more maintenance. They are used by a wide variety of workers, including engineers and automotive designers.

Figure 6.25 A pen plotter

Electrostatic plotter

Whereas pen plotters use pens, **electrostatic plotters** use electrostatic charges to create images made up of tiny dots on specially treated paper (see Figure 6.26). The image is produced when the paper is run through a developer. Electrostatic plotters produce high-resolution images and are much faster than either pen or ink-jet plotters. These plotters, unfortunately, use expensive chemicals that are considered hazardous. Electrostatic plotters are used for applications that require high-volume and high-quality outputs such as in advertising and graphic arts design.

Direct-imaging plotter

Direct-imaging plotters or thermal plotters create images using heat-sensitive paper and electrically heated pins. This type of plotter is comparably priced with electrostatic plotters, quite reliable, and good for high-volume work. However, direct-imaging plotters require expensive paper and typically create only two-colour output. These plotters are typically used for very specific applications such as creating maps.

Figure 6.26 An electrostatic plotter

VOICE-OUTPUT DEVICES

Voice-output devices vocalise prerecorded sounds.

Voice-output devices make sounds that resemble human speech but actually are prerecorded vocalised sounds. With one Macintosh program, the computer speaks the synthesised words 'We'll be right back' if you type in certain letters and numbers. (The characters are *Wiyl biy ray5t bae5k*—the numbers elongate the sounds.) Voice output is not anywhere near as difficult to create as voice input. In fact, there are many occasions when you will hear synthesised speech being used. Examples are found in soft-drink machines, on the telephone, and in cars.

For multimedia applications, the output device is typically a set of stereo speakers or headphones. These devices are connected to a sound card in the system unit (see Figure 6.27). The sound card is used to capture as well as play back recorded sounds.

Voice output is used as a reinforcement tool for learning, such as to help students study a foreign language. It is used in many supermarkets at the checkout counter to confirm purchases. Of course, one of the most powerful capabilities is to assist the physically challenged.

A LOOK AT THE FUTURE

Input and output devices are starting to look like us. Separate devices are being combined, and computers may be controlled by just looking at them.

We can expect some startling developments in input and output in the near future. The major trend is toward *natural* microcomputers or what some call *human-centred* technology. This is an extension or evolution of current devices. It integrates speech and handwriting recognition

Figure 6.27 Stereo speakers: Bose Mediamate computer speakers

and other human-like and natural input and output devices. For example, IBM is developing a *conversational surrogate*, or an animated face, for the computer screen. You provide input by talking directly to the animated face that appears on your display screen. The animated face talks back to you, providing information and assistance.

Another trend is to combine individual input and output devices into a single unit. Sometimes called the *information appliance*, this 'everything-but-the-kitchen-sink' approach is being used by QMS, Inc. QMS, Inc. has developed an all-in-one document-management system. This system combines a printer, scanner, copier, fax machine, and other capabilities into a single device. Rather than purchasing, installing, and maintaining each of these machines, you just have to keep track of one.

Even further down the road, you may be able to control a computer by blinking an eye or twitching a muscle. You may even be able to control a computer by just thinking about it. Using our bodies as an input device is called *biosignal processing*. BioControl Systems has developed a system that connects electrodes to the forehead and cheeks to measure eye movement. The eye movements are then used to control a mouse or robot.

REVIEW QUESTIONS

True/false

1. Input devices translate symbols that people understand into symbols that computers can process.

2. A plotter is a device that can be used to trace or copy a drawing or photograph.

3. Banks use a method called magnetic-ink character recognition (MICR) to automatically read and sort cheques.

4. Laser printers are highly reliable but the quality of their output limits their use to rough drafts and in-house communications.

5. Plotters are special-purpose drawing devices.

Multiple choice

1. Esc, Ctrl, Del, and Ins are _____ keys.
   (a) function
   (b) numeric
   (c) directional arrow
   (d) cursor control
   (e) special-purpose

2. A device that converts images on a page to electronic signals that can be stored in a computer is called a:
   (a) monitor
   (b) scanner
   (c) plotter
   (d) MICR
   (e) POS

3. The type of portable monitor that can display more colours, with better clarity, is called:
   (a) active-matrix
   (b) passive-matrix
   (c) monochrome
   (d) CGA
   (e) VGA

4. The printer that can produce very high quality images using heat elements on heat-sensitive paper is:
   (a) dot-matrix
   (b) laser
   (c) ink-jet
   (d) plotter
   (e) thermal

5. The plotter that creates images using heat-sensitive paper and electrically heated pins is:
   (a) a pen
   (b) ink-jet
   (c) direct imaging
   (d) a scanner
   (e) electrostatic

Fill in the blank

1. Another name for the mouse that has a ball that is controlled with the thumb is _____ .

2. _____ machines are popular office machines because they can transfer documents at electronic speeds.

3. The _____ printer is a reliable, inexpensive printer that forms letters by a series of small pins on a print head.

4. A _____ feed printer has sprockets that advance the paper using holes on the edges.

5. _____ devices make sounds that resemble human speech.

Open ended

1. What are the differences between keyboard entry and direct entry as forms of input?

2. What is a POS terminal? What are two input devices on it that represent the two methods of inputting data?

3. Distinguish among the three kinds of terminals: dumb, smart, intelligent.

4. What are pixels? What do they have to do with screen resolution?

5. What are the differences between personal and shared lasers?

DISCUSSION QUESTIONS AND PROJECTS

1. *Evaluating laser printers* When shopping for an inexpensive personal laser printer, you can't expect to get all of the fancy fonts. Nor can you expect the speedy, sophisticated paper handling more expensive printers offer. At the very least, you'd want crisp, professional-looking output and reasonably fast performance. Evaluate your printer needs in terms of the following criteria:

   (a) output quality

   (b) print speed

   (c) price

   (d) service and support

   (e) design and construction

   (f) font/graphics options

   (g) paper handling

2. *High-definition television (HDTV)* This is a technology that you are certain to become well acquainted with during your lifetime. HDTV is the first major technical change in TV since colour appeared 30 years ago. It produces a sharper and more detailed picture than is available with present TV sets. However, there are presently no world technical standards, and different nations are working on different, and incompatible, systems. Some systems are based on *analog* principles, a technology that is the basis for present television. Others are based on *digital* principles. This approach eliminates image distortions. It also allows television to be integrated with all kinds of other digital technology, such as computerised storage communications.

   Go to the library or other sources to learn more about this evolving technology. Specifically:

   (a) Define HDTV.

   (b) Discuss analog versus digital technology.

   (c) Discuss the potential effect of HDTV, if any, on future computer technology.

CASE STUDY

PETER'S COMPUTER   PART 2

Peter has been using computers at his work for several years. Now he is interested in acquiring one for home use. Since electronics has been his hobby for some time, he has decided to build his own computer. He believes the benefits of this approach are:

• he will learn how computers work and be able to repair same if faults occur; and

• purchasing individual components and assembling them himself would be cheaper than buying a complete pre-assembled system.

After reading some current magazines and speaking to several people, Peter has decided that the open architecture of an IBM-compatible computer is the best choice for his purposes.

Peter compared prices from a number of vendors and has purchased the following components:

• 100 MHz 486DX4 motherboard with 8 Mb RAM (expandable to 64 Mb), and with four 16-bit ISA expansion slots and three VL-bus expansion slots;

• 16-bit I/O card, which contains two serial ports and one parallel port;

• 200 W power supply;

• 101 key keyboard;

• Super VGA colour monitor and VL-bus controller;

• two-button mouse;

• 540 Mb hard-disk drive and VL-bus controller.

QUESTIONS

1. 'Input and output devices are essentially *converters*.' In general terms, explain what this means.

2. Although the keyboard will be Peter's primary form of input, he has also purchased a mouse. Why is a mouse often preferred to a keyboard?

3. Describe the capabilities of Peter's Super VGA colour monitor.

4. Peter has not yet decided on the type of printer he will purchase. He will choose between the following types: dot-matrix, ink-jet and laser. Compare and contrast the characteristics of these three types of printers.

Secondary storage

COMPETENCIES

After you have read this chapter, you should be able to:

- contrast direct access and sequential access storage;

- describe how diskettes and disk drives work and how to take care of them;

- describe the following kinds of disks: internal hard disks, hard-disk cartridges, and hard-disk packs;

- describe ways to improve hard-disk operations: disk caching, data compression, and redundant arrays of inexpensive disks;

- describe the different types of optical discs: CD-ROM, CD-R, and erasable;

- describe magnetic tape streamers and magnetic tape reels.

FROM THE USER'S POINT OF VIEW

Data may be input, processed, and output as information. But one of the best features about using a computer is the ability to save—that is, store—information. Computers can save information permanently, after you turn them off. This way, you can save your work for future use, share information with others, or modify information already available. Secondary storage holds information external from the CPU. Secondary storage allows you to store programs, such as WordPerfect and Lotus 1-2-3. It also allows you to store the data processed by programs, such as text or the numbers in a spreadsheet.

What if you could buy a microcomputer and use your portable audiotape recorder to store programs and data? Actually, this was once advertised as a feature. In the early 1980s there were over 150 kinds of microcomputers being offered. Some inexpensive computers were advertised at that time that could store information on the tape in one's audiotape recorder.

To find a particular song on an audiotape, you may have to play several centimetres of tape. Finding a song on an audio compact disc, in contrast, can be much faster. You select the song, and the disc player moves directly to it. That, in brief, represents the two different approaches to external storage. The two approaches are called *sequential access* and *direct access*.

Magnetic tape is an example of **sequential access storage** media. Information is stored in sequence, such as alphabetically. You may have to search a tape past all the information from A to P, say, before you get to Q. This may involve searching several centimetres, or even metres, which takes time.

Generally speaking, disk storage falls in the category of **direct access storage**. That is, it is like selecting the song you want and then moving directly to it. This form of storage allows you to directly access information. Therefore, retrieving selected data and programs is much faster with disks than with tape.

FOUR KINDS OF SECONDARY STORAGE

Microcomputer secondary storage may be on floppy disk, hard disk, optical disc, or tape.

We described random-access memory (RAM) in Chapter 5. This is the *internal* and *temporary* storage of data and programs in the computer's memory. Once the power is turned off or interrupted, everything in internal storage disappears. Such storage is therefore said to be **volatile**. Thus, we need *external, more permanent*, or **non-volatile**, ways of storing data and programs. We also need external storage because users need much more capacity than is possessed by a computer's primary memory.

The most widely used external storage media are floppy disks, hard disks, optical discs, and magnetic tape. It is important for end users to understand the advantages, disadvantages, and typical uses for each.

Any particular microcomputer could use all of the different media. However, a typical system has a hard-disk drive and one or two other drives. The hard-disk drive is designated as the C drive and is typically used for storing system and application programs. The A drive is generally a floppy-disk drive used for data files. The B drive is typically another floppy-disk drive or an optical drive for data, programs, and reference materials (see Figure 7.1).

FLOPPY DISKS

Floppy disks are removable storage media that are inserted into disk drives.

Floppy disks, often called **diskettes** or simply **disks**, are flat, circular pieces of mylar plastic that rotate within a jacket. Data and programs are stored as electromagnetic charges on a metal oxide film coating the mylar plastic. Data and programs are represented by the presence or absence of these charges, using the ASCII or EBCDIC data representation codes. The two most popular sizes of floppy disks are 3½-inch diameter and 5¼-inch diameter. Larger and smaller sizes are also available, although they are not standard for most microcomputers.

Figure 7.1 Apple's Macintosh Performa 6200 CD with both floppy-disk drive and optical drive

Figure 7.2 A 3½-inch floppy disk

Floppy disks are also called **flexible disks**, and **floppies**. This is because the plastic disk inside the diskette covers is flexible, not rigid. The 3½-inch standard is encased in a hard plastic jacket (Figure 7.2).

The disk drive

The *disk drive* obtains stored data and programs from a floppy disk. It is also used to store data and programs on a floppy disk.

A disk drive consists of a box with a slot into which you insert the floppy disk. Often the slot is covered by a door, called the **drive gate**. A motor inside the drive rotates the floppy disk. As the floppy disk rotates, electronic heads can 'read' data from and 'write' data to it. As we stated earlier, *read* means that the disk drive *copies* data (stored as magnetic impulses) from the floppy disk. *Write* means that the disk drive *transfers* data, the electronic signals in the computer's memory, onto the floppy disk.

It's important to realise that reading makes a copy from the original data; it does not alter the original. Writing, in contrast, *writes over*—and replaces—any data that is already there. This is like recording a new song over an old one on a tape recorder. The same is true of programs on a floppy disk.

How a disk drive works

A floppy disk is inserted into the slot in the front of the disk drive, and the drive gate is closed (see Figure 7.3). Closing the gate positions the floppy disk around a spindle and holds it so that it can revolve without slipping. When the drive is in motion, the floppy disk can turn at about 360 revolutions per minute, depending on the drive.

The magnetic data signals are transferred from floppy disk to computer (and computer to floppy disk) through **read-write heads** (see Figure 7.3). The read-write head is on an **access arm**, which moves back and forth over the floppy disk. To read or write on a particular part of the floppy disk, the access arm moves the read-write head on the floppy disk. This is called the **seek** operation. The drive then rotates the floppy disk to the proper position. This is called the **search** operation.

The parts of a floppy disk

Both 3½-inch and 5¼-inch floppy disks work the same way in principle, although there are some differences.

access arm

read-write head

tracks (invisible)

3½-inch floppy disk

Figure 7.3 Reading from and writing to a floppy disk

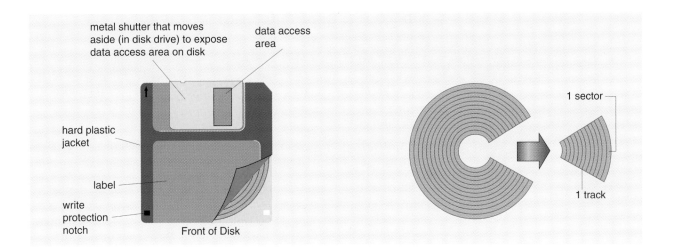

Figure 7.4 The parts of a 3½-inch floppy disk

Data is recorded on a floppy disk in rings called **tracks** (see Figure 7.4). These tracks are closed concentric circles, not a single spiral as on a gramophone record. Unlike a gramophone record, these tracks have no visible grooves. Looking at an exposed floppy disk, you would see just a smooth surface. Each track is divided into invisible wedge-shaped sections known as **sectors**.

Most disks are manufactured without tracks and sectors in place. Called **soft-sectored disks**, they must be adapted to the particular brand of microcomputer and disk drive you are using. Thus, you must put the tracks and sectors on yourself, using a process called *formatting*, or *initialising*.

Storage capacity of floppy disks can vary considerably (see Figure 7.5). For example, you will see boxes of 3½-inch disks labelled 'DS, DD', which means 'double-sided, double-density'. A floppy disk of this sort can store 737 280 bytes or 720 Kb—the equivalent of 450 typewritten pages. The more popular 3½-inch 'DS, HD' ('double-sided, high-density') disks have twice the capacity. Although not nearly as popular, floptical discs can store 21 Mb by using optical technology.

The two most popular sizes of floppy disks have distinct differences in how the jacket and the write-protect notch are handled:

3½-inch The 3½-inch version is the sturdier of the two (refer back to Figure 7.4). The exterior **jacket** is made of hard plastic to protect the flexible disk inside. The **write-protect notch** is covered by a sliding shutter. When you open the shutter, the write-protect notch prevents the computer from accidentally writing over information on the disk that you want to keep.

5¼-inch On the 5¼-inch version, the exterior jacket is made of flexible plastic or cardboard. The disk is protected by a paper envelope, or sleeve, when it is not in the disk drive. The write-protect notch can be covered with a removable tab, which comes with the disk when you buy it.

Taking care of floppy disks
Taking care of floppy disks boils down to four rules:

1. *Don't bend the disks, put heavy weights on them, or use sharp objects on them.* For 5¼-inch disks, do not write on them with ballpoint pens. Use a felt-tip pen when writing on the index label.

FLOPPY DISK CAPACITY

Description	Capacity
3½-inch	
Double-sided, double-density	720 Kb
Double-sided, high-density	1.44 Mb
Floptical	21 Mb
5¼-inch	
Double-sided, double-density	360 Kb
Double-sided, high-density	1.2 Kb

Figure 7.5 Typical floppy disk capacities

2. *Don't touch anything visible through the protective jacket* (such as the data access area).

3. *Keep disks away from strong magnetic fields* (like motors or telephones). Also, *keep them away from extreme heat* (like a car boot) *and chemicals* (such as alcohol and solvents). Keep 5¼-inch disks in their paper envelopes and store them in a file box when they are not in use.

4. *Store disks in a sturdy plastic storage box.* Even though the 3½-inch disks have a hard plastic jacket, they can be damaged.

Of course, the best protection is to make a *backup*, or duplicate, copy of your disk.

Despite these cautions, you will find floppy disks are actually quite durable. For instance, you can send them through the mail if you enclose them in cardboard or use special rigid mailing envelopes. They usually can also be put through the X-ray machines at airport security checkpoints without loss of data.

Hard disks

Hard disks are of three types: internal hard disk, hard-disk cartridge, and hard-disk pack.

Hard disks consist of metallic rather than plastic platters. They are also tightly sealed to prevent any foreign matter from getting inside.

Hard disks are extremely sensitive instruments. The read-write head rides on a cushion of air about 0.000025 millimetres thick. It is so thin that a smoke particle, fingerprint, dust, or human hair could cause what is known as a head crash (see Figure 7.6). A **head crash** happens when the surface of the read-write head or particles on its surface contact the magnetic disk surface. A head crash is a disaster for a hard disk. It means that some or all of the data on the disk is destroyed. Hard disks are assembled under sterile conditions and sealed from impurities within their permanent containers.

Hard disks come in three forms: *internal hard disk, hard-disk cartridge,* and *hard-disk pack.*

Internal hard disk

An **internal hard disk** consists of one or more metallic platters sealed inside a container. The container includes the motor for rotating the disks. It also contains an access arm and read-write heads for writing

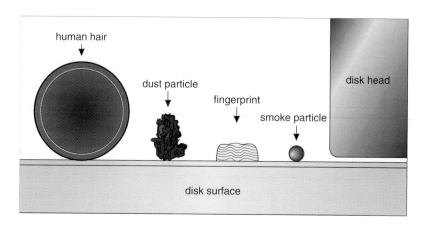

Figure 7.6 Materials that can cause a head crash

data to and reading data from the disks. Like a floppy-disk drive, an internal hard-disk drive has a seek operation and a search operation for reading and writing data in tracks and sectors. From the outside of a microcomputer, an internal hard disk looks like part of a front panel on the system cabinet. Typically, inside is a 3½-inch metallic platter with an access arm that moves back and forth (see Figure 7.7).

Internal hard disks have two advantages over floppy disks: capacity and speed. A hard disk can hold many times the information of a similar size floppy disk. One 850 Mb internal hard disk, for instance, can hold as much information as 590 3½-inch double-sided, high-density floppy disks. Some *external* hard-disk drives for microcomputers (drives that are not built into the system cabinet) can store thousands of megabytes. Moreover, access is faster: a hard disk spins 10 times faster than a floppy disk. For these reasons, most of today's powerful applications are designed to be stored and run from an internal hard disk. Adequate capacity or size of a microcomputer's internal hard disk is essential.

Hard-disk cartridges

The disadvantage of hard disks is that they have only a fixed amount of storage and cannot be easily removed. Hard-disk cartridges have the advantage of being as easy to remove as a cassette from a videocassette recorder (see Figure 7.8). They can give microcomputer systems fast access to very large quantities of data. The amount of storage available is limited only by the number of cartridges. For instance, one self-contained removable hard-disk cartridge has a storage capacity of 340 Mb. While a regular hard-disk system has a fixed storage capacity, a removable hard-disk cartridge system is unlimited—you can just buy more removable cartridges. One removable 20 Mb palm-sized hard disk available weighs only 200 grams and may be moved easily from laptop to laptop.

Hard-disk packs

Microcomputers that are connected to other microcomputers, minicomputers, or mainframes often have access to external hard-disk packs (see Figure 7.9). Microcomputer hard-disk drives typically have only one or two disk platters and one or two access arms. In contrast, **hard-disk packs** consist of several *platters* aligned one above the other, thereby offering much greater storage capacity. These hard-disk packs resemble a stack of gramophone records. The difference is that

disk spindle
disk platter

movable access arm with read-write head

Figure 7.7 The inside of a hard-disk drive

Figure 7.8 Removable hard-disk cartridge

Figure 7.9 Hard-disk packs

there is space between the disks to allow the access arms to move in and out (see Figure 7.10). Each access arm has two read-write heads. One reads the disk surface above it; the other reads the disk surface below it. A disk pack with 11 disks provides 20 recording surfaces. This is because the top and bottom outside surfaces of the pack are not used.

All the access arms move in and out together. However, only one of the read-write heads is activated at a given moment. **Access time** is the time between the computer's request for data from secondary storage and the completion of the data transfer. Access time for most disk drives is under 25 milliseconds.

You may well use your microcomputer to gain access to information over a telephone or other communications line. (We show this in the next chapter.) Such information is apt to be stored on disk packs. One large information service (named Dialog), for example, has over 300 databases. These databases cover all areas of science, technology, business, medicine, social science, current affairs, and humanities. All of these are available through a telephone link with your desktop computer. There are more than 100 million items of information, including references to books, patents, directories, journals, and newspaper articles. Such an information resource may be of great value to you in your work.

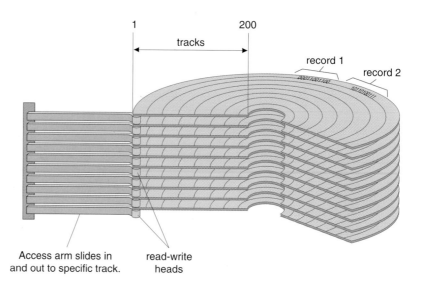

Figure 7.10 How a disk pack works

Access arm slides in and out to specific track.

read-write heads

Performance enhancements

Three ways to improve the performance of hard disks are disk caching, data compression, and redundant arrays of inexpensive disks.

Disk caching improves hard-disk performance by anticipating data needs. It requires a combination of hardware and software. During idle processing time, frequently used data is read from the hard disk into memory (cache). When needed, the data is then accessed directly from memory. The transfer rate from memory is much faster than from hard disk. Thus, overall system performance is often increased by as much as 30 percent.

Data compression and **decompression** increase storage capacity by reducing the amount of space required to store data and programs. In data compression, entering data is scanned for ways to reduce the amount of required storage. One way is to search for repeating patterns. The repeating patterns are replaced with a token, leaving enough space so that the original can be rebuilt or decompressed. Data compression and decompression can be accomplished through the use of special software and/or hardware. An example is add-on boards inserted into the computer's expansion slots. Many times the software is included in the operating system, as is the case with DOS 6.0. Also available are specialised programs (see Figure 7.11).

Data compression can regain or free as much as 80 percent of a microcomputer's hard disk. The major tradeoff is performance: a great deal of compression may slow down processing.

Redundant arrays of inexpensive disks (RAIDs) improve performance by expanding external storage. Groups of inexpensive hard-disk drives are related or grouped together using networks and special software. These grouped disks are treated as a single large-capacity hard disk. They can outperform single disks of comparable capacities.

OPTICAL DISCS

Optical discs are used for storing great quantities of data.

An **optical disc** can hold 650 Mb of data—the equivalent of hundreds of floppy disks (see Figure 7.12). Moreover, an optical disc makes an immense amount of information available on a microcomputer. Optical

Figure 7.11 Data compression software, Stacker version 4.0

129

1 book   147 books   451 books

1 book = 720 pages

1.44 MB floppy   212 MB hard disk   650 MB CD-ROM

Figure 7.12 Comparison of disk storage capacities

discs are having a great impact on storage technology today, but we are probably only beginning to see their effects.

In optical-disc technology, a laser beam alters the surface of a plastic or metallic disc to represent data. To read the data, a laser scans these areas and sends the data to a computer chip for conversion. Optical discs are made in diameters of 3½, 4¾, 5¼, 8, 12, and 14 inches.

There are three kinds of optical discs available: *CD-ROM, CD-R,* and *erasable optical discs.*

CD-ROM

CD-ROM stands for *compact disc—read-only memory.* Industry sources estimate that half of the microcomputers sold in 1997 will contain a CD-ROM drive. And the number of installed CD-ROM drives will continue to increase every year (see Figure 7.13).

Unlike floppy and hard disks, which use magnetic charges to represent 1s and 0s, optical discs use reflected light. On a CD-ROM disc, 1s and 0s are represented by flat areas and bumpy areas (called 'pits') on its bottom surface. The CD-ROM disc is read by a laser that projects a tiny beam of light on these areas. The amount of reflected light determines whether the area represents a 1 or a 0 (see Figure 7.14).

Like a commercial CD found in music stores, a CD-ROM is a 'read-only' disc. **Read-only** means it cannot be written on or erased by the user. Thus, you as a user have access only to the data imprinted by the publisher. CD-ROM discs are used to distribute large databases and references. An example is the *Grolier Electronic Encyclopedia,* a

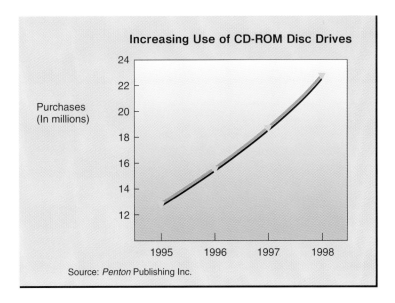

Figure 7.13 CD-ROM disc drives in use—past, present, and future

CD-ROM containing the *Academic American Encyclopedia*, with over 9 million words and 1500 pictures (see Figure 7.15 for other CD-ROM titles).

CD-ROMs are also used to distribute large software application packages. For example, Microsoft Office for Windows 95 is available on a single CD-ROM or on over twenty floppy disks. One advantage of the CD-ROM version is that installation from one CD-ROM to the internal hard disk is much faster and easier.

Figure 7.14 How a CD-ROM works

LEADING CD-ROM TITLES

Title	Description
Grolier Electronic Encyclopaedia	21 volumes of the Academic American Encyclopedia, with over 9 million words and 1500 pictures
Microsoft Bookshelf	8 complete reference books, including the *American Heritage Dictionary*, *Roget's II Electronic Thesaurus*, *Bartlett's Familiar Quotations*, and a ZIP code directory
US History on CD-ROM	107 books on US history, with over 1000 photos, maps, and tables
Crompton's Multimedia Encyclopaedia	*Compton's Encyclopaedia*, including 15 000 illustrations and audio of speeches by Martin Luther King, Jr, and John F. Kennedy
Mammals: A Multimedia Encyclopaedia	45 documentary video clips from *National Geographic* and animal audio sound tracks

Figure 7.15 Leading CD-ROM reference materials

A single CD-ROM disc can store 650 Mb of data. That is equivalent to 147 floppy disks. With that much information on a single disc, the time to retrieve or access the information is very important. An important characteristic of CD-ROM drives is their access rate (see Figure 7.16).

CD-R

CD-R stands for *CD-Recordable*. Also known as **WORM** or *write once, read many*, CD-R discs can be written to once. After that they can be read many times without deterioration and cannot be written on or

CD-ROM DRIVES

Type	Description
Single-speed	The original drive introduced in the mid 1980s; transfer rate of 150 Kb per second; data retrieval was slow; poor sound and video capabilities
Double-speed	Introduced in 1991; transfer rate of 300 Kb per second; widely used standard; acceptable data retrieval and sound production; video capabilities limited; too slow for most multimedia applications
Triple-speed	Introduced in 1993; transfer rate of 450 Kb per second; also not quite fast enough for full-motion video
Quad-speed	Also introduced in 1993; transfer rate of 600 Kb; acceptable for full-motion video
Six-speed	Recently introduced with faster speeds expected soon

Figure 7.16 Access speeds for CD-ROM drives

erased. A typical 5¼-inch CD-R disc can store between 600 and 650 Mb of data.

Because the data cannot be erased, CD-R discs are ideal for use as archives to permanently store large amounts of important information. CD changers or CD Jukeboxes (see Figure 7.17) are used to give quick access to several CDs, allowing billions of bytes of data to be easily retrieved.

Erasable optical discs

Erasable optical discs, also known as **rewriteable optical discs**, are like CD-Rs except that they can be written to many times. That is, a disc that has been written on can be erased and used over and over again. The most viable disc of this type runs on a *magneto-optical* (MO) disc drive, which borrows from both magnetic and optical technologies. A typical 5¼-inch MO disc can store from 600 Mb to 1000 Mb (1 gigabyte) of data.

For a summary of optical disc storage capacities, see Figure 7.18.

Figure 7.17 CD jukebox

MAGNETIC TAPE

Magnetic tape streamers and magnetic tape reels are used primarily for backup purposes.

We mentioned the alarming consequences that can happen if a hard disk suffers a head crash. You will lose some or all of your data or programs. Of course, you can always make copies of your hard-disk files on floppy disks. However, this can be time-consuming and may require many floppy disks. Here is where magnetic tape storage becomes important. Magnetic tape falls into the category of sequential access storage and is therefore slower than direct access storage. However, it is an effective way of making a *backup*, or duplicate, copy of your programs and data.

There are two forms of tape storage. These are *magnetic tape streamers*, for use with microcomputers, and *magnetic tape reels*, for use with minicomputers and mainframes.

Magnetic tape streamers

Many microcomputer users with hard disks use a device called a **magnetic tape streamer** or a **backup tape cartridge unit** (see Figure 7.19). This enables you to duplicate or make a backup of the data on your hard disk onto a tape cartridge. Typical capacities of such tape cartridges are 120 megabytes to 5 gigabytes. Advanced forms of backup technology known as **digital audiotape (DAT) drives**, which use 2- by 3-inch cassettes, store 4 gigabytes or more. If your internal hard disk fails, you can have it repaired (or get another hard disk). You can restore all your lost data and programs in a matter of minutes from the backup tapes.

Magnetic tape reels

The cassette tapes you get for an audiotape recorder are only about 200 feet long. They record 200 characters to the inch. A reel of magnetic tape used with minicomputer and mainframe systems, by contrast, is ½-inch wide and ½-mile long. It stores 1600 to 6400 characters to the inch. Such tapes are run on **magnetic tape drives** or **magnetic tape units** (see Figure 7.20). You may never actually see these devices yourself. However, as a microcomputer user sharing

OPTICAL DISCS	
Technology	**Capacity**
CD-ROM	650 MB
CD-R	600–650 MB
Erasable	600–1000 MB

Figure 7.18 Typical capacities for optical discs

133

Figure 7.19 Backup software copying files to magnetic tape

take-up reel

supply reel

read-write head

erase head

tape

Figure 7.20 Data is recorded on magnetic tape on tape reels

storage devices with others, you may have access to them through a minicomputer or mainframe.

For the typical microcomputer user, the four storage options—floppy disk, hard disk, optical disc, and magnetic tape—are complementary, not competing. Almost all microcomputers today have at least one floppy-disk drive and one hard-disk drive. For those users who need access to vast amounts of data, an optical drive is added. Lastly, for those who need to back up lots of data and programs, magnetic tape drives are added.

For a summary comparison of the four storage options, see Figure 7.21.

A LOOK AT THE FUTURE

Three storage technologies of the future: wet disks, glass disks, and holograms.

The principal trend now in evidence—that of packing more and more data in less and less space—will doubtless continue. Three

Figure 7.21 Summary of storage options

SECONDARY STORAGE

Type	Advantage	Disadvantage	Typical Use	Cost/ Megabyte
Floppy disk	Inexpensive, direct access removable	Low capacity, slow access	Store files for word processors and spreadsheets	$1.00
Hard disk	Fast, dirct access	Limited capacity	Store programs and data	$0.40 to $0.80
CD-ROM	High capacity, direct access	Slow access	Reference material	$0.04 to $1.00
Magnetic tape	High capacity	Slow sequential data access	Backup programs and data	$0.10 to $0.40

technologies that promise to greatly expand disk capacities are 'wet' disks, glass disks, and holograms.

Wet disk technology replaces the air cushion between the disk and the drive head with a liquid. This allows the drive head to get closer to the disk and to read more closely packed data. Wet disks have approximately twice the capacity of today's disks; however, special liquid-resistant parts are required. The leader in developing this technology, Conner Peripherals Inc., recently introduced a wet-disk drive.

Traditional hard disks are made of aluminium. Developers have found that by replacing aluminium with glass, more data can be stored on a disk. Unfortunately, the cost to manufacture the glass disks is higher. But all that might change in the near future. An advantage over wet disks is that glass disks can be used with traditional hard-disk-drive technologies. Hewlett-Packard already has a commercial glass disk called Kittyhawk Personal Storage Module.

A bit further on the horizon is holographic storage, in which information is stored on holograms. Holograms, as you may know, are those shimmering, three-dimensional images often seen on credit cards and the like. Holographic systems store data equivalent to thousands of books in three dimensions inside a box made of special material the size of a sugar cube. Data stored in a holographic system is retrievable in 1 second. Tamarack Storage Devices expects to have a holographic drive available within the next few years.

REVIEW QUESTIONS

True/false
1. Secondary storage holds information within the CPU.

2. Floppy disks are also known as flexible disks and as floppies.

3. Sectors are wedge-shaped sections on a disk.

4. CD-R discs can be erased and used over and over again.

5. Laser beams are used to record data on optical discs.

Multiple choice
1. Which of the following is exclusively a sequential access storage media?
   (a) floppy disk
   (b) hard disk
   (c) magnetic tape
   (d) CD-ROM
   (e) WORM

2. On a floppy-disk drive, data signals are transferred to the computer through:
   (a) read-write heads
   (b) access arms
   (c) drive gate
   (d) drive A
   (e) sectors

3. The disk with the greatest capacity is:
   (a) 5¼-inch double-sided, double-density
   (b) 5¼-inch double-sided, high-density
   (c) 3½-inch double-sided, double-density
   (d) 3½-inch double-sided, high-density
   (e) CD-ROM

4. The hard-disk type that has several platters aligned one above the other is a:
   (a) internal hard disk
   (b) hard-disk pack
   (c) floppy-disk array
   (d) hard-disk cartridge
   (e) disk cache

5. The method of improving hard-disk performance by anticipating data needs is:
   (a) disk compression
   (b) disk caching
   (c) disk decompression
   (d) RAIDs
   (e) virtual processing

Fill in the blank

1. A _____ disc is read by a laser projecting a beam of light.

2. Data is recorded on a disk in rings called _____.

3. Internal hard disks have two advantages over floppy disks: _____ _____ and speed.

4. Data _____ time measures how long it takes to move data from the hard-disk track to memory.

5. The two forms of tape storage are magnetic tape streamers and magnetic tape _____.

Open ended

1. Explain the difference between direct access storage and sequential access storage. Which is more apt to be identified with magnetic disk and which with magnetic tape?

2. What are the four kinds of secondary storage? What are their relative advantages and disadvantages?

3. State the four primary rules about taking care of floppy disks.

4. What is so disastrous about a head crash?

5. What are the three types of hard-disk drives? Discuss their differences and similarities.

DISCUSSION QUESTIONS AND PROJECTS

1. *What type of storage system?* Suppose for the past few years you have owned a computer with two floppy-disk drives but no hard-disk drive. Your several file boxes of floppy disks include all kinds of research data comprising a college career. This is research that may be quite valuable later in college or in your career. You also have several disks containing important information about non-college matters—for example, your family history, your music collection, and your personal finances.

   Suppose that you're beginning to lose control and are no longer able to find things when you want them. A hard-disk drive would help. However, if a hard-disk drive suffers a head crash or other accident, you could lose all the programs and data on it. What kind of storage system should you get—hard disk, hard disk and magnetic tape backup (tape streamer), hard-disk cartridge, data-compression software and hardware, or optical disc?

2. *Looking for the right CD-ROM* Perhaps you have had the difficulty of dealing with competing standards of media for something you want. Was a film you wanted to see available on Betamax but not on VHS videotape? Did a musical group have songs available on an LP or tape but not CD? Now you face a similar difficulty in evaluating the new storage medium of CD-ROM, for which competing versions exist. To help resolve the confusion, determine:

   (a) How the CD-ROMs used for computer storage differ from those used as adjuncts to television sets, such as the CD-1 and CDTV.

   (b) How the CD-ROMs normally associated with desktop computers differ from those used in the small electronic 'book' players, such as the Data Discman put out by Sony.

   (c) The difference between the CD-ROMs available for Macintosh and those available for IBM and IBM-compatible micro-computers.

3. *Obtaining a CD-ROM drive* Suppose you have a microcomputer system that does not have a CD-ROM drive and that you would like to have one. You have three options: (1) purchase an external CD-ROM drive that connects to one of the ports in the back of your system unit; (2) purchase and install an internal CD-ROM directly into your system unit; or (3) purchase a new microcomputer system that has a CD-ROM drive.

   Research each of the three options and prepare a set of written guidelines that could be used to make the best choice.

CASE STUDY

WELD-RITE ENGINEERING

Weld-Rite Engineering is a medium sized manufacturing company that produces pressure vessels such as boilers. The managing director of Weld-Rite is Alex, and he is responsible for making decisions on which products to support, marketing strategies, determining major client requirements and ensuring the profitability of the enterprise. The firm has a well-equipped engineering shop where up to 25 workers cut out and assemble the product line. Graham is the engineering manager and his major role includes purchasing, scheduling and the design of components and boiler systems. The supervisor of the factory floor is Carmel. She is in charge of work allocation and overseeing all welding and other engineering work. The manager of the administration section of Weld-Rite is Beryl and she allocates duties involving invoicing, payment of wages, the servicing of accounts as well as general secretarial requirements.

Over the past ten years computer facilities have been purchased without an overall strategy. Graham uses an old Unix microcomputer system to provide job costings, engineering calculations and work scheduling. He uses a number of software packages, which were specifically written in the Unix operating system for Weld-Rite, by a company that has now closed down.

An MS-DOS style AT computer is located in the engineering shop and is connected to an electronic bar-code reader. As in a library or video store, the workers have cards with printed bar codes. The workers use these cards to clock on and off jobs. The information from the bar codes is used to calculate employees' salaries and to record details that identify who has worked on particular jobs in the event of customer complaints. The AT computer is also used by the workers to generate production and quality assurance reports.

A CD-ROM drive was connected to the AT computer to allow Graham to use a product called TechSpecs. This is a CD-ROM based package that enables him to look up the specifications of construction materials used in manufacturing at Weld-Rite. Graham copies the numerical data from TechSpecs onto a scrap of paper and takes it back to his Unix machine.

Alex uses an old Macintosh Plus computer to type out personal memos and confidential letters. He has found the 'point and click' technology to be easy to learn and simple to use. A few years ago Alex was a reluctant user of computer technology, but now recognises the improvements he has gained in efficiency and quality from the use of information technology.

Alex has proposed to the Board of Directors that the current outdated computer hardware be replaced. He successfully argued that for the firm to remain competitive, a consistent system interface be installed on all computers and industry standard 'off-the-shelf' application software be used. This will allow mobility of data and personnel within the organisation and will use new employee software knowledge to advantage. Temporary staff are often hired during busy periods, and their training time will be reduced if standardised software is used.

A computer system is required that consists of a common operating platform for the manufacturing and accounting sides of the business. This system must be easy to use and run common business software. Existing procedures to determine employee hours worked is to remain. Alex requires a replacement computer enabling him to read data files from employees, and allow him to save his confidential and personal material to a storage device that cannot be accessed by any other computer in the business.

Graham has undertaken courses in using CAD, and wishes to start doing some design work using a sophisticated graphics package. The computing system provided for his use should support this new aspect of his work.

The following list of computers is being considered as possible upgrade machines for Weld-Rite Engineering:

- MS-DOS computer running Windows, 486 66 MHz, 4 Mb RAM, 120 Mb hard disk;

- MS-DOS computer, XT 12 MHz, 1 Mb RAM, 20 Mb hard disk;

- MS-DOS computer running Windows, 486 100 MHz, 16 Mb RAM, 1 Gb hard disk;

- Macintosh Plus computer, 2 Mb RAM, 40 Mb hard disk.

QUESTIONS

1. Currently, Weld-Rite Engineering has a CD-ROM that stores much of the vital data needed in the engineering section of the business. This has information such as metal strengths, stress capacity, structure diagrams, and so on.

   (a) Describe two advantages of storage on CD-ROM.

   (b) What are two of the major limitations of storage on CD-ROM?

   (c) What four different types of data can be stored on CD-ROM? Briefly explain the different memory requirements of each type.

   (d) Briefly explain the difference between the way information is retrieved from a hard-disk drive and a CD-ROM.

2. Make recommendations for the most practical method of backing up data for the:

   (a) managing director

   (b) engineering manager

   Justify your recommendations.

3. (a) Define the validation information processing phase.

   (b) Describe two possible ways that Graham could validate the data on construction materials that he currently enters into his UNIX machine.

4. Graham and Beryl are both acquiring new computers to process the data into information. For each person, describe what data they will be processing.

Communications and connectivity

COMPETENCIES

After you have read this chapter, you should be able to:

- describe available communications resources and online services;

- describe communications hardware, such as types of modems;

- describe the cable and air communications channels—telephone, coaxial, and fibre-optic cables— microwave relays, and satellites;

- discuss bandwidth, serial versus parallel transmission, direction of flow, modes of transmission, and protocols;

- explain network architecture— configurations and strategies;

- describe local area, metropolitan area, and wide area networks.

FROM THE USER'S POINT OF VIEW

A familiar instrument—the telephone—has extended our uses for the microcomputer enormously. With the telephone or other kinds of communications equipment, you can connect your microcomputer to other people and to other, larger computers. As we've mentioned earlier, this *connectivity* puts the power of a mainframe on your desk. The result is increased productivity—for you as an individual and for the groups and organisations of which you are a member. Connectivity has become particularly important in business, where individuals now find themselves connected in networks to other individuals and departments.

Imagine: you are a real estate salesperson, and the telephone in your car rings. It is a client who is on the phone in his car across town. He asks you about a certain property, and you agree to meet him there. After you go back to look at the property, you connect your laptop computer to your car phone. You then dial the multiple listing service and get information on the property. This is an example of the use of communications to expand computer capabilities.

In Chapter 2, you learned about communications software. In this chapter, you will learn about communications systems. **Data communications systems** are the electronic systems that transmit data over communications lines from one location to another. You might use data communications through your microcomputer to send information to a friend using another computer. You might work for an organisation whose computer system is spread throughout a building, or even throughout the country or world. That is, all the parts—input and output units, processor, and storage devices—are in different places and linked by communications. Or you might use *telecommunications* lines—telephone lines—to tap into information located in an outside data bank. You could then transmit it to your microcomputer for your own reworking and analysis.

Data communications is now considered essential in business. As we will see, an important part of communications is the *network*, a system connecting two or more computers. A popular form of network is the *local area network (LAN)*. In a LAN, computers are connected together within a limited area, such as within the same building. In one survey in the United States, over 80 percent responded that there was a local area network within their company or organisation. There are many occasions when you and coworkers need a network to gain access to one another's information. Such information may be on sales, customers, prices, schedules, or products. The list is nearly endless.

COMMUNICATIONS AND CONNECTIVITY

With communications capability, microcomputer users can transmit and receive data and gain access to electronic information resources.

You may have a desktop microcomputer next to a telephone. You may (or may someday) have a laptop microcomputer and a cellular phone in your car. Or you may have a microcomputer that is directly connected to other computers without telephone lines at all. Whatever the case, communications systems present many opportunities for transmitting and receiving information, giving you access to many resources. This brings up the important revolution represented by this chapter, that of connectivity.

Connectivity means you can connect your microcomputer by telephone or other telecommunications links to other computers and information sources almost anywhere. With this connection, you are linked to the world of larger computers. This includes minicomputers and mainframes and their large storage devices, such as disk packs, and their enormous volumes of information. Thus, computer competence becomes a matter of knowing not only about microcomputers. You should also know something about larger computer systems and their information resources.

Let us consider the options that connectivity makes available to you. These include *fax machines, electronic bulletin boards, electronic mail, voice-messaging systems, shared resources,* and *online services* (Figure 8.1).

Fax machines

Fax machines—facsimile transmission machines—are now extremely popular in offices (see Figure 8.2). Indeed, they have become essential machines in many workplaces. As we mentioned earlier, these devices scan the image of a document. They convert the image to signals that can be sent over a telephone line to a receiving machine. This machine prints the image out on paper. Microcomputers, using fax/modem circuit boards, can be used to send and receive fax messages.

Sending a document by fax is certainly faster—it arrives immediately—than any delivery service. It also is often cheaper than overnight delivery, unless you're sending more than 50 pages of a document. Almost every fax machine can exchange messages with every other fax machine. All you need is the receiving machine's phone number. It can transmit photographs and other artwork, as well as text in various typefaces.

If you are in the business of meeting deadlines—as most people are—a fax machine can be invaluable. Construction engineers can get

Figure 8.1 Connectivity options

cost estimates to major contractors. Lawyers can get contracts to other lawyers. Advertising people can get prospective ad layouts to their clients. Just as important, because people often respond better to pictures than to text, fax can get a picture to them quickly.

Electronic bulletin board systems

This is an activity you can utilise yourself if you have access to a microcomputer and the necessary telephone links. **Electronic bulletin board systems (BBS)** are like public bulletin boards. You can post and read messages. These messages can be personal or intended for a group. The difference is that all the messages are electronic, and you need a microcomputer, telephone connection, and the electronic bulletin board's telephone number. The board's number connects you to a computer that receives messages, posts messages, and handles the details of administering the BBS. Such bulletin boards have been popular with microcomputer hobbyists and enthusiasts for many years. They are rapidly gaining favour with other people, too.

Bulletin boards exist for almost any subject. Many are concerned with new developments and problems related to particular brands of microcomputers. Others have to do with hobbies, such as rock music, science fiction, or genealogy. Still others serve special interests, such as political causes, or professional groups, such as lawyers. Finally, some companies offer bulletin boards as a means by which customers can get advice from other customers. They can also get advice from the company itself regarding a particular service or product. Finally, some companies use bulletin boards to communicate with employees working at home.

Figure 8.2 A fax machine

Electronic mail

Also called **e-mail, electronic mail** resembles bulletin boards (see Figure 8.3). Often it uses a special communications line rather than a telephone line. In addition, electronic mail offers confidentiality. A **user name** and **password**—special number or letter sequences that limit access—are required to get into the 'mailbox'. The mailbox is simply a file stored on a computer system. Passwords are not limited to electronic mail. They are widely used to control access and use of restricted data and resources.

To send an electronic message, you dial the special number, specify the user name, password, and mailbox number, and type the message. You can also put the same message in several mailboxes at the same time. To access your own mailbox, dial the number of the e-mail system and type in your user name and password. You can look through the list of file names and transmission times of the messages. You then transfer to your own computer the messages you want to keep.

Electronic mail is used within companies to help employees exchange memos, set up meetings, and the like. It may also be used between companies. Sometimes outside electronic bulletin board services are used for these business purposes. We will discuss electronic mail in the Internet Guide.

Voice-messaging systems

Voice-messaging systems are computer systems linked to telephones that convert the human voice into digital bits. They resemble conventional answering machines and also resemble electronic mail systems. However, they can receive large numbers of incoming calls and route them to the appropriate 'voice mailboxes'. They can deliver the same message to many people. They allow callers to leave 'voice mail'—recorded voice messages. They can forward calls to your home or hotel, if you wish. When you check for your messages, you can speed through them or slow them down. You can dictate replies into the phone, and the system will send them out.

Figure 8.3 Microsoft Network's In-box

Shared resources

An important option that connectivity gives microcomputer users is that it lets them share expensive hardware. We have mentioned many of these: laser printers, chain printers, disk packs, and magnetic tape storage. Only in rare instances would a single microcomputer user need the use of, say, a disk pack. However, several microcomputers linked in a network make this option not only feasible but in many cases even essential. Communications networks also permit microcomputer users to share workstations, minicomputers, and mainframes. This is why we have stressed that it's important to know what these machines are.

Another important option of connectivity is the ability to share data. As we saw in Chapter 2, with a microcomputer you can have your own personal database. An example of such a database might be a collection of names and addresses. A *database*, as we mentioned, is a collection of integrated data. By 'integrated', we mean the data consists of logically related files and records.

Your personal database might consist of data that only you use. However, it may also be data you share with others. The data might be stored on your microcomputer's hard disk. Or it might be located somewhere else. That is, you might use a shared database, like one a company might provide for its employees so they can share information. This could be information stored on disk packs and accessible from the company's mainframe. You could gain access by using your microcomputer linked to your telephone and **downloading** selected data. That is, you could transfer the data from the larger computer to your microcomputer. Then you could process and manipulate the data as you chose. The reverse is **uploading**— transferring from your microcomputer to a mainframe or minicomputer. For example, a salesperson could record daily sales on a portable computer and upload monthly sales data to the company's mainframe.

Online services

Several businesses offer services specifically for microcomputer users. Four well-known service providers are Oz-Email, CompuServe, Microsoft Network, and AT&T Interchange (see Figure 8.4).

Teleshopping You dial into a database listing prices and descriptions of products such as appliances and clothes. You then order what you want and charge the purchase to a credit card number. The merchandise is delivered later by a package delivery service.

Home banking If you arrange it with your bank, you may be able to use your microcomputer to pay some bills. Such bills include those owed to big department stores and utility companies. You can also make loan repayments and transfer money between accounts.

Investing You can get access to current prices of stocks and bonds and enter buy and sell orders.

Travel reservations Just like a travel agent, you can get information on airline schedules and fares. You can also order tickets, charging the purchase to your credit card.

See Figure 8.5 for a summary of the many connectivity options.

Figure 8.4 CompuServe's basic services

CONNECTIVITY OPTIONS

Option	Function
Fax machines	Convert images to signals and send them over telephone lines to receiving fax machines
Electronic bulletin boards	Provide forums on a variety of subjects available to telephone linked microcomputer users
Electronic mail	Systems resembling bulletin boards but are restricted in access by passwords
Voice-mail systems	Convert a voice message to digital bits and distribute to many locations over telephone lines
Shared resources	Microcomputer users may share expensive hardware, data, and information
Online services	Provide wide range of activities including teleshopping, home banking, investments, and travel reservations services

Figure 8.5 Summary of connectivity options

NATIONAL INFORMATION HIGHWAY AND INTERNET

Internet is the foundation for future communication networks. Four applications: transfer electronic mail, participate in public discussions, copy files, and run programs. Two utilities: Gopher and World Wide Web.

The **National Information Highway (NIH)** is also known as the **National Information Infrastructure (NII)** and as the **information**

superhighway. These popular phrases are used to describe the future of communication networks and computers. In the United States, legislation proposed and championed by Vice President Gore has laid the foundation for this billion-dollar project. Because of this legislation, Congress is now encouraging private investment, competition, and two-way universal access for the NIH. Such access would make computing resources available to everyone.

Internet

At the forefront of today's NIH is the **Internet**. It is a huge computer network available to nearly everyone who has a microcomputer and a means to connect to it. Once on the Internet it seems like you are on a single giant computer that branches all over the world. It is an unprecedented resource for information about an infinite number of topics. Also, it connects people as close as the next office and as far as halfway around the world (see Figure 8.6).

Technically, the Internet is a network connecting thousands of other networks and millions of computers; however, it represents much more. It is today's means to access and share knowledge. It is also tomorrow's foundation for a global community of users.

Applications

There are any number of uses for the Internet. The four most common applications are transferring electronic mail (e-mail), participating in public discussion groups, copying files, and running programs on a remote computer.

Electronic mail Sending and receiving e-mail is the most popular Internet service. You can send e-mail to anyone in the world if you know their e-mail address and have access to the Internet. You can even send and receive e-mail from other commercial service networks like Oz-Email.

Figure 8.6 Internet connections around the world

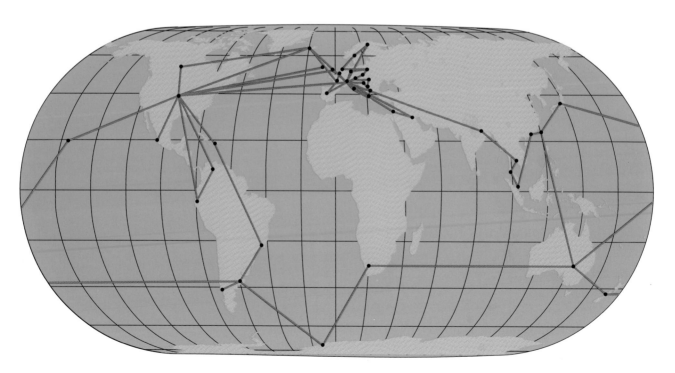

Public discussion groups You can join and listen to discussions and debates on a wide variety of topics on the Internet. This application is a variation of e-mail that uses a system called **UseNet**. This system creates an electronic forum of interested parties in a particular subject known as a *newsgroup*. There is an enormous number of newsgroups. They range from general interest topics such as current events and movie reviews, to specialised forums like computer trouble-shooting and Star Trek.

Files from remote databases The Internet service called **FTP** (file transfer protocol) lets you look at the names of files and copy files from other computers on the Internet. There are over 1500 FTP sites that have access to millions of publicly available files. These files can be downloaded to your microcomputer. FTP allows access to a large number of databases, from stock market quotations to personal income census data.

Programs on remote computers The Internet service called **Telnet** makes your computer a terminal for other computers on the Internet. It enables you to run selected programs from other computers. For example, you could access the NASA SPACElink computer. This Telnet link was originally designed for science teachers and is now available to the general public through the Internet. With it, you can learn about NASA's history, read about many exploration plans, view animated clips, and perform other space-related activities. Of course, not all Telnet connections are free. Medline, for example, is a fee-based application containing over 4000 medical journals and publications. You may have access to this application and others through a library or university near you.

See Figure 8.7 for a summary of Internet applications.

Utilities
Fortunately, there are several programs or utilities available to help you locate and use the Internet resources. Two of the most widely used Internet utility programs are gopher and World Wide Web.

Gopher **Gophers** are programs that help individuals on the Internet access other computers on the Internet. There are two types of gopher

INTERNET APPLICATIONS	
Application	**Description**
Electronic mail	Send and receive e-mail from around the world
Public discussion	Participate in discussions and debate on general and special interest topics using UseNet newsgroups
File transfer	Locate and copy selected files using FTP from over 1500 FTP sites across the Internet
Run programs	Allow terminal access to locate and run programs on thousands of computers on the Internet using Telnet

Figure 8.7 Summary of common Internet applications

programs. One type, called the gopher client, runs on the computer requesting access. This program uses Telnet to request access. Once access is granted, the second type—the *gopher server*—displays a menu system allowing access to the computer's available resources. There are hundreds of public computer systems on the Internet that can be accessed using gopher software.

World Wide Web The **World Wide Web** is also known as **WWW, W3**, and the **Web**. Like gopher, WWW helps users search for and retrieve information on the Internet. It uses clients and servers to provide menus to access a computer's resources. However, WWW goes one step further by providing **hypertext links** that allows users to effortlessly jump from one computer's resources to another computer's resources. This is accomplished using special software called **browsers**. Three well-known browsers are Lynx, Mosaic, and Netscape.

USER CONNECTION

Microcomputers require modems to send and receive messages over telephone lines.

A great deal of computer communications is over telephone lines. However, because the telephone was originally designed for voice transmission, telephones typically send and receive **analog signals** (see Figure 8.8). Computers, in contrast, send and receive **digital signals**. These represent the presence or absence of an electronic pulse—the on/off binary signals we mentioned in Chapter 5. To convert the digital signals of your microcomputer to analog and vice versa, you need a modem.

Modems

The word *modem* is short for '*mo*dulator-*dem*odulator'. **Modulation** is the name of the process of converting from digital to analog. **Demodulation** is the process of converting from analog to digital. The modem enables digital microcomputers to communicate across analog telephone lines. Both voice communications and data communications can be carried over the same telephone line.

The speed with which modems transmit data varies. Communications speed is often measured in **baud rate**. Baud rate represents the number of changes in the electrical state in the line per second. Unfortunately, this measure can be misleading. At low speeds, baud rate is equivalent to *bits per second (bps)*. However, at higher speeds, baud rate is not equal to bits per second. For this reason, most communications professionals prefer to measure modem speed in bits per second.

The most popular microcomputer speeds are 9600, 14 400, and 28 800 bps. The higher the speed, the faster you can transmit a document—and therefore the cheaper your line costs. For example, transmitting a 20-page single-spaced report could take nearly 1½ minutes at 9600 bps and less than 30 seconds at 28 800 bps.

Types of modems

The four types of modems are external, internal, wireless, and fax:

• The **external modem** stands apart from the computer and is connected by a cable to the computer's serial port. Another cable

Figure 8.8 Analog versus digital signals

telephone
wall jack

external modem   microcomputer   external modem

telephone
line

connects the modem to the telephone wall jack (see Figure 8.9). Some modems weigh as little as 85 grams, making them practical for use with portable computers.

Figure 8.9 An external direct-connect modem

The **internal modem** consists of a plug-in circuit board inside the system unit. A cable directly connects the computer's serial port to the telephone wall jack. Internal modems are frequently used in portable computers where uploading and downloading files is common. They are generally less expensive than external modems.

The **wireless modem** is very similar to the external modem (see Figure 8.10). It connects to the computer's serial port. Unlike an external modem, it does not connect to telephone lines. Rather, wireless modems receive through the air. This is a new type of modem using new technology. Although not as fast as the other modems, wireless modems are becoming popular with users of portable computers.

A **fax modem** is a special modem that allows you to send and/or receive faxes. With the other modems, signals represent bits—0s and 1s combined to signify letters and numbers typically using an ASCII code. A fax modem uses the signals to represent a graphic image of a page. When a fax is received, the data is stored on the hard disk. The fax can be viewed on the screen or printed out.

Not all computer communications require a modem to convert from digital to analog and back. Computer systems connected by coaxial or fibre-optic cables can transmit digital data directly through these channels.

COMMUNICATIONS CHANNELS

Data may flow through five kinds of communications channels: telephone lines, coaxial cable, fibre optic cable, microwave, and satellite.

The two ways of connecting microcomputers with each other and with other equipment are through the cable and through the air. Specifically, five kinds of technology are used to transmit data. These are telephone lines (twisted pair), coaxial cable, fibre-optic cable, microwave, and satellite. The diameters and transmission capacities of the three kinds of cable are compared in Figure 8.11.

Figure 8.10 A wireless modem

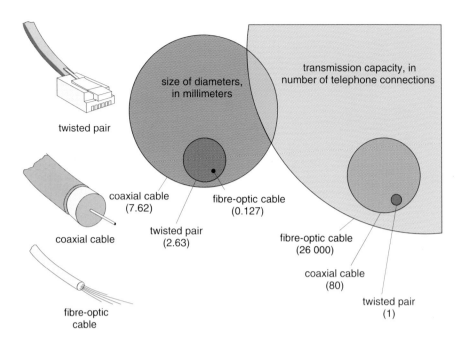

Figure 8.11 Comparing cable size and capacity

Telephone lines

Most telephone lines you see strung on poles consist of cables made up of hundreds of copper wires, called **twisted pairs**. A single twisted pair culminates in a wall jack into which you can plug your phone. Telephone lines have been the standard transmission medium for years for both voice and data. However, they are now being phased out by more technically advanced and reliable media.

Coaxial cable

Coaxial cable, a high-frequency transmission cable, replaces the multiple wires of telephone lines with a single solid copper core. In terms of number of telephone connections, a coaxial cable has 80 times the transmission capacity of a twisted pair. Coaxial cable is often used to link parts of a computer system in one building.

Fibre-optic cable

In **fibre-optic cable**, data is transmitted as pulses of light through tubes of glass. In terms of number of telephone connections, fibre-optic cable has 26 000 times the transmission capacity of a twisted pair (see Figure 8.11). However, it is significantly smaller. Indeed, a fibre-optic tube can be half the diameter of a human hair. Although limited in the distance they can carry information, fibre-optic cables have several advantages. Such cables are immune to electronic interference, which makes them more secure. They are also lighter and less expensive than coaxial cable and are more reliable at transmitting data. They transmit information using beams of light at light speeds instead of pulses of electricity, making them far faster than copper cable. Fibre-optic cable is rapidly replacing twisted-pair telephone lines.

Microwave

In this communications channel the medium is not a solid substance but rather the air itself. **Microwaves** are high-frequency radio waves that travel in straight lines through the air. Because the waves cannot bend with the curvature of the earth, they can be transmitted only over short distances. Thus, microwave is a good medium for sending data between buildings in a city or on a large college campus. For longer distances, the waves must be relayed by means of 'dishes', or antennas. These can be installed on towers, high buildings, and mountaintops, for example (see Figure 8.12).

Satellites

Orbiting about 22 000 miles above the earth, **satellites** are also used as microwave relay stations. Many of these are offered by Intelsat, the *In*ternational *Tele*communications *Sat*ellite Consortium, which is owned by 114 governments and forms a worldwide communications system. Teledesic Corporation announced plans to launch 840 satellites with the capability of linking 95 percent of the earth's surface. Satellites rotate at a precise point and speed above the earth. This makes them appear stationary so they can amplify and relay microwave signals from one transmitter on the ground to another (see Figure 8.13). Thus, satellites can be used to send large volumes of data. Their only drawback is that bad weather can sometimes interrupt the flow of data.

Figure 8.12 Microwave transmission

DATA TRANSMISSION

Several technical matters affect data communications. They are bandwidth, serial versus parallel transmission, direction of flow, modes of transmission, and protocols.

Several factors affect how data is transmitted. They include speed or bandwidth, serial or parallel transmission, direction of data flow, modes of transmitting data, and protocols.

Bandwidth

The different communications channels have different data transmission speeds. This bits-per-second transmission capability of a channel is called its **bandwidth**. Bandwidth may be of three types:

Voiceband The **voiceband** is the bandwidth of a standard telephone line and used often for microcomputer transmission; typical speeds are

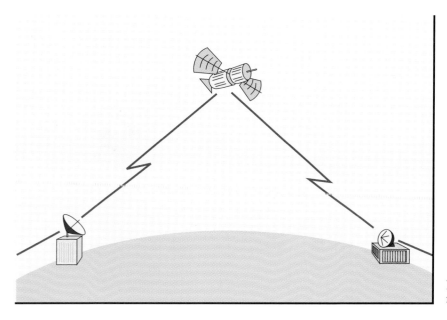

Figure 8.13 Satellite relaying microwave signals from earth

serial

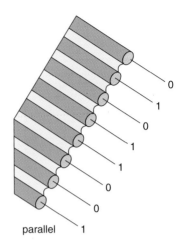

parallel

Figure 8.14 Serial versus parallel transmission

9600 to 14 400, although with special equipment much higher speeds are possible.

Medium band The **medium band** is the bandwidth of special leased lines used mainly with minicomputers and mainframe computers; the bps is 56 000–264 million.

Broadband The **broadband** is the bandwidth that includes microwave, satellite, coaxial cable, and fibre-optic channels. It is used for very high speed computers whose processors communicate directly with each other. It is in the range of 56 000–30 billion bps.

Serial and parallel transmission

Data travels in two ways: serially and in parallel (see Figure 8.14).

- In **serial data transmission**, bits flow in a series or continuous stream, like cars crossing a one-lane bridge. Each bit travels on its own communications line. Serial transmission is the way most data is sent over telephone lines. Thus, the plug-in board making up the serial connector in a microcomputer's modem is usually called a *serial port*. More technical names for the serial port are **RS-232C connector** and **asynchronous communications port**.

- With **parallel data transmission**, bits flow through separate lines simultaneously. In other words, they resemble cars moving together at the same speed on a multilane freeway. Parallel transmission is typically limited to communications over short distances and is not used over telephone lines. It is, however, a standard method of sending data from a computer's CPU to a printer.

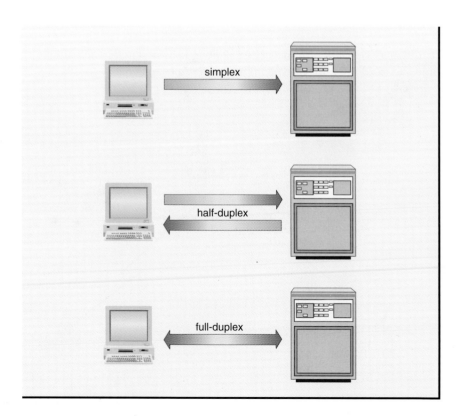

Figure 8.15 Simplex, half-duplex, and full-duplex communication

Direction of data transmission

There are three directions or modes of data flow in a data communications system (see Figure 8.15):

- **Simplex communication** resembles the movement of cars on a one-way street. Data travels in one direction only. It is not frequently used in data communications systems today. One instance in which it is used may be in point-of-sale (POS) terminals in which data is being entered only.

- In **half-duplex communication**, data flows in both directions, but not simultaneously. That is, data flows in only one direction at any one time. This resembles traffic on a one-lane bridge. Half-duplex is very common and is frequently used for linking microcomputers by telephone lines to other microcomputers, minicomputers, and mainframes. Thus, when you dial into an electronic bulletin board through your microcomputer, you may well be using half-duplex communication.

- In **full-duplex communication**, data is transmitted back and forth at the same time, like traffic on a two-way street. It is clearly the fastest and most efficient form of two-way communication. However, it requires special equipment and is used primarily for mainframe communications. An example is the weekly sales figures and delivery schedules that a supermarket or regional office sends to and receives from its corporate headquarters in another state.

Modes of transmitting data

Data may be sent by asynchronous or synchronous transmission (see Figure 8.16).

- In **asynchronous transmission**, the method frequently used with microcomputers, data is sent and received one byte at a time. Asynchronous transmission is often used for terminals with slow speeds. Its advantage is that the data can be transmitted whenever convenient for the sender. Its disadvantage is a relatively slow rate of data transfer.

- **Synchronous transmission** is used to transfer great quantities of information by sending several bytes or a block at a time. For the

Figure 8.16 Asynchronous and synchronous communication

153

data transmission to occur, the sending and receiving of the blocks of bytes must occur at carefully timed intervals. Thus, the system requires a synchronised clock. Its advantage is that data can be sent very quickly. Its disadvantage is the cost of the required equipment.

Protocols

For data transmission to be successful, sender and receiver must follow a set of communication rules for the exchange of information. These rules for exchanging data between computers are known as the line **protocol**. A communications software package like Crosstalk helps define the protocol, such as speeds and modes, for connecting with another microcomputer.

When different types of microcomputers are connected in a network, the protocols can become very complex. Obviously, for the connections to work, these network protocols must adhere to certain standards. The first commercially available set of standards was IBM's Systems Network Architecture (SNA). This works for IBM's own equipment, but other machines won't necessarily communicate with them. The International Standards Organization has defined a set of communications protocols called the Open Systems Interconnection (OSI). The purpose of the OSI model is to identify functions provided by any network. It separates each network's functions into seven 'layers' of protocols, or communication rules. When two network systems communicate, their corresponding layers may exchange data. This assumes that the microcomputers and other equipment on each network have implemented the same functions and interfaces.

NETWORK ARCHITECTURE

Network architecture describes how a computer network is configured and what strategies are used.

Communications channels can be connected in different arrangements, or *networks*, to suit different users' needs. A *computer network* is a communications system connecting two or more computers that work together to exchange information and share resources. **Network architecture** describes how the network is arranged and how the resources are co-ordinated and shared.

Terms

There are a number of specialised terms that describe computer networks. Some terms often used with networks are the following:

Node A node is any device that is connected to a network. It could be a computer, printer, or communication or data storage device.

Client A client is a node that requests and uses resources available from other nodes. Typically, a client is a user's microcomputer.

Server A server is a node that shares resources with other nodes. Depending on the resources shared, it may be called a file server, printer server, communication server, or database server.

Network operating system (NOS) Microcomputer operating systems like DOS and Windows NT interact with an application and a computer. On the other hand, network operating systems control and co-ordinate the activities between computers on a network. These activities include electronic communication and the sharing of information and resources.

Distributed processing In a distributed processing system, computing power is located and shared at different locations. This type of system is common in decentralised organisations where divisional offices have their own computer systems. The computer systems in the divisional offices are networked to the organisation's main or centralised computer.

Host computer A host computer is a large centralised computer, usually a minicomputer or a mainframe.

A network may consist only of microcomputers, or it may integrate microcomputers or other devices with larger computers. Networks can be controlled by all nodes working together equally or by specialised nodes co-ordinating and supplying all resources. Networks may be simple or complex, self-contained or dispersed over a large geographical area.

Configurations

A network can be arranged or configured in several different ways. This arrangement is called the network's **topology**. The four principal network topologies are star, bus, ring, and hierarchical.

In a **star network**, a number of small computers or peripheral devices are linked to a central unit (see Figure 8.17). This central unit may be a *host computer* or a *file server*.

All communications pass through this central unit. Control is maintained by **polling**. That is, each connecting device is asked ('polled') whether it has a message to send. Each device is then in turn allowed to send its message.

One particular advantage of the star form of network is that it can be used to provide a **time-sharing system**. That is, several users can share resources ('time') on a central computer. The star is a common arrangement for linking several microcomputers to a mainframe that allows access to an organisation's database.

In a **bus network**, each device in the network handles its own communications control. There is no host computer. All communications travel along a common connecting cable called a **bus** (see Figure 8.18). As the information passes along the bus, it's examined by each device to see if the information is intended for it.

The bus network is typically used when only a few microcomputers are to be linked together. This arrangement is common in systems for electronic mail or for sharing data stored on different microcomputers. The bus network is not as efficient as the star network for sharing common resources. (This is because the bus network is not a direct link to the resource.) However, a bus network is less expensive and is in very common use.

In a **ring network**, each device is connected to two other devices, forming a ring (see Figure 8.19). There is no central file server or computer. Messages are passed around the ring until they reach the correct destination. With microcomputers, the ring arrangement is the least frequently used of the four networks. However, it often is used to link mainframes, especially over wide geographical areas. These mainframes tend to operate fairly autonomously. They perform most

Figure 8.17 A star network

Figure 8.18 A bus network

Figure 8.19 A ring network

Figure 8.20 A hierarchical network

or all of their own processing and only occasionally share data and programs with other mainframes.

A ring network is useful in a decentralised organisation because it makes possible a *distributed data processing system*. That is, computers can perform processing tasks at their own dispersed locations. However, they can also share programs, data, and other resources with each other.

The **hierarchical network** consists of several computers linked to a central host computer, just like a star network. However, these other computers are also hosts to other, smaller computers or to peripheral devices (see Figure 8.20).

Thus, the host at the top of the hierarchy could be a mainframe. The computers below the mainframe could be minicomputers, and those below, microcomputers. The hierarchical network—also called a **hybrid network**—allows various computers to share databases, processing power, and different output devices.

A hierarchical network is useful in centralised organisations. For example, different departments within an organisation may have individual microcomputers connected to departmental minicomputers. The minicomputers in turn may be connected to the corporation's mainframe, which contains data and programs accessible to all.

Strategies

Every network has a strategy or way of co-ordinating the sharing of information and resources. The most common network strategies are terminal, peer-to-peer, and client/server systems.

In a **terminal network system**, processing power is centralised in one large computer, usually a mainframe. The nodes connected to this host computer are terminals with little or no processing capabilities. The star and hierarchical networks are typical configurations with UNIX as the operating system.

Most airline reservation systems are terminal systems. A large central computer maintains all the airline schedules, rates, seat availability, and so on. Travel agents use terminals to connect to the central computer and use it to schedule reservations. Although the tickets may be printed along with travel itineraries at the agent's desk, nearly all processing is done at the central computer.

Some of the advantages of terminal network systems are centralised location and control of technical personnel, software, and data. One disadvantage is the lack of control and flexibility for the end user. Another disadvantage is that terminal systems do not use the processing power available with microcomputers. Once very popular, most new systems do not use the terminal strategy.

In a **peer-to-peer network system**, nodes can act as both servers and clients. For example, one microcomputer can *obtain* files located on another microcomputer and can also *provide* files to other microcomputers. A typical configuration for a peer-to-peer system is the bus network. Commonly used network operating systems are Artisoft LANtastic, Apple's Macintosh Peer-to-Peer LANs, Novell's NetWare Lite, and Microsoft's Windows for Workgroups.

There are several advantages to using this type of strategy. The networks are inexpensive and easy to install, and they usually work well for smaller systems with less than ten nodes. As the number of nodes increases, however, the performance of the network declines. Another disadvantage is the lack of powerful management software to effectively monitor a large network's activities. For these reasons, peer-to-peer networks are typically used by small networks.

Client/server network systems use one powerful computer to co-ordinate and supply services to all other nodes on the network. The server provides access to centralised resources such as databases, application software, and hardware. This strategy is based on specialisation. Server nodes co-ordinate and supply specialised services, and client nodes request the services. Commonly used network operating systems are Novell's NetWare, IBM's LAN Server, Banyan Vines, and Microsoft's LAN Manager and Windows NT.

One advantage of client/server network systems is their ability to handle very large networks efficiently. Another advantage is the powerful network management software that monitors and controls the network's activities. The major disadvantages are the cost of installation and maintenance.

Computer networks in organisations have evolved over time. Most large organisations have a wide range of different network configurations, operating systems, and strategies. These organisations are moving toward integrating or connecting all of these networks together. That way, a user on one network can access resources available throughout the company. This is called **enterprise computing.**

NETWORK TYPES

Communications networks differ in geographical size. Three important types are LANs, MANs, and WANs.

Clearly, different types of channels—cable or air—allow different kinds of networks to be formed. Telephone lines, for instance, may connect communications equipment within the same building. In fact, many new buildings—called *smart buildings*—have coaxial or fibre-optic cable installed inside the walls. This makes it easy to form communications networks.

Networks may also be city-wide and even international, using both cable and air connections. Here let us distinguish among three types: *local area networks, metropolitan area networks,* and *wide area networks.*

Local area networks

Networks with computers and peripheral devices in close physical proximity—within the same building, for instance—are called **local area networks (LANs)**. Linked by cable—telephone, coaxial, or fibre-optic—LANs often use a bus form of organisation.

Our illustration shows an example of a LAN (see Figure 8.21). This typical arrangement has two benefits. People can share different equipment, which lowers the cost of equipment. For instance, here the four microcomputers share the laser printer and the file server, which are expensive pieces of hardware. (Individual microcomputers many times also have their own less expensive printers, such as the dot-matrix printer shown in our illustration.) Other equipment may also be added to the LAN—for instance, mini- or mainframe computers or optical-disc storage devices.

Note that the LAN shown in our illustration also features a **network gateway.** A LAN may be linked to other LANs or to larger networks in this manner. With the gateway, one LAN may be connected to the LAN of another office group. It may also be connected to others in the

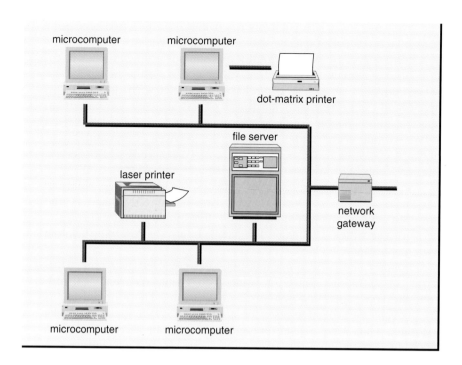

Figure 8.21 A local area network that includes a file server and network gateway

wider world, even if their configurations are different. Alternatively, a network bridge would be used to connect networks with the same configurations.

Experts predict great growth of microcomputer LANs (see Figure 8.22).

Metropolitan area networks

The next step up from the LAN might be the **MAN**—the **metropolitan area network**. These networks are used as links between office buildings in a city. *Cellular phone systems* expand the flexibility of MAN by allowing links to car phones and portable phones.

Wide area networks

Wide area networks (WANs) are countrywide and worldwide networks. Among other kinds of channels, they use microwave relays

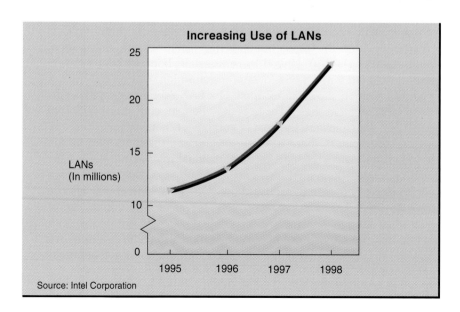

Figure 8.22 Local area network usage—past, present, and future

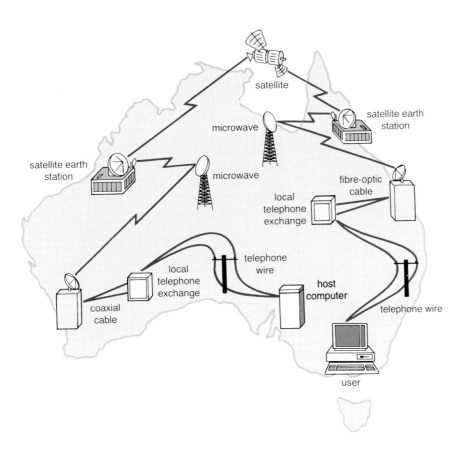

and satellites to reach users over long distances—for example, from Sydney to Perth (see Figure 8.23). One of the most widely used WANs is the Internet, which allows users to connect to other users and facilities worldwide.

The primary difference between a LAN, MAN, and WAN is the geographical range. Each may have various combinations of hardware, such as microcomputers, minicomputers, mainframes, and various peripheral devices.

Figure 8.23 Wide area network

A LOOK AT THE FUTURE

New developments in hardware, the telephone system, and the National Information Highway suggest new trends: fewer 'standalone computers', the era of the portable office, and downsized applications.

The next decade will see phenomenal changes in the area of communications. Two important developments will be the expansion of the Integrated Services Digital Network (ISDN) and Asynchronous Transfer Mode (ATM). In use in the United States since 1988, ISDN utilises a set of technologies and international-exchange standards that will completely digitise today's telephone system. ATM extends ISDN's capability by providing even faster data transfer using public telephone lines. In early 1994, long distance telephone providers US West and Sprint agreed to supply ATM services countrywide. These developments promise to support data, voice, and video transmission across the country. ATM is expected to be widely used by multimedia specialists. ISDN is expected to have more general use in smaller organisations and home offices.

What do these trends suggest? First, the 'standalone' computer—one that isn't connected to any network—will become a thing of the past. Second, we have arrived at the era of the *portable office*. Hooking a portable computer or fax machine to a network while you are travelling makes you more efficient. Third, we are clearly at the point of so-called *downsized applications*. That is, many applications that were once available only on mainframes and minicomputers are now possible on network-linked microcomputers.

REVIEW QUESTIONS

True/false

1. A local area network connects two or more computers within a limited area, such as within the same building.

2. Modems are used to convert data on a CD-ROM to an internal hard disk.

3. Frequently, computer communications over telephone lines require a modem.

4. In half-duplex communication, data flows in both directions at the same time.

5. In a client/server system, each node on the network has equal responsibility for co-ordinating the network's activities.

Multiple choice

1. A special sequence of numbers or letters that limits access to electronic mailboxes is a:
   (a) combination
   (b) code
   (c) fax
   (d) password
   (e) modem

2. Transferring data from a larger computer to your microcomputer is called:
   (a) a LAN
   (b) time-sharing
   (c) downloading
   (d) networking
   (e) uploading

3. What communications channel transfers data as pulses of light?
   (a) telephone lines
   (b) coaxial cable
   (c) fibre-optic cable
   (d) microwave
   (e) satellite

4. Rules for exchanging data on a network are called:
   (a) protocol
   (b) asynchronous transmission
   (c) configuration
   (d) channel
   (e) serial transmission

5. A system frequently used in decentralised organisations in which computing power is located and shared at different sites is:
   (a) a client/server
   (b) a ring
   (c) centralised
   (d) mainframe
   (e) distributed

Fill in the blank

1. _____ systems are computer systems linked to telephones that convert the human voice into digital bits.

2. Transferring data from your microcomputer to a minicomputer or mainframe is called _____ .

3. Because _____ travel in straight lines through the air and cannot bend with the curvature of the earth, they can transmit data only over short distances.

4. A _____ _____ system controls and co-ordinates the activities on a network.

5. _____ are countrywide and worldwide networks that connect users over long distances.

Open ended

1. What are electronic bulletin boards? How do they differ from electronic mail systems?

2. List and describe the five kinds of communications channels.

3. What are the differences between a terminal, peer-to-peer, and a client/server system?

4. Describe the differences between simplex, half-duplex, and full-duplex communication.

5. Discuss the four basic network configurations.

DISCUSSION QUESTIONS AND PROJECTS

1. *Electronic bulletin boards* Unquestionably there is an area of personal interest to you that is available on an electronic bulletin board. A glance at one local microcomputer publication shows bulletin boards available on such subjects as sports, restaurants, politics, religion, business opportunities, music, mental health, drug recovery, alternative lifestyles, and many other topics.

   What kind of electronic bulletin board would be of interest to you? See if you can find a printed list of bulletin boards in a local microcomputer publication. Or try contacting a users' group for help. Users' groups are clubs or volunteer organisations. Their members meet to help each other solve problems or share interests regarding particular personal computers.

2. *The rise of telecommuting* Over 9 million US employees work full- or part-time at home. This number is expected to increase to 25 million by the year 2000. Discuss what you think would be some of the positive and negative consequences of this trend on:

(a) employee accessibility

(b) information security

(c) productivity

(d) communication

CASE STUDY

DAVID BROS PROPERTY DEVELOPMENT OFFICE

David Bros is a retail chain of stores with a large store in the central business district and a number of suburban branches. The property development office (PDO), which is based at the head office of David Bros, designs and creates new store interiors. The remodel of a store may be a full store remodel or, as is more often the case, a departmental remodel only.

The PDO manager, Ian Thomas, is responsible to the general manager of David Bros and is in charge of the following staff:

• A branch liaison officer, who deals with the branch management to ensure a smooth operation once the remodel is under way.

• Three designers, who are responsible for creating the floor plans and drawings that are necessary to facilitate the changes to store interiors.

• Two full-time carpenters, who each supervise a team of part-time staff who are responsible for the physical changes to the stores.

• A full-time secretary, Julie Hender, who types all correspondence that goes to the suburban branches and to the other departments within the head office. Julie also acts as courier between the PDO, the other head office departments and the suburban branches.

Previously, the PDO has used a manual system to produce floor plans. Recently, a computer system has been purchased together with the 'off-the-shelf' computer-aided design package 'HAWK'. The CAD program HAWK allows the user to create 2D and 3D drawings. The computer system consists of a local area network of six PCs attached to a central file server. The file server is a 75 MHz Pentium IBM-compatible system with 16 Mb of RAM and a 1.2 Gb hard disk. An electrostatic plotter was purchased to enable the designers to print the complex diagrams generated. The computer system has been implemented to aid the interior designing of stores. Its main functions are to:

• draw accurate and concise two-dimensional (2D) floor plans of a store's present structural layout;

• convert present two-dimensional floor plans into a scaled three-dimensional (3D) drawing of the store's interior;

• remodel present store interior (3D) plans, while working within the restrictions of the permanent building structure (2D) plans.

One of the designers, Jennifer Webster, has been largely responsible for the purchase and implementation of the new computer system. She has trained the other designers in the use of the software and feels that she can now leave the company. She has been offered a permanent position as chief designer but has decided to go back to university to further her studies.

The general manager has just instigated a staffing study under the name Project Centre. Project Centre aims to rationalise staffing at David Bros, in particular staffing at the head office. Ian Thomas has been instructed to find ways in which he could change the structure of his department in order to reduce staffing costs.

Ian has the following suggestions for implementing staff reductions:

* Install a LAN that would link the various departments within the head office.

* Instigate an e-mail system that would enable easy interdepartmental contact within the head office.

* Equip the branch liaison officer with a laptop computer with an internal modem to enable him to access the head office network.

Ian needs you to answer the following questions before he submits his proposal.

QUESTIONS

1. The property development office manager, Ian Thomas, has suggested that a LAN be installed at the head office.

    (a) State what LAN stands for and then explain the important features of a LAN.

    (b) Explain the advantages of a LAN in relation to the PDO and the other departments within the head office.

    (c) For each of the five kinds of communications channels, explain why they would be suitable, or unsuitable, for use with the suggested LAN.

2. Ian has suggested an e-mail system be installed at the head office.

    (a) What will the e-mail system be used for?

    (b) How will an e-mail system affect the staff within the PDO?

3. Jennifer is a very competent designer who is the most efficient user of the CAD program. Ian is of the opinion that if she stayed with the company, she could replace one of the existing designers. Working half-time would allow Jennifer to continue her university studies. Ian has suggested that Jennifer could work from home.

    (a) What hardware and software would Jennifer need to enable her to continue her design work at home?

    (b) What facilities would need to be provided at the head office to allow Jennifer access to the LAN?

4. Assuming that the company decides to implement all of the suggestions, including those in questions 1 to 3:

    (a) What personnel changes could take place?

    (b) Who would take over the role of the staff who are retrenched?

5. There is a possibility that the LAN could be expanded to form a WAN.

    (a) What is a WAN?

    (b) What would be the advantages for the property development office if a WAN was installed?

    (c) What hardware and software would need to be installed at each branch to enable full utilisation of a WAN?

Files and databases

FROM THE USER'S POINT OF VIEW

Like a library, the purpose of secondary storage is to store information. How is such information organised? What are files and databases, and why know anything about them? Perhaps the answer is: to become competent at making use of information in the Information Age, you have to know how to *find* that information.

At one time, it was not important for microcomputer users to have to know much about files and databases. However, the recent arrival of very powerful microcomputer chips and their availability to communications networks has changed that. To attain true computer competency, you need to know how to gain access to the files and databases on your personal computer. You also need to be able to access those available from other sources. Communications lines extend the reach of your microcomputer well beyond the desktop.

FILES

Understanding how files work means understanding data organisation, key fields, batch versus real-time processing, master versus transaction files, and file organisation.

You want to know your final grades for the semester. You call your school's registrar after your last semester exams to find out your grade point average. Perhaps you are told, 'Sorry, that's not in the computer yet'. Why can't they tell you? How is the school's computer system different from, say, your bank's, where deposits and withdrawals seem to be recorded right away?

Data organisation

To be processed by the computer or stored in secondary storage, data is typically organised into groups or categories. Each group is more complex than the one before:

COMPETENCIES

After you have read this chapter, you should be able to:

- describe how data is organised: characters, fields, records, and files;

- understand the difference between batch processing and real-time processing;

- describe the difference between master files and transaction files;

- define and describe the three types of file organisation; sequential, direct, and index sequential;

- describe the advantages of a database;

- describe the two essential parts of a database management system (DBMS);

- describe three ways of organising a DBMS: hierarchical, network, and relational;

- distinguish among individual, company, distributed, and proprietary databases;

- discuss some issues of productivity and security.

Character A character is a single letter, number, or special character such as a punctuation mark or $.

Field A field contains a set of related characters. On a college registration form or a driver's licence, a person's first name is a field. Last name is another field, street address another field, city yet another field, and so on.

Record A record is a collection of related fields. Everything on a person's college registration form or driver's licence, including identification number, is a record.

File A file is a collection of related records. All the dog licences issued in one local council could be a file.

Database A database is a collection of related files. All the dog licence files for the state could be a database.

An example of how data is organised is shown in the illustration (see Figure 9.1). Note that a student's name is not one field, but three: first name, middle initial, and last name.

The key field

Our illustration also shows the student's identification number. Is such a number really necessary? Certainly most people's names are different enough that at a small college, say, you might think identification numbers wouldn't be necessary. However, as anyone named John Smith or Linda Williams knows, there are plenty of other people around with the same name. Sometimes they even have the same middle initial. This is the reason for the student identification number: the number is unique, whereas the name may not be.

This distinctive number is called a *key field*. A **key field** is the particular field of a record that is chosen to uniquely identify each record. The key may be social security number, employee identification number, or part number.

Batch versus real-time processing

Traditionally data is processed in two ways. These are *batch processing*, what we might call 'later', and *real-time processing*, what we might call 'now'. These two methods have been used to handle common record-keeping activities such as payroll and sales orders.

Figure 9.1 How data is organised

Batch processing In **batch processing**, data is collected over several hours, days, or even weeks. It is then processed all at once—as a 'batch'. If you have a bank credit card, your bill probably reflects batch processing. That is, during the month, you buy things and charge them to your credit card. Each time you charge something, a copy of the transaction is sent to the credit card company. At some point in the month, the company's data processing department puts all those transactions (and those of many other customers) together. It then processes them at one time. The company then sends you a single bill totalling the amount you owe.

Real-time processing Totalling up the sales charged to your bank credit card is an example of batch processing. You might use another kind of card—your bank's automatic teller machine (ATM) card—for the second kind of processing. **Real-time processing** occurs when data is processed at the same time the transaction occurs. As you use your ATM card to withdraw cash, the system automatically computes the balance remaining in your account.

At one time, only tape storage, and therefore only sequential access storage (as we discussed in Chapter 7), was available. All processing then was batch processing and was done on mainframe computers. Even today, a great deal of mainframe time is dedicated to this kind of processing. Many smaller organisations, however, use microcomputers for this purpose.

Real-time processing is made possible by the availability of disk packs and direct access storage (as we described in Chapter 7). Direct access storage enables the user to quickly go directly to a particular record. (In sequential access storage, by contrast, the user must wait for the computer to scan several records one at a time. It continues scanning until it comes to the one that's needed.) Not long ago, specialised terminals were used to enter data and perform real-time processing. Today, however, more and more microcomputers are being used for this purpose. As we have stated, microcomputers have become increasingly more powerful. Thus, smaller companies and departments of large companies use these machines by themselves for many real-time processing needs. That is, they use them without connecting to a mainframe.

Master versus transaction files

Two types of files are commonly used to update data—a *master file* and a *transaction file*:

- The **master file** is a complete file containing all records current up to the last update. An example is the data file used to prepare your last month's telephone bill or credit card bill.

- The **transaction file** contains *recent* changes to records that will be used to update the master file. An example could be a temporary 'holding' file that accumulates telephone charges or credit card charges through the present month.

File organisation

File organisation may be of three types: *sequential, direct,* and *index sequential.*

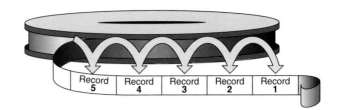

Figure 9.2 Sequential file
organisation

Sequential file organisation The simplest organisation is **sequential file organisation**, in which records are stored physically one after another in predetermined order. This order is determined by the key field on each record, such as a student identification number (see Figure 9.2).

This organisation is very efficient whenever all or a large portion of the records need to be accessed—for example, when final grades are to be mailed out. There is also an equipment cost advantage because magnetic tapes and tape drives can be used. Both are less expensive than disks and disk drives. One disadvantage is that the records must be ordered in a specific way, and that can be time-consuming.

The major disadvantage, however, is that access to a particular record can be very slow. For example, to find the record about a particular student, the registrar's office would sequentially search through the records. It would search them one at a time until the student's number was found. If the number is 4315, the computer will start with record number 0000. It will go through 0001, 0002, and so on until it reaches the student's number.

Direct file organisation To obtain particular records, **direct file organisation** is much better. Records are not stored physically one after another. Rather, they are stored on a disk in a particular address or location that can be determined by their key field. This address is calculated by a technique known as **hashing**. Hashing programs use mathematical operations to convert the key field's numeric value to a particular storage address. These programs are used to initially store records and later to relocate them (see Figure 9.3).

Unlike sequential access files, which are stored on either magnetic tape or disk, direct files can only be stored on disk. The primary advantage is that direct file organisation can locate specific records very quickly. If your grades were stored in a direct file, the registrar could access them quickly using only your student identification number.

Figure 9.3 Direct file
organisation

Figure 9.4 Index sequential file organisation

The disadvantage of direct file organisation is cost. It needs more storage space on disk. It also is not as good as sequential file organisation for large numbers of updates or for listing large numbers of records.

Index sequential file organisation **Index sequential file organisation** is a compromise between sequential and direct file organisations. It stores records in a file in sequential order. However, an index sequential file also contains an index. The index lists the key to each group of records stored and the corresponding disk address for that group. When the user seeks a particular record, the computer starts searching sequentially by looking at the beginning of the record group (see Figure 9.4). *Note:* The disk addresses listed in Figure 9.4 represent the actual locations, which are identified by specific track and sector locations.

For example, the college registrar could index certain ranges of student identification numbers—0000 to 1999, 2000 to 3999, and so on. For the computer to find your number (for example, 4315), it would first go to the index. The index would give the location of the range in which your number appears on the disk (for example, 4000 to 4999). The computer would then search that range (A4) sequentially to find your number.

Index sequential file organisation requires disks or other direct access storage devices. It is faster than sequential but not as fast as direct access. It's best used when large batches of transactions must occasionally be updated, yet users also want frequent, quick access to data. For example, every month a bank will update bank statements to send to its customers. However, customers and bank tellers need to be able to have up-to-the-minute information about cheque accounts.

See Figure 9.5 for a summary of the advantages and disadvantages of each type of file organisation.

DATABASES

A database consolidates multiple files of duplicate information.

Many organisations have multiple files on the same subject or person. For example, records for the same customer may appear in different files in the sales department, billing department, and credit department. If the customer moves, then the address in each file must be updated. If one file is overlooked, it can cause embarrassment. For

FILE ORGANISATION

Type	Advantages	Disadvantages
Sequential	Efficient access to all or large part of records, cost	Slow access to specific records
Direct	Fast access to specific records	Inefficient access to all or large part of records, cost
Index sequential	Faster than sequential, more efficient than direct	Not quite as efficient as sequential, not quite as fast as direct, cost

Figure 9.5 Summary of the three types of file organisation

example, a product ordered might be sent to the new address, but the bill might be sent to the old address.

Moreover, data spread around in different files is not as useful. The marketing department, for instance, might want to do special promotions to customers who order large quantities of merchandise. However, they may be unable to do so because that information is in the billing department. A database can make the needed information available.

A *database* is defined as a collection of integrated data. By 'integrated', we mean the data consists of logically related files and records.

The need for databases

For both individuals and organisations, there are many advantages to having databases:

Sharing In organisations, information from one department can be readily shared with others, as we saw in the example above.

Security Users are given passwords or access only to the kind of information they need to know. Thus, the payroll department may have access to employees' pay rates, but other departments would not.

Fewer files With several departments having access to one file, there are fewer files. Excess storage, or what is called 'data redundancy', is reduced. Microcomputers linked by a network to a file server, for example, could replace the hard disks located in several individual microcomputers.

Data integrity Older filing systems many times did not have 'integrity'. That is, a change made in the file in one department might not be made in the file in another department. As you might expect, this can cause serious problems and conflicts when data is used for important decisions affecting both departments.

Software for a database management system

In order to create, modify, and gain access to the database, special software is required. This software is called a *database management system*, which is commonly abbreviated DBMS.

Some DBMSs, such as dBASE, are designed specifically for microcomputers. Other DBMSs are designed for minicomputers and mainframes. Once again, increased processing power and the wide use of communications networks linked to file servers are changing everything. Now microcomputer DBMSs have become more like the ones used for mainframes—and vice versa.

DBMS software is made up of a data dictionary and a query language.

Data dictionary

A **data dictionary** contains a description of the structure of the data used in the database. For a particular item of data, it defines the names used for a particular field. It defines what type of data that field is (alphabetic, numeric, or alphanumeric, date, time, or logic). It also specifies the number of characters in each field and whether that field is a key field. An example of a data dictionary appears in the illustration (see Figure 9.6).

Query language

Access to most databases is accomplished with a **query language**. This is an easy-to-use language understandable to most users. The most widely used query language is **SQL** or **Structured Query Language.**

Query languages have commands such as DISPLAY, ADD, COMPARE, LIST, SELECT, and UPDATE. For example, imagine you wanted the names of all salespeople in an organisation whose sales were greater than their sales quotas. You might type the statement 'DISPLAY ALL FOR SALES > QUOTA'.

DBMS ORGANISATION

The three principal DBMS organisations are hierarchical, network, and relational.

The purpose of a database is to integrate individual items of data—that is, to transform isolated facts into useful information. We saw that files

Figure 9.6 Data dictionary: Access for Windows 3.1, version 2.0

171

can be organised in various ways (sequentially, for example) to best suit their use. Similarly, databases can also be organised in different ways to best fit their use. Although other arrangements have been tried, the three most common formats are *hierarchical, network,* and *relational.*

The hierarchical database

In a **hierarchical database**, fields or records are structured in **nodes**. Nodes are points connected like the branches of an upside-down tree. This is sometimes described as a one-to-many relationship. Each entry has one **parent node**, although a parent may have several **child nodes**. To find a particular field you have to start at the top with a parent and trace down the tree to a child.

The nodes farther down the system are subordinate to the ones above, like the hierarchy of managers in a corporation. An example of a hierarchical database for part of a nationwide airline reservations system is shown in our illustration (see Figure 9.7). The parent node is the 'departure' city, Los Angeles. This parent has four children, labelled 'arrival'. New York, one of the children, has three children of its own. They are labelled 'flight number'. Flight 110 has three children, labelled 'passenger'.

The problem with a hierarchical database is that if one parent node is deleted, so are all the subordinate child nodes. Moreover, a child node cannot be added unless a parent node is added first. The most significant limitation is the rigid structure: one parent only per child, and no relationships between the child nodes themselves.

The network database

A **network database** also has a hierarchical arrangement of nodes. However, each child node may have more than one parent node. This is sometimes described as a many-to-many relationship. There are additional connections—called **pointers**—between parent nodes and child nodes. Thus, a node may be reached through more than one path. It may be traced down through different branches.

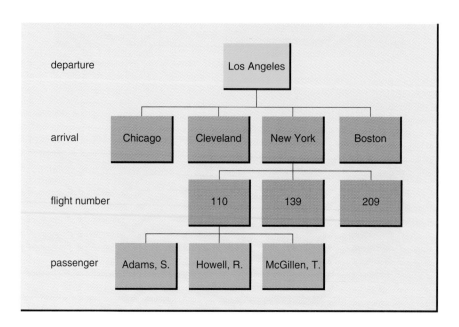

Figure 9.7 Example of a hierarchical database

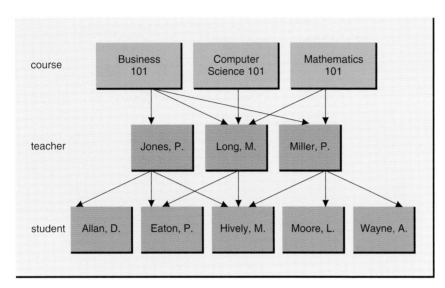

Figure 9.8 Example of a network database

An example of the use of a network organisation is that shown in our illustration for students taking courses (see Figure 9.8). If you trace through the logic of this organisation, you can see that each student can have more than one teacher. Each teacher can also teach more than one course. Students may take more than a single course. This demonstrates how the network arrangement is more flexible and in many cases more efficient than the hierarchical arrangement.

The relational database

The most flexible type of organisation is the **relational database**. In this structure, there are no access paths down a hierarchy to an item of data. Rather, the data elements are stored in different tables, each of which consists of rows and columns. A table is called a **relation**.

An example of a relational database is shown in our illustration (see Figure 9.9). The address table contains the names, drivers' licence numbers, and addresses for all registered drivers in a particular state. Within the table, a row resembles a record—for example, information about one driver. A column entry resembles a field. The driver's name is one field; the driver's licence number is another field. All related tables must have a *common data item* (a key field). Thus, information stored on one table can be linked with information stored on another table. One key field might be a person's name. Another might be a driver's licence number.

Thus, police officers who stop a speeding car can radio the driver's licence number and the car's licence plate number to the department of motor vehicles. They can use the driver's licence number as the key field. With it they can find out about any unpaid traffic violations (such as parking tickets). Also using the licence plate number they can obtain the car owner's name and address. If the owner's name and address do not match the driver who has been stopped, the police officer may further check for a stolen vehicle.

The most valuable feature of relational databases is their simplicity. Entries can be easily added, deleted, and modified. The hierarchy and network databases are more rigid. The relational organisation is common for microcomputer DBMSs, such as Access, Paradox, dBASE, and R:Base. Relational databases are also becoming very popular for mainframe- and minicomputer-based systems.

Figure 9.9 Example of a relational database

TYPES OF DATABASES

There are four kinds of databases: individual, company, distributed, and proprietary.

Databases may be small or large, limited in accessibility or widely accessible. Databases may be classified into four types: *individual, company* (or shared), *distributed,* and *proprietary.*

The individual database
The **individual database** is also called a **microcomputer database**. It is a collection of integrated files primarily used by just one person. Typically, the data and the DBMS are under the direct control of the user. They are stored either on the user's hard-disk drive or on a LAN file server.

There may be many times in your life when you will find this kind of database valuable. If you are in sales, for instance, a micro-computer database can be used to keep track of customers. If you are a sales manager, you can keep track of your salespeople and their performance. If you're an advertising account executive, you can keep track of what work and how many hours to charge each client.

The company, or shared, database
Companies, of course, create databases for their own use. The **company database** may be stored on a mainframe and managed by a computer professional (known as a database administrator). Users throughout the company have access to the database through their microcomputers linked to local area networks or wide area networks.

Company databases are of two types:

- The **commonly operational database** contains details about the operations of the company, such as inventory, production, and sales.

It contains data describing the day-to-day operations of the organisation.

• The **common user database** contains selected information both from the common operational database and from outside private (proprietary) databases. Managers can tap into this information on their microcomputers or terminals and use it for decision making.

As we will see in the next chapter, company databases are the foundation for management information systems. For instance, a department store can record all sales transactions in the database. A sales manager can use this information to see which salespeople are selling the most products. The manager can then determine year-end sales bonuses. Or the store's buyer can learn which products are selling well or not selling and make adjustments when reordering. A top executive might combine overall store sales trends with information from outside databases about consumer and population trends. This information could be used to change the whole merchandising strategy of the store.

The distributed database

Many times the data in a company is stored not in just one location but in several locations. It is made accessible through a variety of communications networks. The database, then, is a **distributed database**. That is, it is located in a place or places other than where users are located. Typically, database servers on a client/server network provide the link between users and the distant data.

For instance, some database information can be at regional offices. Some can be at company headquarters, some down the hall from you, and some even overseas. Sales figures for a chain of department stores, then, could be located at the various stores. But executives at district offices or at the chain's headquarters could have access to these figures.

The proprietary database

A **proprietary database** is generally an enormous database that an organisation develops to cover particular subjects. It offers access to this database to the public or selected outside individuals for a fee. Sometimes proprietary databases are also called *information utilities* or *data banks*. An example is CompuServe, which sells a variety of consumer and business services to microcomputer users (see Figure 9.10).

Some important proprietary databases are the following:

CompuServe Offers consumer and business services, including electronic mail.

Dialog Information Services Offers business information, as well as technical and scientific information.

Dow Jones News Retrieval Provides world news and information on business, investments, and stocks.

Prodigy Offers news and information on business and economics, as well as leisure services.

There are also specialised proprietary databases for investors and financial analysts, such as Chase Econometric Associates.

Figure 9.10 Proprietary database: CompuServe's consumer reports

Costs

If you have a microcomputer, modem, and phone at home, many of these proprietary databases are available to you. Usually you pay a start-up fee, an hourly charge for searching the database, and the phone company or telecommunications line charges.

As you might expect, fees and charges are high during the normal nine-to-five business hours. Dialog Information Services offers comprehensive coverage of journals, abstracts, research reports, reviews, news, tax information, and bibliographies. Topics covered range from agriculture to social science.

See Figure 9.11 for a summary of the four types of databases.

TYPES OF DATABASES

Type	Description
Individual	Integrated files used by just one person
Company	Common operational or commonly used files shared in an organisation
Distributed	Database spread geographically and accessed using database server
Proprietary	Information utilities or data banks available to users on wide range of topics for a subscription fee

Figure 9.11 Summary of the four types of databases

DATABASE USES AND ISSUES

Databases help users keep up to date and plan for the future, but keeping them secure is important. Databases may be supervised by a database administrator.

Databases offer great opportunities for productivity. In fact, in corporate libraries, electronic databases are now considered more valuable than books and journals. However, maintaining databases means users must make constant efforts to keep them from being tampered with or misused.

Data for strategic uses

Databases help users keep up to date and plan for the future. Among the hundreds of databases available to help users with both general and specific business purposes are the following:

* *business directories* providing addresses, financial and marketing information, products, and trade and brand names;

* *demographic data*, such as rural and city statistics, current estimates on population and income, employment statistics, census data, and so on;

* *business statistical information*, such as financial information on publicly traded companies, market potential of certain retail stores, and other business data and information;

* *text databases* providing articles from business publications, press releases, reviews on companies and products, and so on.

Importance of security

Precisely because databases are so valuable, their security has become a vital issue. One concern is that personal and private information about people stored in databases will be used for the wrong purposes. For instance, a person's credit history or medical records might be used to make hiring or promotion decisions.

Another concern is with preventing unauthorised users from gaining access to a database. For example, there have been numerous instances in which a **computer virus** has been launched into a database or network. Computer viruses are hidden instructions that 'migrate' through networks and operating systems and become embedded in different programs and databases. Some are relatively harmless, but others may destroy data. Computer viruses and other security issues are discussed in detail in Chapter 13.

Security can require putting guards on company computer rooms and checking the identification of everyone admitted. Some security systems electronically check fingerprints (see Figure 9.12). It can also include storing backup tapes or disks of all valuable information in another location. Security concerns are particularly important to organisations using WANs. Violations can occur without the violator actually entering secured areas.

The database administrator

Librarians have had to be trained in the use of electronic databases so that they can help their coporate users. However, corporate databases of all sorts—not just those in the library—have become extremely important. Hence, many large organisations employ a **database administrator (DBA)**. He or she helps determine the structure of the

Figure 9.12 Security: electronic fingerprint pads

large databases and evaluates the performance of the DBMS. For shared databases, the DBA also determines which people have access to what kind of data; these are called **processing rights**. In addition, the DBA is concerned with such significant issues as security, privacy, and ethics.

A LOOK AT THE FUTURE

Large databases give us everything from specialty phone books to census maps. Risks are increased compromises of privacy and security. Products are available to sift information.

The collection and use of data are sure to get more and more sophisticated. Microcomputer users now, for instance, can get computerised *specialty phone books* loaded with corporate names, telephone numbers, and other data. A database project of awesome proportions is the huge national computer map developed by the US Census Bureau. Known as *TIGER* (for *T*opologically *I*ntegrated *G*eographic *E*ncoding and *R*eference system), it will have 23 million street intersections. TIGER can be coupled with statistics that provide a numerical or income profile of every block in the United States. *Taxi* is a recently developed software package that uses a computer map database for six major cities. Users are provided with detailed maps including individual street addresses, and hotel and restaurant locations.

Global Positioning Systems (GPS) combine databases like TIGER with satellite communications. GPS allow a vehicle to be precisely tracked as it travels to its destination. Oldsmobile is offering a GPS navigation system in the Los Angeles area.

Big databases have not only great potential payoffs in productivity but also great risks for privacy and security. Your name probably passes through 50 different databases in a day. One worry is that corporations and governments may use them to create unnecessary or dangerous confidential files (dossiers) about private citizens. People also worry about disasters disrupting a local communications or computer system. A fire, earthquake, computer virus, or sabotage could have nationwide or worldwide effects on such a computer system.

Finally, the mountains of information generated by databases have now created a new industry. We now have products that sift the information to give us what we really want to know. These products range from personal newsletters to filtering technology that scans data for key words specified by the user.

REVIEW QUESTIONS

True/false

1. A record is a collection of related files.

2. In batch processing, data is processed at the same time the transaction occurs.

3. A data dictionary describes the structure of the data in a database.

4. A distributed database has data located in more than one location.

5. Processing rights are typically determined by the database administrator to specify which people have access to what kind of data.

Multiple choice

1. A collection of related fields is called a:
   (a) byte
   (b) word
   (c) character
   (d) record
   (e) file

2. A temporary file containing recent changes to records is:
   (a) master
   (b) data
   (c) transaction
   (d) indexed
   (e) batch

3. The database organisation in which fields and records are structured in nodes with each child node having only one parent is called:
   (a) hierarchical
   (b) network
   (c) proprietary
   (d) relational
   (e) individual

4. The type of database that is sometimes called an information utility or a data bank is:
   (a) individual
   (b) common operational
   (c) common user
   (d) distributed
   (e) proprietary

5. Hidden instructions that 'migrate' through networks and operating systems are:
   (a) file servers
   (b) viruses
   (c) nodes
   (d) relation
   (e) pointer

Fill in the blank

1. The _____ field uniquely identifies each record.

2. _____ file organisation is best for locating specific records.

3. A database is a collection of _____ data.

4. _____ databases are more flexible and easier to use than hierarchical and network databases.

5. Large organisations employ database _____ to help determine database structures and evaluate database performance.

Open ended

1. Describe how data is organised and give an example.

2. What are the differences between sequential, direct, and index sequential file organisations?

3. What are databases, and why are they needed?

4. Discuss the three principal ways of organising a database.

5. Describe each of the four types of database.

DISCUSSION QUESTIONS

1. *Useful information utilities* What are your main subjects? What kinds of information are you apt to be required to obtain for research papers, projects, and assignments? Imagine you work in the health field; you may be required to learn about diet, exercise, drug recovery, and the like. If you're in marketing, you may need to know about sales forecasting and product marketing.

   Take a few minutes to list the areas of information required in your field. Then go to the library and look up which information utilities or data banks would be most valuable to you. Examples are CompuServe, Dialog or The Knowledge Index, Dow Jones News Retrieval, and Prodigy.

2. *Electronic publishing by telephone companies?* In the United States, a dispute has been going on among the seven regional telephone companies (the 'Baby Bells') and the newspaper industry. Following the 1984 breakup of American Telephone & Telegraph (AT&T), the regional phone companies were sharply limited from entering 'electronic publishing'. They were prohibited from selling database information services like news headlines, stock quotations, and computerised *Yellow Pages* over their phone lines. Then some 1991 court rulings reversed this prohibition. Now the phone companies are laying plans to enter the $100-billion-a-year information services market.

   Newspapers complain that the phone companies will monopolise their hold over residential phone lines and dictate what information reaches homes. In reply, critics point out that most newspapers are monopolies as well and that, unlike the phone companies, they are unregulated. In addition, they observe that newspapers have, through their editorial pages, a monopoly on the dissemination of opinion.

   Probably these struggles between the Baby Bells and the newspaper industry will continue. What do you think? Discuss the pros and cons with classmates.

3. *Your school's database* Almost all organisations keep information about their employees and customers in databases. Surely your school does also. Without conducting extensive research, respond to each of the following:

(a) What information about you do you think is stored in your school's database?

(b) How do you suppose the data is organised? Specifically, give an example of a database, file, record, field, and character.

(c) Which type of file organisation do you think is used, and why?

(d) Which type of DBMS organisation is likely used, and why?

CASE STUDY

GRAHAM JOHNS REAL ESTATE LTD

Graham Johns Real Estate Ltd is a small real estate agency servicing the south-eastern suburbs. The managing director, Graham, is in charge of the general operation of the company. His secretary, Julie, completes all the clerical tasks and is in charge of the payroll. Four salespeople working in three departments are responsible for residential sales, commercial sales and rentals, and residential rentals.

- James and Mary handle all the residential sales and auctions. They deal with customers who are either buying or selling houses, flats or units.

- Amy as the commercial manager deals with small business rentals and sales.

- Karen is in charge of all the residential rental properties.

The sales staff are on confidential negotiated salary contracts. Julie keeps the details of the contracts on file in her office. She needs to refer to these contracts monthly when she calculates the salaries of the staff.

The three departments all keep records of their past and current clients. They each keep their own alphabetical card index of personal data of clients. At the daily staff meeting information is exchanged. For example, a business client may be a prospective client in the residential area. Often, however, the required information is hard to find and potential sales have been lost to other real estate agents.

Graham Johns has recently had a computer network installed at the office. Julie has been the only person at the company with access to a computer. She has been using a Macintosh computer for some time to maintain a staff database and to handle all the correspondence of the company. The company now has 5 Apple Macintosh computers connected to form a local area network. The decision to purchase Macintoshes was made to take advantage of Julie's considerable expertise with the Macintosh operating system and her knowledge of programs available on the Macintosh.

Graham has decided to implement a DBMS that will enable all the sales staff to enter clientele information into the one database. He wants a system flexible enough to allow his staff easy access to all the information on the database.

Graham is undecided how to train his staff in the use of the DBMS. He realises that the following training options are open to him:

- Send his staff to a training course at one of several independent providers.

- Hire a trainer to spend time at the office training his staff.

- Send one of his staff to a training course. This person would in turn train other staff.

- Give his staff the manuals and let them train themselves.

QUESTIONS

1. Graham Johns has decided to implement a DBMS.

    (a) What does DBMS stand for?

    (b) What is a DBMS used for?

2. (a) Explain the difference between batch and real-time processing.

    (b) Would Graham Johns Real Estate use batch or real-time processing? Why?

3. (a) What are the four advantages of using databases?

   (b) How would they relate to Graham Johns Real Estate?

4. (a) What are the three principal database organisations?

   (b) Which of the three formats would best suit Graham Johns Real Estate? Why?

5. Graham is considering a database of client information and a database of staff information that would include information on salaries.

   (a) Briefly describe the four types of databases.

   (b) What type of database would be suitable for the client database?

   (c) Who at Graham Johns Real Estate would have access to the database of clients?

   (d) What kind of database would be suitable for the staff database?

   (e) Who at Graham Johns Real Estate would have access to the staff database?

6. What are the two reasons why database security is important?

7. Which of the training options would you recommend to Graham? Why?

Information systems

COMPETENCIES

After you have read this chapter, you should be able to:

- explain how organisations can be structured according to five functions and three management levels;

- describe how information flows in an organisation;

- distinguish among a transaction processing system, a management information system, a decision support system, and an executive support system;

- distinguish between office automation systems and knowledge work systems;

- explain the difference between data workers and knowledge workers.

FROM THE USER'S POINT OF VIEW

Communications links and databases connect you with information resources far beyond the surface of your desk. The microcomputer offers you access to a greater *quantity* of information than was possible a few years ago. In addition, you also have access to a better *quality* of information. As we show in this chapter, when you tap into a computer-based information system, you not only get information—you also get help in *making* decisions.

Why are computers used in organisations? No doubt you can easily state one reason: to keep records of events. However, another reason might be less obvious: to help make decisions. For example, point-of-sale terminals do more than record sales. They also record which salesperson made each sale. This information can be used for decision making. For instance, it can help the sales manager decide which salespeople will get year-end bonuses for doing exceptional work.

Keeping accurate records and making good decisions are extremely important in running any successful organisation, small or large. Let us see how some organisations are structured and how information flows within them.

HOW INFORMATION FLOWS IN AN ORGANISATION

Information flows up and down among managers and sideways among departments.

An **information system** (as we discussed in Chapter 1) is a collection of *hardware*, *software*, *people*, *procedures*, and *data*. They all work together to provide information essential to running an organisation. This is information that will successfully produce a product or service and, for profit-oriented enterprises, derive a profit.

In large and medium-sized organisations, computerised information systems don't just keep track of transactions and day-to-day business operations. They also support the flow of information within the organisation. This information flows both vertically and horizontally. In order to understand this, we need to understand how an organisation is structured. One way to examine an organisation's structure is to view it from a functional perspective. That is, you can study the different basic functional areas in organisations and the different types of people within these functional areas.

As we describe these, you might consider how they apply to any organisation you are familiar with. Or consider how they apply to a hypothetical manufacturer of sporting goods in the United States, the HealthWise Group. Think of this as a large company that manufactures equipment for sports and physical activities, including those that interest you. These goods range from every type of ball imaginable (from golf to tennis to soccer) to hockey pads, leotards, and exercise bicycles.

Functions

Depending on the services or products they provide, most organisations have departments that specialise in one of five basic functions. These are *accounting, production, marketing, human resources*, and *research*. Even in very small organisations these functions must be performed—often by one person, the owner (see Figure 10.1). Their purposes are as follows:

Accounting This department keeps track of all financial activities. It pays bills, records payments, issues pay cheques, and compiles periodic financial statements. At HealthWise, for example, this department performs two major activities. First, it records bills and other financial transactions with sporting goods stores and produces financial statements. Second, it produces financial budgets and forecasts of projected financial performance to help managers run the business.

Production This department makes the product (see Figure 10.2). It takes in raw materials and puts people to work to turn out finished goods (or services). The department may be a manufacturing activity or, in the case of a retail store, for example, an operations activity. It manages purchases, inventories, and flows of goods and services. At HealthWise, this department is a big purchaser of steel and aluminium, materials used in weight-lifting and exercise machines.

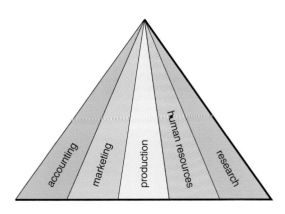

Figure 10.1 The five functions of an organisation

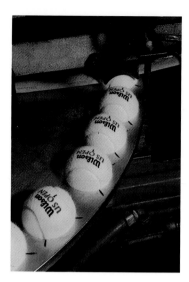

Figure 10.2 Production: this department is responsible for making products—in this case, tennis balls

Marketing Advertising, promotion, and sales are handled by this department (see Figure 10.3). The people in this department plan, price, promote, sell, and distribute goods and services to customers. At HealthWise they even get involved in what colours to put on the equipment that is sold.

Human resources This department finds and hires people and handles matters such as sick leave and retirement benefits. In addition, it is concerned with evaluation, compensation, and professional development. As you might imagine, HealthWise has rather good health benefits.

Research The research (or research and development) department has two tasks. First, it does product research. That is, it does basic research and relates new discoveries to the firm's current or new products. For instance, research people at HealthWise might look into new ideas from exercise physiologists about muscle development. They might use this knowledge in designing new physical fitness machines. Second, it does product development. That is, it develops and tests new products created by research people. It also monitors and troubleshoots new products as they are being produced.

Suppose you are now an employee. Whatever your job in an organisation, it is likely to be in one of these departments. Within the department, you may also be at one of the management levels.

Management levels

Most people who work in an organisation are not managers, of course. At the base of the organisational pyramid are the assemblers, painters, welders, drivers, and so on. These people produce goods and services. Above them, however, are various levels of managers—people with titles such as supervisor, director, regional manager, and vice president. These are the people who do the planning, leading, organising, and controlling necessary to see that the work gets done.

Figure 10.3 Marketing: this department handles advertising, promotion, and sales

At HealthWise, for example, the northwest district sales manager directs and co-ordinates all the salespeople in her area. Other job titles might be vice president of marketing, director of human resources, or production manager. In smaller organisations, these titles are often combined.

Management in many organisations is divided into three levels: supervisors, middle-level, and top-level (see Figure 10.4). They may be described as follows:

Supervisors **Supervisors** manage and monitor the employees or workers, those who actually produce the goods and services. Thus, these managers have the responsibility relating to *operational matters.* They monitor day-to-day events and immediately take corrective action, if necessary. For example, at HealthWise, a production supervisor monitors the materials needed to build exercise bicycles. If parts begin to run low, the supervisor must take action immediately.

Middle management **Middle-level managers** deal with *control, planning* (also called *tactical planning*), and *decision-making.* They implement the long-term goals of the organisation. For example, the HealthWise regional sales manager for the Northwest sets sales goals for district sales managers in three American cities. He or she also monitors their sales performance and takes corrective action if necessary.

Top management **Top-level managers** are concerned with *long-range planning* (also called *strategic planning*). They need information that will help them to plan the future growth and direction of the organisation. For example, the HealthWise vice president of marketing might need to determine the demand and the sales strategy for a new product. Such a product might be a stationary exercise bicycle with a biometric feedback mechanism.

Information flow

Each level of management has different information needs. Top-level managers need information that is summarised in capsule form to reveal the overall condition of the business. They also need information from outside the organisation, because top-level managers need to forecast and plan for long-range events. Middle-level managers need

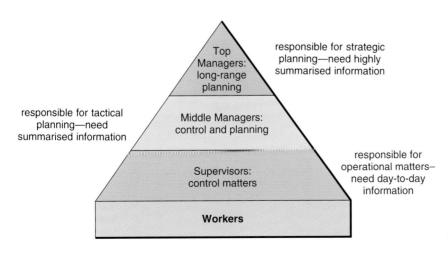

Figure 10.4 Three levels of management

summarised information—weekly or monthly reports. They need to develop budget projections as well as to evaluate the performance of supervisors. Supervisors need detailed, very current day-to-day information on their units so that they can keep operations running smoothly.

To support these different needs, information *flows* in different directions (see Figure 10.5). The top-level managers, such as the chief executive officer (CEO), need information from below and from all departments. They need information from outside the organisation as well. For example, at HealthWise, they are deciding whether to introduce a line of hockey equipment in the southwestern United States. The vice president of marketing must look at relevant data. Such data might include availability of ice rinks and census data about the number of young people. It might also include sales histories on related cold-weather sports equipment.

For middle-level managers, the information flow is both horizontal and vertical across functional lines within the organisation. For example, the regional sales managers at HealthWise set their sales goals by co-ordinating with middle managers in the production department. They are able to tell sales managers what products will be produced, how many, and when. An example of a product might be an exercise bicycle. The regional sales managers also must co-ordinate with the strategic goals set by the top managers. They must set and monitor the sales goals for the supervisors beneath them.

For supervisory managers, information flow is primarily vertical. That is, they communicate mainly with their middle managers and with the workers beneath them. For instance, at HealthWise, production supervisors rarely communicate with people in the accounting department. However, they are constantly communicating with production-line workers and with their own managers.

Now we know how a large organisation is usually structured and how information flows within the organisation. But how is a computer-based information system likely to be set up to support its needs? And what do you, as a microcomputer user, need to know to use it?

COMPUTER-BASED INFORMATION SYSTEMS

There are four kinds of computer-based information systems: transaction processing system, management information system, decision support system, and executive support system.

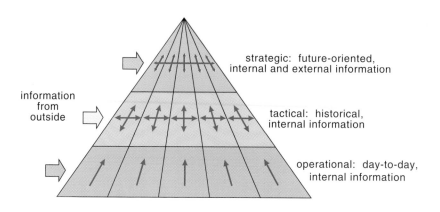

Figure 10.5 Information flow within an organisation

Inputs

some summarised reports, some processed transaction data, other internal data plus external data

processed transaction data, other internal data

transaction data

Outputs

high-level decisions: introduce new product, start company-wide cost control program, etc.

flexible, on-demand reports to make decisions about unstructured problems: possible effects of strikes, rising interest rates, etc.

summarised, structured reports: budget summaries, production schedules, etc.

processed transactions: bills, pay cheques, orders, etc.

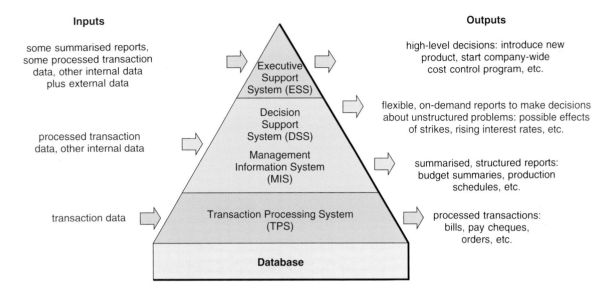

Executive Support System (ESS)

Decision Support System (DSS)

Management Information System (MIS)

Transaction Processing System (TPS)

Database

Figure 10.6 The three levels of information systems

All large organisations have computer-based information systems. Some systems record routine activities: employees hired, materials purchased, products produced, and the like. Such recorded events are called **transactions**. Other systems use these recorded events to help managerial planning and control. The systems form a pyramid, each primarily (but not exclusively) supporting one level of management (see Figure 10.6).

Transaction processing system The **transaction processing system (TPS)** records day-to-day transactions such as customer orders, bills, inventory levels, and production output. The transaction processing system helps supervisors by generating databases that act as the foundation for the other information systems.

Management information systems The **management information system (MIS)** summarises the detailed data of the transaction processing system in standard reports for middle-level managers. Such reports might include production schedules and budget summaries.

Decision support system The **decision support system (DSS)** provides a flexible tool for analysis. The DSS helps middle-level managers and others in the organisation analyse a wide range of problems, such as the effect of events and trends outside the organisation. Like the MIS, the DSS draws on the detailed data of the transaction processing system.

Executive support system The **executive support system (ESS)**, also known as the **executive information system (EIS)**, is an easy-to-use system that presents information in a very highly summarised form. It helps top-level managers oversee the company's operations and develop strategic plans. The ESS combines the internal data from TPS and MIS with external data.

Let us describe these four kinds of information systems in more detail.

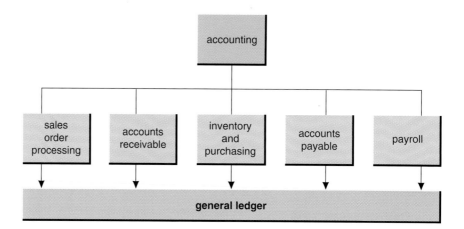

Figure 10.7 Transaction processing system for accounting

TRANSACTION PROCESSING SYSTEMS

A transaction processing system records routine operations.

A *transaction processing system (TPS)* helps an organisation keep track of routine operations and records these events in a database. For this reason, some firms call this the **data processing system (DPS)**. The data from operations—for example, customer orders for HealthWise's products—makes up a database that records the transactions of the company. This database of transactions is used to support an MIS, DSS, and ESS.

One of the most essential transaction processing systems for any organisation is in the accounting area (see Figure 10.7). Every accounting department handles six basic activities. Five of these are sales order processing, accounts receivable, inventory and purchasing, accounts payable, and payroll. All of these are recorded in the general ledger, the sixth activity. We explain these below.

Let us take a look at these six activities. They will make up the basis of the accounting system for almost any office you might work in:

- The **sales order processing** activity records the customer requests for the company's product or service (see Figure 10.8). When an order comes in—a request for a set of barbells, for example—the warehouse is alerted to ship a product.

Figure 10.8 Sales order processing for Canadian Airlines International

- The **accounts receivable** activity records money received from or owed by customers. HealthWise keeps track of bills paid by sporting goods stores and by gyms and health clubs to which it sells directly.

- The parts and finished goods that the company has in stock are called **inventory**—all exercise machines in the warehouse, for example. An *inventory control system* keeps records of the number of each kind of part or finished good in the warehouse. **Purchasing** is buying of materials and services. Often a purchase order is used. This is a form that shows the name of the company supplying the material or service and what is being purchased.

- **Accounts payable** refers to money the company owes its suppliers for materials and services it has received—steel and aluminium, for example.

- The **payroll** activity is concerned with calculating employee pay cheques. Amounts are generally determined by the kind of job, hours worked, and kinds of deductions (such as taxes, social security, medical insurance). Pay cheques may be calculated from employee time cards or, in some cases, supervisors' time sheets.

- The **general ledger** keeps track of all summaries of all the foregoing transactions. A typical general ledger system can produce income statements and balance sheets. *Income statements* show a company's financial performance—income, expenses, and the difference between them for a specific time period. *Balance sheets* list the overall financial condition of an organisation. They include assets (for example, buildings and property owned), liabilities (debts), and how much of the organisation (the equity) is owned by the owners.

MANAGEMENT INFORMATION SYSTEMS

A management information system produces summarised, structured reports.

A *management information system (MIS)* is a computer-based information system that produces standardised reports in summarised, structured form. It is used to support middle managers. An MIS differs from a transaction processing system in a significant way. Whereas a transaction processing system *creates* databases, an MIS *uses* databases. Indeed, an MIS can draw from the databases of *several* departments (see Figure 10.9). Thus, an MIS requires a *database management system* that integrates the databases of the different departments. Middle managers need summary data often drawn from across different functional areas.

An MIS produces reports that are *predetermined*. That is, they follow a predetermined format and always show the same kinds of content. Although reports may differ from one industry to another, there are three common categories of reports:

- **Periodic reports** are produced at regular intervals—weekly, monthly, or quarterly, for instance (see Figure 10.10). Examples are HealthWise's monthly sales or production reports. The sales reports from district sales managers are combined into a monthly report for the regional sales managers. For comparison purposes, a regional manager is also able to see the sales reports of other regional managers.

Figure 10.9 MIS uses databases created by various departments

- **Exception reports** call attention to unusual events. An example is a sales report that shows that certain items are selling significantly above or below marketing department forecasts. For instance, if fewer exercise bicycles are selling than were predicted for the northwest sales region, the regional manager will receive an exception report. That report may be used to alert the district managers and salespeople to give this product more attention.

- The opposite of a periodic report, a **demand report**, is produced on request. An example is a report on the numbers of, and jobs held by, women and minorities. Such a report is not needed periodically, but it may be required when requested by the government. At HealthWise, many government contracts require this information. It's used to certify that HealthWise is achieving certain government equal-opportunity guidelines.

DECISION SUPPORT SYSTEMS

A DSS helps decision makers analyse unanticipated situations.

Managers often must deal with unanticipated questions. For example, the HealthWise manager in charge of manufacturing might ask, how would a strike affect production schedules? A *decision support system*

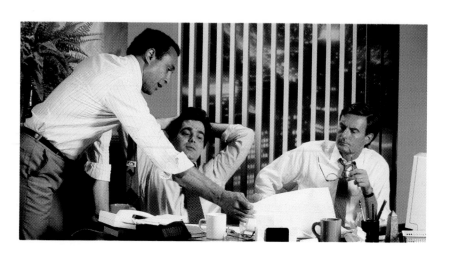

Figure 10.10 Periodic reports may be produced weekly, monthly, or quarterly

(DSS) enables managers to get answers to unexpected and generally non-recurring kinds of problems. Frequently, a team is formed to address large problems. A **group decision support system (GDSS)** is then used to support this collective work. They do this using interactive terminals (or microcomputers) and software. **Interactive** means that there is immediate communication between the user and the computer system. That is, when input data is entered into the computer, it is processed immediately. The output results are promptly displayed on the screen.

A DSS, then, is quite different from a transaction processing system, which simply records data. It is also different from a management information system, which summarises data in predetermined reports. A DSS is used to *analyse* data. Moreover, it produces reports that do not have a fixed format. This makes the DSS a flexible tool for analysis.

Many DSSs are designed for large computer systems. However, microcomputers, with their increased power and sophisticated software, such as spreadsheet and database programs, are being used for DSS. Users of a DSS are managers, not computer programmers. Thus, a DSS must be easy to use—or most likely it will not be used at all. Commands need to be in English-like language: 'SEARCH' or 'FIND', for instance. A HealthWise marketing manager might want to know which territories are not meeting their sales quotas and need additional advertising support. To find out, the executive might type 'FIND ALL FOR SALES < QUOTA'.

How does a decision support system work? Essentially, it consists of four parts: the user, system software, data, and *decision models*.

The user

The user could be you. In general, the user is someone who has to make decisions—a manager, often a middle-level manager.

System software

The system software is essentially the operating system—programs designed to work behind the scenes to handle detailed operating procedures. In order to give the user a good, comfortable interface, the software typically is menu- or icon-driven. That is, the screen presents easily understood lists of commands or icons, giving the user several options.

The data

The data in a DSS is stored in a database and consists of two kinds. *Internal data*—data from within the organisation—consists principally of transactions from the transaction processing system. *External data* is data gathered from outside the organisation. Examples are data provided by marketing research firms, trade associations, and the government (such as customer profiles, census data, and economic forecasts).

The decision models

The **decision models** give the DSS its analytical capabilities. There are three basic types of models: strategic, tactical, and operational. *Strategic models* assist top-level managers in long-range planning, such as stating company objectives or planning plant locations. *Tactical models* help middle-level managers control the work of the organisation, such as financial planning and sales promotion planning.

Such models help middle-level managers implement top managers' long-range plans. *Operational models* help lower-level managers accomplish the organisation's day-to-day activities, such as evaluating and maintaining quality control.

EXECUTIVE SUPPORT SYSTEMS

Executive support systems are specially designed, simplified systems for top executives.

Using a DSS requires some training. Many top managers have other people in their offices running DSSs and reporting their findings. Top-level executives also want something more concise than an MIS—something that produces very focused reports.

Executive support systems (ESSs) consist of sophisticated software that, like an MIS or a DSS, can draw together data from an organisation's databases in meaningful patterns. However, an ESS is specifically designed to be easy to use. This is so that a top executive with little spare time can obtain essential information without extensive training. Thus, information is often displayed in very condensed form and in bold graphics.

Consider an executive support system used by the president of HealthWise. It is available on his microcomputer. The first thing each morning, the president calls up the ESS on his display screen, as shown in the left-hand illustration (see Figure 10.11). Note that the screen gives a condensed account of activities in the five different areas of the company. (These are Accounting, Marketing, Production, Human Resources, and Research.) On this particular morning, the ESS shows business in four areas proceeding smoothly. However, in the first area, Accounting, the percentage of late-paying customers—past due accounts—has increased 3 percent. Three percent may not seem like much. But HealthWise has had a history of problems with late payers, which has left the company at times short of cash. The president decides to find out the details. To do so, he presses *1* (corresponding to Accounting) on his keyboard.

The right-hand screen shows information about past due accounts expressed in graphic form (see Figure 10.11). The status of today's late payers is shown in blue. The status of late payers at this time a year ago is shown in yellow. The differences between today and a year

Figure 10.11 An executive information system. Left: information in condensed text form. Right: details in graphic form

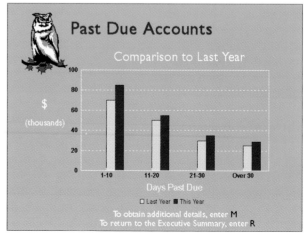

ago are very clearly presented. The differences are significant. For example, approximately $70 000 was late 1 to 10 days last year. This year, over $80 000 was late. The president knows that he must take some action to speed up customer payments. (For example, he might call this to the attention of the vice president of accounting. The vice president might decide to offer discounts to early payers or charge more interest to late payers.)

ESSs permit a firm's top executives to gain direct access to information about the company's performance. Some also have electronic mail setups that allow managers to communicate directly with other executives. Some systems even have structured forms to help managers streamline their thoughts before sending electronic memos. In addition, an ESS may be organised to retrieve information from databases outside the company, such as business-news services. This enables a firm to watch for stories on competitors and stay current on relevant news events that could affect its business. For example, news of increased sports injuries caused by running and aerobic dancing, and the consequent lessened interest by people in these activities, might cause HealthWise to alter its sales and production goals for its line of fitness-related shoes.

OTHER INFORMATION SYSTEMS

Information workers use office automation systems and knowledge work systems.

We have discussed only four information systems: TPS to support lower-level managers, MIS and DSS to support middle-level managers, and ESS to support top-level managers. There are many other information systems to support different individuals and functions. The fastest-growing are information systems designed to support information workers.

Information workers create, distribute, and communicate information. They are the secretaries, clerks, engineers, and scientists, to name a few, in the organisation. Some are involved with distribution and communication of information (like the secretaries and clerks). They are called *data workers*. Others are involved with the creation of information (like the engineers and scientists). They are called *knowledge workers*.

Two systems to support information workers are:

Office automation systems **Office automation systems (OASs)** are designed primarily to support data workers. These systems focus on managing documents, communicating, and scheduling. Documents are managed using word processing, desktop publishing, and other image technologies. Communications use e-mail, voice-messaging, and videoconferencing (see Figure 10.12).

Knowledge work systems Knowledge workers use OAS systems. Additionally, they use specialised information systems called **knowledge work systems (KWSs)** to create information in their areas of expertise. For example, engineers involved in product design and manufacturing use **CAD/CAM (computer-aided design/computer-aided manufacturing)** systems (see Figure 10.13). These KWSs consist of powerful microcomputers running special programs that integrate the design and manufacture activities. CAD/CAM is widely used in the manufacture of automobiles and other products.

Figure 10.12
Videoconferencing: individuals see and share information with one another

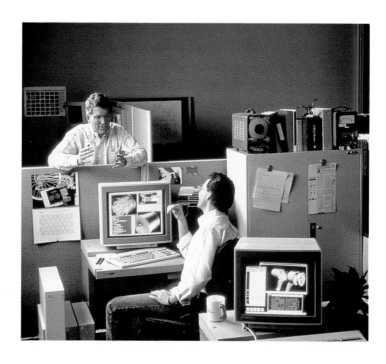

Figure 10.13 CAD/CAM: knowledge work systems used by design and manufacturing engineers

A LOOK AT THE FUTURE

Information from executive support systems will be made available in conference-room microcomputers and eventually in laptops.

Executive support systems, still being developed in many companies, are definitely the wave of the future. Already, however, forward-looking executives are using *laptop* and *palmtop computers* to get ESS information while they are travelling.

Before use of laptop ESSs becomes popular, experts think, large companies will equip their conference rooms with microcomputers that have speedy communications with corporate computers around the world. These meeting-room computers will become part of management presentations, as well as serve executives visiting from elsewhere.

As executive support systems become more a part of corporate life, something else will happen. Competent computer end users (perhaps yourself) who have risen through the management ranks will begin to demand more from their ESS. Thus, the relatively simple kinds of ESS often seen in use today will be replaced by systems that offer much more power and many more options. Additionally, ESS will become more widely noted by middle-level managers.

REVIEW QUESTIONS

True/false

1. For small companies, keeping accurate records and making good decisions are extremely important.

2. The production department takes in raw materials and puts people to work to turn out finished goods (or services).

3. In smaller organisations such titles as vice president of marketing and director of human resources are often combined.

4. CEO stands for chief executive officer.

5. Decision support systems summarise the detailed data of the transaction processing system in standard reports.

Multiple choice

1. An information system is a collection of hardware, software, procedures, data, databases, and:
   (a) people
   (b) functions
   (c) managers
   (d) accounting systems
   (e) information

2. This department finds and hires people and handles such matters as sick leave and retirement benefits:
   (a) accounting
   (b) production
   (c) marketing
   (d) human resources
   (e) research

3. The level of manager who deals with control and planning is:
   (a) executive
   (b) top management
   (c) middle management
   (d) supervisors
   (e) vice presidents

4. The level of manager whose information is primarily vertical is:
   (a) supervisors
   (b) top management
   (c) middle management
   (d) executive
   (e) vice presidents

5. The information system that provides a flexible tool for analysis is a:
   (a) database information system
   (b) transaction processing system
   (c) management information system
   (d) executive information system
   (e) decision support system

Fill in the blank

1. The _____ department relates new discoveries and does product development.

2. _____ managers are concerned with long-range planning.

3. _____ _____ systems record day-to-day activities such as customer orders and inventory levels.

4. _____ information systems are specially designed, simplified systems for top-level executives.

5. _____ workers use office automation and knowledge work systems.

Open ended

1. What are the five departments found in medium-sized and large organisations? Discuss the function of each department.

2. What are the three levels of management? What are the responsibilities of managers at each level?

3. Explain the differences between the three types of reports produced by a management information system.

4. Discuss the three types of decision models used in a DSS.

5. Explain what an executive support system is. Give an example.

DISCUSSION QUESTIONS AND PROJECTS

1. *The functions and transactions of an organisation* What is the equivalent of 'production' in a hotel or 'marketing' in a college? The five functions or departments of an organisation—accounting, production, marketing, human resources, and research—clearly exist in a for-profit organisation such as an apparel manufacturer. However, they would not be found—at least not in the same form— in an employment agency, a department store, or a hospital. Nevertheless, these organisations do offer products or services, and they probably (if large enough) have three management levels.

   Choose an organisation, such as your school, and interview someone to find out what might constitute departments and management layers. Summarise your findings in a drawing identifying the departments and the levels of management. See if you can discover the transactions that go into the database of one of the departments—for example, registrar, housing, fund raising, financial aid, or student affairs.

2. *Systems to collect and use data* Almost all organisations collect and use data. Large organisations typically have formal names for the systems designed to collect and use the data. Although different organisations may use different names, the most common names are transaction processing, management information, decision support, and executive information systems.

   Choose an organisation, such as a college, and consider the data and information needs. Describe each of the following:

   (a) The transaction processing system—identify the data collected and briefly describe the six basic activities of the accounting department.

   (b) The management information system—describe a typical periodic report, exception report, and demand report.

   (c) The decision support system—discuss a problem that might be addressed.

   (d) The executive support system—present a typical display the president would see first thing each morning.

3. *Do computers really make use more productive?* The basic reason for installing and learning computers is that they help us increase our productivity. But do they really? Research has shown some of the following problems: (1) People in organisations spend more time fine-tuning their word-processing documents when such polishing is not necessary. (2) They devote time to unnecessarily putting spreadsheet information into graphic form. (3) They fill up ordinary memos with facts gleaned from expensive computer searches. (4) They create unnecessary pressure by transmitting messages via modem or fax when regular mail would do. These are serious problems that you will run across in the workplace. Discuss the following:

   (a) Who or what creates this information overload?

   (b) What would you do to prevent these problems if you were a supervisor in an office?

   (c) What can you do to prevent becoming a contributor to these problems yourself?

CASE STUDY

CAR BUILDERS INC.

Car Builders Inc. is an Australian company that designs, manufactures and markets a range of small four cylinder cars. Their present range consists of:

- the Shopper: small three-door hatch with basic fittings and features only;

- the Coupe: larger three-door hatch with better equipment and finish; and

- the Family: four-door sedan with a range of different equipment and feature options.

The head office of Car Builders Inc. is located in Melbourne. This office houses all top-level management and their support staff together with the design and market research divisions. All plastic fittings and accessories are manufactured in their Plastics Division factory in Adelaide. Car bodies and all other components constructed from steel are made in their Steels Division plant in Sydney. All parts made interstate are transported by rail to the Melbourne factory for final assembly and testing. There are dealerships for these cars in all Australian capital cities and many large regional centres.

There are three middle-level managers each in charge of one of the factories. Middle-level managers are responsible for ensuring their factories run smoothly. This entails co-ordinating ordering required materials and ensuring work schedules and deadlines are adhered to.

Within each factory there are several supervisors who take their instructions directly from the factory manager. They are responsible for monitoring all work done on the factory floor. They usually receive their instructions on Monday morning with details of production targets for the week. The supervisors 'report back' to their respective managers by entering details of the work completed into a computerised transaction processing system at the end of each shift. The head office and each of the three factories all have their own accounting and personnel departments.

All computer systems used in the factories are linked by a Wide Area Network so that:

- each factory manager can communicate with the other middle-level managers regarding work in progress and the order and supply of goods; and

- factory managers have easy access to summaries of the detailed data contained in the transaction processing system via a management information system;

- top-level management can monitor the business via a computerised decision support system.

QUESTIONS

1. Explain the responsibilities of the three levels of management in Car Builders Inc.:

   (a) top-level management

   (b) middle-level management—factory managers

   (c) supervisors

2. This question deals with the flow of information in this organisation.

   (a) Who does top-level management communicate with directly?

   (b) Who do the factory managers communicate with?

   (c) Who do the supervisors communicate with?

   (d) Who do the factory workers communicate with?

3. How does a computerised transaction processing system help this business?

4. How does a computerised management information system help this business?

5. What is the purpose of the decision support system used by top-level management?

6. In what ways would the introduction of an executive support system benefit Car Builders Inc.?

Systems analysis and design

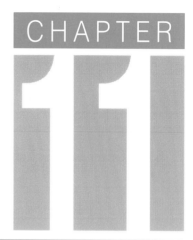

COMPETENCIES

After you have read this chapter, you should be able to:

• describe the six phases of the systems life cycle;

• discuss how problems or needs are identified during Phase 1, preliminary investigation;

• explain how the current system is studied and new requirements are specified in Phase 2, systems analysis;

• describe how a new or alternative information system is designed in Phase 3, systems design;

• explain how new hardware and software are acquired, developed, and tested in Phase 4, systems development;

• discuss how a new information system is installed and users are trained in Phase 5, systems implementation;

• describe Phase 6, systems maintenance, the systems audit and ongoing evaluation, to see if a new system is doing what it's supposed to;

• understand prototyping.

FROM THE USER'S POINT OF VIEW

Most people in an organisation are involved with an information system of some kind, as we saw in the previous chapter. Assuredly, most microcomputer users in the future will have access to such a system, and they will also be part of it. For an organisation to *establish* a system and for users to make it truly useful, considerable thought and effort are needed. Fortunately, there is a six-step problem-solving process for accomplishing this. It is known as *systems analysis and design.*

Big organisations can make big mistakes. For example, General Motors spent $40 billion putting in factory robots and other high technology in its automaking plants. It then removed much of this equipment and reinstalled that basic part of the assembly line—the conveyor belt. Why did the high-technology production systems fail? The probable reason was that GM didn't devote enough energy to training its work force in using the new systems.

The government also can make big mistakes. In one year, in the United States, the Internal Revenue Service computer system was so overwhelmed it could not deliver tax refunds on time. The reason? Despite extensive testing of much of the system, not all testing was completed. Thus, when the new system was phased in, the IRS found it could not process tax returns as quickly as it had hoped. Many tax refunds were delayed.

Both of these examples show the necessity for thorough planning—especially when an organisation is trying to implement a new kind of system. Despite the spectacular failures above, there is a way to reduce the chances for such mistakes. It is called *systems analysis and design.*

Why should you, as a computer end user rather than a computer professional, know anything about this procedure? There are four reasons:

• If you work for a large organisation, a systems analysis and design study will sometime undoubtedly focus on your job. Knowing how the procedure works will enable you to deal with it better.

• You can use the steps in systems analysis and design to improve your own productivity within the organisation. That is, you can use the procedure to solve problems within your own corner of the organisation. Or you can use it to assist professionals in solving larger problems within the organisation.

• You can use this procedure to reduce the risk of a new project failing. Many new information systems fail or do not work well for a variety of reasons. If you use systems analysis and design, you can minimise the chances of these flaws occurring.

• You can use this procedure to choose an entire microcomputer system for any small business or for yourself.

SYSTEMS ANALYSIS AND DESIGN

Systems analysis and design is a six-phase problem-solving procedure for examining and improving an information system.

We described different types of information systems in the last chapter. Now let us consider: what, exactly, is a **system**? We can define it as a collection of activities and elements organised to accomplish a goal. As we saw in the last chapter, an *information system* is a collection of hardware, software, people, procedures, and data. These work together to provide information essential to running an organisation. This information helps to produce a product or service and, for profit-oriented businesses, derive a profit.

Information—about orders received, products shipped, money owed, and so on—flows into an organisation from the outside. Information—about what supplies have been received, which customers have paid their bills, and so on—also flows inside the organisation. In order to avoid confusion, these flows of information must follow some system. However, from time to time, organisations need to change their information systems. Reasons include organisational growth, mergers and acquisitions, new marketing opportunities, revisions in governmental regulations, availability of new technology, or other changes.

Systems analysis and design is a six-phase problem-solving procedure for examining and improving an information system.

The six phases make up the **systems life cycle** (see Figure 11.1). The phases are as follows:

1. *Preliminary investigation* The information problems or needs are identified.

2. *Systems analysis* The present system is studied in depth. New requirements are specified.

3. *Systems design* A new or alternative information system is designed.

4. *Systems development* New hardware and software are acquired, developed, and tested.

5. *Systems implementation* The new information system is installed and adapted to the new system, and people are trained to use it.

6. *Systems maintenance* In this ongoing phase, the system is periodically evaluated and updated as needed.

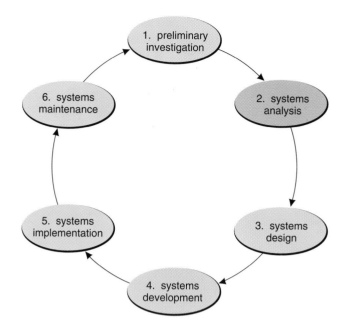

Figure 11.1 The six-phase systems life cycle

In organisations, the six-phase systems life cycle is used by computer professionals known as **systems analysts**. These people study an organisation's systems to determine what actions to take and how to use computer technology to assist them. A 1995 survey by *Money* magazine compared salary, prestige, and security of 100 widely held jobs. The top job classification was computer engineer, followed by computer systems analyst.

As an employee, you may well find yourself working with a systems analyst. Or, you may even become one yourself. It's important that you understand how the six phases work. After all, you better than anyone should understand what is needed in your part of the organisation. And you should be best able to express that need. Developing a large computer-based information system requires the close collaboration of end users and systems analysts.

The procedure is also one that *you* as an end user can perform, working alone or with a systems analyst. In fact, you may *have* to use the procedure. More and more end users are developing their own information systems. This is because in many organisations there is a three-year backlog of work for systems analysts. For instance, suppose you recognise that there is a need for certain information within your organisation. Obtaining this information will require the introduction of new hardware and software. You go to seek expert help from systems analysts in studying these information needs. At that point you discover they are so overworked it will take them three years to get to your request! You can see, then, why many managers are learning to do these activities themselves. In any case, learning these six steps will raise your computer competency. It will also give you skills to solve a wide range of problems. These steps can make you more valuable to an organisation.

Let us now describe each phase in the systems life cycle.

PHASE 1: PRELIMINARY INVESTIGATION

In the preliminary investigation phase, the problems are briefly identified and a few solutions are suggested.

The first phase is a **preliminary investigation** of a proposed project to determine the need for a new information system (see Figure 11.2). This usually is requested by an end user or a manager who wants something done that is not presently being done. For example, suppose you work for Advantage Advertising, a fast-growing advertising agency. Advantage Advertising produces a variety of different ads for a wide range of different clients. The agency employs both regular staff people and on-call freelancers. One of your responsibilities is keeping track of the work performed for each client and the employees who performed the work. In addition, you are responsible for tabulating the final bill for each project.

How do you figure out how to charge which clients for which work done by which employees? This kind of problem is common to many service organisations (such as lawyers' and contractors' offices). Indeed, it is a problem in any organisation where people charge for their 'time' and clients need proof of hours worked.

In Phase 1, the systems analyst—or the end user—is concerned with three tasks. These are (1) briefly defining the problem, (2) suggesting alternative solutions, and (3) preparing a short report. This report will help management decide whether to pursue the project further. (If you are an end user employing this procedure for yourself, you may not produce a written report. Rather, you would report your findings directly to your supervisor.)

Defining the problem

Defining the problem means examining whatever current information system is in use. Determining what information is needed, by whom, when, and why, is accomplished by interviewing and making

Figure 11.2 Phase 1: preliminary investigation

observations. If the information system is large, this survey is done by a systems analyst. If the system is small, the survey can be done by the end user.

For example, suppose Advantage Advertising account executives, copywriters, and graphic artists currently just record the time spent on different jobs on their desk calendars. (Examples might be 'Client A, telephone conference, 15 minutes'; 'Client B, design layout, 2 hours'.) This approach is somewhat helter-skelter. Written calendar entries look somewhat unprofessional to be shown to clients. Moreover, a large job often has many people working on it. It is difficult to pull together all their notations to make up a bill for the client. Some freelancers work at home, and their time slips are not readily available. These matters constitute a statement of the problem: the company has a manual time-and-billing system that is slow and difficult to implement.

As an end user, you might experience difficulties with this system yourself. You're in someone else's office, and a telephone call comes in for you from a client. Your desk calendar is back in your own office. You have two choices. You can always carry your calendar with you. As an alternative, you can remember to note the time you spent on various tasks when you return to your office. The secretary to the account executive is continually after you (and everyone else at Advantage) to provide photocopies of your calendar. This is so that various clients can be billed for the work done on various jobs. Surely, you think, there must be a better way to handle time and billing.

Suggesting alternative systems

This step is simply to suggest some possible plans as alternatives to the present arrangement. For instance, Advantage could hire more secretaries to collect the information from everyone's calendars (including telephoning those working at home). Or it could use the existing system of network-linked microcomputers that staffers and freelancers presently use. Perhaps, you think, there is already some off-the-shelf packaged software available that could be used for a time-and-billing system. At least there might be one that would make your own job easier.

Preparing a short report

For large projects, the systems analyst writes a short report summarising the results of the preliminary investigation and suggesting alternative systems. The report may also include schedules for further development of the project. This document is presented to higher management, along with a recommendation to continue or discontinue the project. Management then decides whether to finance the second phase, the systems analysis.

For Advantage Advertising, your report might point out that billing is frequently delayed. It could say that some tasks may even 'slip through the cracks' and not get charged at all. Thus, as the analyst has noted, you suggest the project might pay for itself merely by eliminating lost or forgotten charges.

PHASE 2: ANALYSIS

In the systems analysis phase, the present system is studied in depth, and new requirements are specified.

In Phase 2, **systems analysis**, data is collected about the present system. This data is then analysed, and new requirements are determined. We are not concerned with a new design here, only with determining the *requirements* for a new system. The design itself will be done in Phase 3. Systems analysis is concerned with gathering and analysing the data. It usually is completed by documenting the analysis in a report.

Gathering data

Here the systems analyst—or the end user doing systems analysis— expands on the data gathered during Phase 1. He or she adds details about how the current system works. Data is obtained from observation and interviews. It is also obtained from studying documents that describe the formal lines of authority and standard operating procedures. One document is the **organisation chart**, which shows levels of management and formal lines of authority (see Figure 11.3, top). You might note that an organisation chart resembles the hierarchy of three levels of management we described in Chapter 10. The levels are top managers, middle managers, and supervisors (see Figure 11.3, bottom). In addition, data may be obtained from questionnaires given to people using the system.

Note in our illustration that we have preserved the department labelled 'Production' (see Figure 11.3, top). (However, the name in an

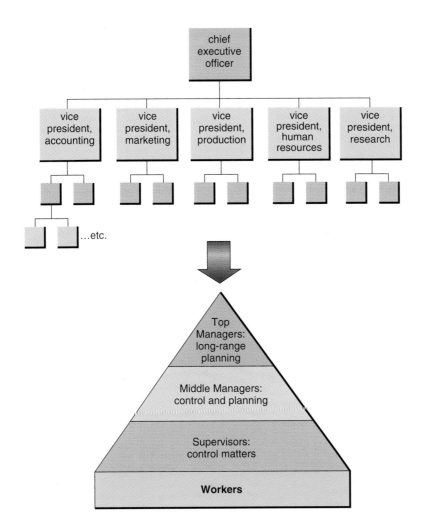

Figure 11.3 Example of an organisation chart—and how it corresponds to the management pyramid

advertising agency might be something like 'Creative Services'.) Obviously, the products an advertising agency produces are ads: radio and television commercials, magazine and newspaper ads, billboard ads, and so on. In any case, if the agency is working on a major advertising campaign, people from several departments might be involved. There might also be people from different management levels within the departments. Their time charges will vary depending on how much they are paid.

Analysing the data

In this step, the data is analysed to learn how information currently flows and to pinpoint why it isn't flowing appropriately. The whole point of this step is to apply *logic* to the existing arrangement to see how workable it is. Many times the current system is not operating correctly because prescribed procedures are not being followed. That is, the system may not really need to be redesigned. Rather, the people in it may need to be shown how to follow correct procedures.

Many different tools are available to assist systems analysts and end users in the analysis phase. Some of the principal ones are as follows:

Checklists Numerous checklists are available to assist in this stage. A **checklist** is a list of questions. It is helpful in guiding the systems analyst and end user through key issues for the present system.

For example, one question might be 'Can reports be easily prepared from the files and documents currently in use?' Another might be 'How easily can the present time-and-billing system adapt to change and growth?'

Top-down analysis methodology The **top-down analysis methodology** is used to identify the top-level components of a complex system. Each component is then broken down into smaller and smaller components. This approach makes each component easier to analyse and deal with.

For instance, the systems analyst might look at the present kind of bill submitted to a client for a complex advertising campaign. The analyst might note the categories of costs—employee salaries, telephone and mailing charges, travel, supplies, and so on.

Grid charts A **grid chart** shows the relationship between input and output documents. An example is shown in Figure 11.4, which indicates the relationship between the data input and the outputs.

For instance, a time sheet is one of many inputs that produces a particular report, such as a client's bill. (Other inputs might be forms having to do with supplies, travel, and other costs of an advertising

	Reports (output)		
Forms (input)	Client Billing	Personnel expense	Support cost
Time sheet	✓	✓	
Telephone log	✓		✓
Travel log	✓		✓

Figure 11.4 Example of a grid chart

	Decision rules			
	1	2	3	4
Conditions:				
1. Project less than $10,000	Y	Y	N	N
2. Good credit history	Y	N	Y	N
Actions:				
1. Accept project	✓	✓	✓	
2. Require deposit		✓	✓	
3. Reject project				✓

Figure 11.5 Example of a decision table

campaign.) Horizontal rows represent inputs, such as time card forms. Vertical rows represent output documents, such as different clients' bills. A checkmark at the intersection of a row and column means that the input document is used to create the output document.

Decision tables A **decision table** shows the decision rules that apply when certain conditions occur. Figure 11.5 shows a decision table to evaluate whether to accept a client's proposed advertising project. The first decision rule applies if both conditions are met. If the project is less than $10 000 and if the client has a good credit history, the firm will accept the project without requiring a deposit.

System flowcharts **System flowcharts** show the flow of input data to processing and finally to output, or distribution of information. An example of a system flowchart keeping track of time for advertising 'creative people' is shown in Figure 11.6. The explanation of the

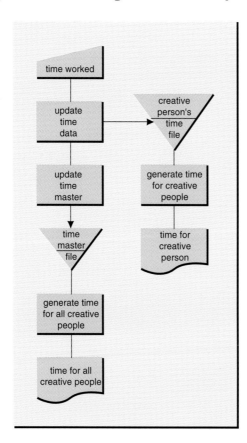

Figure 11.6 Example of a system flowchart

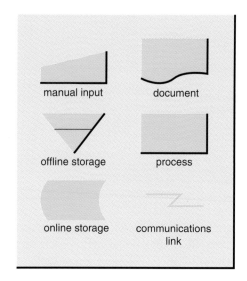

Figure 11.7 System flowchart symbols

symbols used (and others not used) appears in Figure 11.7. Note that this describes the present manual, or non-computerised, system. (A *system* flowchart is not the same as a *program* flowchart, which is very detailed. Program flowcharts are discussed in the next chapter.)

Data flow diagrams **Data flow diagrams** show the data or information flow within an information system. The data is traced from its origination through processing, storage, and output. An example of a data flow diagram is shown in Figure 11.8.

Automated design tools **Automated design tools** are software packages that evaluate hardware and software alternatives according to requirements given by the systems analyst. They are also called **computer-aided software engineering tools**, or **CASE tools**. These

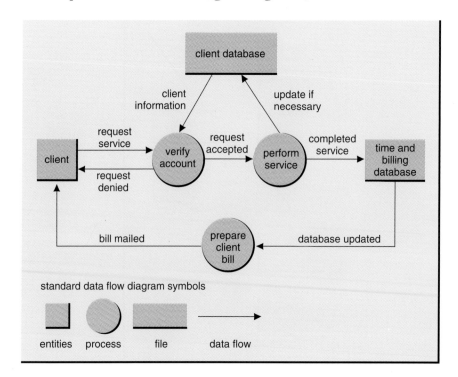

Figure 11.8 Example of a data flow diagram

ANALYSIS TOOLS

Tool	Description
Checklist	Provides a list of questions about key issues
Top-down analysis	Divides a complex system into components, beginning at the top
Grid chart	Shows relationships between inputs and outputs
Decision table	Specifies decision rules and circumstances when specific rules are to be applied
System flowchart	Shows movement of input data, processing, and output or distribution of information
Data flow diagram	Shows data flow within an organisation or application
CASE	Automates the analysis, design, and development of information systems

Figure 11.9 Summary of analysis tools

tools are not limited to systems analysis. They are used in system design and development as well. CASE tools relieve the systems analysts of many repetitive tasks, develop clear documentation, and, for larger projects, co-ordinate team-member activities.

For a summary of the analysis tools, see Figure 11.9.

Documenting the systems analysis stage

In larger organisations, the systems analysis stage is typically documented in a report for higher management. The systems analysis report describes the current information system, the requirements for a new system, and a possible development schedule. For example, at Advantage Advertising, the system flowcharts show the present flow of information in a manual time-and-billing system. Some boxes in the system flowchart might be replaced with symbols showing where a computerised information system could work better. For example, in our flowchart, the offline storage symbol ('time master file') might be replaced by an online storage symbol (refer back to Figure 11.6). That is, the information in the file would be instantly accessible.

Management studies the report and decides whether to continue with the project. Let us assume your boss and higher management have decided to continue. You now move on to Phase 3, systems design.

PHASE 3: DESIGN

In the systems design phase, a new or alternative information system is designed.

Phase 3 is **systems design** (see Figure 11.10). It consists of three tasks: (1) designing alternative systems, (2) selecting the best system, and (3) writing a systems design report.

Figure 11.10 Phase 3: design

Designing alternative systems

In almost all instances, more than one design can be developed to meet the information needs. Systems designers evaluate each alternative system for feasibility. By 'feasibility' we mean three things:

Economic feasibility Will the costs of the new system be justified by the benefits it promises?

Technical feasibility Are reliable hardware, software, and training available to make the system work?

Operational feasibility Can the system actually be made to operate in the organisation, or will people—employees, managers, clients—resist it?

Selecting the best system

When choosing the best design, managers must consider these four questions: (1) Will the system fit in with the organisation's overall information system? (2) Will the system be flexible enough so it can be modified in the future? (3) Can it be made secure against unauthorised use? (4) Are the benefits worth the costs?

For example, one aspect you have to consider at Advantage Advertising is security. Should freelancers and outside vendors enter data directly into a computerised time-and-billing system, or should they keep submitting time slips manually? In allowing these outside people to directly input information, are you also allowing them access to files they should not see? Do these files contain confidential information, perhaps information of value to rival advertising agencies?

Writing the systems design report

The report is prepared for higher management and describes the alternative designs. It presents the costs versus the benefits and outlines the effect of alternative designs on the organisation. It usually concludes by recommending one of the alternatives.

PHASE 4: DEVELOPMENT

In the systems development phase, new hardware and software are developed, acquired, and tested.

Phase 4 is **systems development** (see Figure 11.11). It has three steps: (1) developing software, (2) acquiring hardware, and (3) testing the new system.

Developing software

Application software for the new information system can be obtained in two ways. It can be purchased as off-the-shelf packaged software and possibly modified, or it can be custom designed. If any of the software is being specially created, the steps we will outline on programming (in Chapter 12) should be followed.

With the systems analyst's help, you have looked at time-and-billing packaged software designed for service organisations. Such organisations might include advertising agencies, law firms, and building contractors. The systems analyst points out the importance of time-and-billing data being collected in an appropriate manner so that it can be used for a variety of purposes. Such a system will not only help supervisory and middle managers do their jobs but also help top managers make decisions.

Unfortunately, you find that none of the packaged software will do. Most of the packages seem to work well for one person (you). However, none seem to be designed for many people working together. It appears, then, that software will have to be custom designed. (We discuss the process of developing software in Chapter 12 on programming.)

Acquiring hardware

Some new systems may not require new computer equipment, but others will. The kinds needed and the places they are to be installed must be determined. This is a very critical area. Switching or upgrading equipment can be a tremendously expensive proposition. Will a microcomputer system be sufficient as a company grows? Are networks expandable? Will people have to undergo costly training?

The systems analyst tells you that there are several different makes and models of microcomputers currently in use at Advantage Advertising. Fortunately, all are connected by a local area network to a file server that can hold the time-and-billing data. To maintain security, the systems analyst suggests that an electronic mailbox can be installed for freelancers and others outside the company. They can use this electronic mailbox to post their time charges. Thus, it appears that existing hardware will work just fine.

Figure 11.11 Phase 4: development

Testing the new system

After the software and equipment have been installed, the system should be tested. Sample data is fed into the system. The processed information is then evaluated to see whether results are correct. Testing may take several months if the new system is complex.

For this step, you take some time and expense charges from an ad campaign that Advantage ran the previous year. You then ask some people in Creative Services to test it on the system. You observe that time is often charged in fractions of minutes and that the software ignores these fractions of time. You also see that some of the people in Creative Services have problems knowing where to enter their times. To solve the first problem, you must see that the software is corrected to allow for fractional minutes. To solve the second problem, you must see that the software is modified so that it displays an improved user entry screen. After the system has been thoroughly tested and revised as necessary, you are ready to put it into use.

PHASE 5: IMPLEMENTATION

In the systems implementation phase, the new information system is installed, and people are trained to use it.

Another name for Phase 5, **systems implementation**, is **conversion** (see Figure 11.12). It is the process of changing—converting—from the old system to the new.

Types of conversion

There are four approaches to conversion: *direct, parallel, pilot,* and *phased*:

- In the **direct approach**, the conversion is done simply by abandoning the old and starting up the new. This can be risky. If anything is still wrong with the new system, the old system is no longer available to fall back on.

  The direct approach is not recommended precisely because it is so risky. Problems, big or small, invariably crop up in a new system. In a large system, a problem might just mean catastrophe.

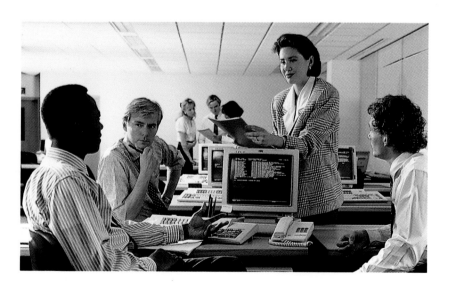

Figure 11.12 Phase 5: implementation

SYSTEMS ANALYSIS AND DESIGN

- In the **parallel approach**, old and new systems are operated side by side until the new one has shown it is reliable.

  This approach is low-risk. If the new system fails, the organisation can just switch to the old system to keep going. However, keeping enough equipment and people active to manage two systems at the same time can be very expensive. Thus, the parallel approach is used only in cases in which the cost of failure or of interrupted operation is great.

- In the **pilot approach**, the new system is tried out in only one part of the organisation. Once the system is working smoothly in that part, it is implemented throughout the rest of the organisation.

  The pilot approach is certainly less expensive than the parallel approach. It also is somewhat riskier. However, the risks can be controlled because problems will be confined to only certain areas of the organisation. Difficulties will not affect the entire organisation.

- In the **phased approach**, the new system is implemented gradually over a period of time.

  The entire implementation process is broken down into parts or phases. Implementation begins with the first phase and once it is successfully implemented, the second phase begins. This process continues until all phases are operating smoothly. This is an expensive proposition, because the implementation is done slowly. However, it is certainly one of the least risky approaches.

In general, the pilot and phased approaches are the most favoured methods. Pilot is preferred when there are many people in an organisation performing similar operations—for instance, all salespersons in a department store. Phased is more appropriate for organisations in which people are performing different operations.

You and the systems analyst succeed in convincing the top managers of Advantage Advertising to take a pilot approach. The reason is that it is easy to select one trial group—the group of which you are a member. Moreover, this group is eager to try the new system. Thus, the new time-and-billing system is tried first with a handful of people in your particular department.

Training

Training people is important, of course. Unfortunately, it is one of the most commonly overlooked activities. Some people may begin training early, even before the equipment is delivered, so that they can adjust more easily. In some cases, a professional software trainer may be brought in to show people how to operate the system. However, at Advantage Advertising the time-and-billing software is simple enough that the systems analyst can act as the trainer.

PHASE 6: MAINTENANCE

Systems maintenance is first a systems audit and then an ongoing evaluation to see whether a system is performing productively.

After implementation comes **systems maintenance**, the last step in the systems life cycle (see Figure 11.13). This phase is a very important and ongoing activity. Most organisations spend more time and money on this phase than any of the others. Maintenance has two parts—a *systems audit* and *periodic evaluation*.

Figure 11.13 Phase 6: maintenance

In the **systems audit**, the system's performance is compared with the original design specifications. This is to determine if the new procedures are actually furthering productivity. If they are not, some further redesign may be necessary.

After the systems audit, the new information system is periodically evaluated and further modified, if necessary. All systems should be evaluated from time to time to see if they are meeting the goals and providing the service they are supposed to.

For example, over time the transaction database at Advantage Advertising is expanded. After a year or two, the systems analyst might suggest that the time-and-billing part of it be re-evaluated. For instance, the analyst might discover that telephone and mailing charges need to be separated. This might be because, with more people using the electronic mailbox and more people sharing data, telephone charges are now higher.

The six-step systems life cycle is summarised in Figure 11.14.

PROTOTYPING

Prototyping consists of devising a model of a new system for users to try out.

Is it necessary to follow every phase of the six phases of systems analysis and design? It may be desirable, but often there is no time to do so. For instance, hardware may change so fast that there is no opportunity for the evaluation, design, and testing just described.

Figure 11.14 Summary of systems life cycle

SYSTEM DEVELOPMENT LIFE CYCLE

Phase	Activity
1. Preliminary investigation	Define problem Suggest alternatives Prepare short report
2. Systems analysis	Gather data Analyse data Document
3. Systems design	Design alternatives Select best alternative Write report
4. Systems development	Develop software Acquire hardware Test system
5. Systems implementation	Convert Train
6. Systems maintenance	Perform system audit Evaluate periodically

A faster alternative is prototyping. **Prototyping** means to build a model, or prototype (pronounced '*proh*-toh-type'), that can be modified before the actual system is installed. For instance, the systems analyst for Advantage Advertising might develop a menu as a possible screen display for the time-and-billing system. Users could try it before the system is put into place.

Prototyping is considered a 'quickie' way of building a system. It allows users to find out right away how a change in the system can help their work. However, relying on prototyping alone can be risky. It might lead to a system being changed or installed without all costs and other matters being considered.

A LOOK AT THE FUTURE

The systems life cycle will be shortened using a method called rapid applications development.

The traditional systems life cycle can take a long time—sometimes years, in the case of large projects for large organisations. Because the pace of business is increasing, to stay competitive, corporations must shorten development life cycles so that products can be produced more quickly.

In the future, we will probably see increasing use of a new method called *rapid applications development (RAD)*, which is intended to reduce development to months instead of years. RAD uses powerful development software (such as CASE), small teams, and highly trained people to produce applications much faster and with higher-quality results than traditional methods do.

REVIEW QUESTIONS

True/false
1. Systems analysis and design is a way to reduce the chance of creating an ineffective information system.

2. In large organisations, the person who uses the systems life cycle the most is called a database administrator.

3. Defining the problem is a task in Phase 2, design.

4. Software is either purchased or developed in the implementation phase.

5. In pilot conversion, one part of the organisation initially tries out the new system.

Multiple choice
1. A collection of hardware, software, people, procedures, and data is called:
   (a) analysis and design
   (b) a system
   (c) a network
   (d) a microcomputer
   (e) design

2. This phase in the systems life cycle focuses on evaluating and determining the need for a new information system:
   (a) preliminary investigation
   (b) systems design
   (c) systems development
   (d) systems implementation
   (e) systems maintenance

3. Phase 2, analysis, involves gathering data, analysing the data, and:
   (a) designing the new system
   (b) creating programs
   (c) auditing the existing information system
   (d) documenting the systems analysis stage
   (e) training

4. The evaluation of economic, technical, and operational feasibility is made during this phase:
   (a) preliminary investigation
   (b) systems design
   (c) systems development
   (d) systems implementation
   (e) systems maintenance

5. The final step in Phase 4, development, is:
   (a) designing alternative systems
   (b) selecting the best system
   (c) developing software
   (d) acquiring hardware
   (e) testing the new system

Fill in the blank
1. The six-phase problem-solving procedure for systems analysis and design is the _____ _____ _____ .

2. Defining the problem, suggesting alternative systems, and preparing a short report are all parts of _____ _____ .

3. _____ _____ diagrams trace data from its origination through processing, storage, and output.

4. Once the new system is operational, a _____ _____ is performed to compare the original design specifications with the actual system.

5. A _____ is a model of a system.

Open ended
1. What is the purpose of systems analysis and design? Who is involved with this process?

2. What are the six phases in the systems life cycle? Briefly describe each phase.

3. Describe top-down analysis methodology.

4. Explain the three steps in Phase 4, systems development.

5. Describe the four possible ways of implementing a system. Which one would you recommend?

DISCUSSION QUESTIONS

1. *Using systems analysis in your life* Will the systems life cycle approach work in the real world? Will it work for you? To find out, try one of the following activities:

   (a) Interview a systems analyst, perhaps one working at the computer centre or in the information systems department of a university. Ask the analyst's opinion of the systems approach as applied to ordinary, non-computer-related problems.

   (b) Apply the systems life cycle to activities at school that you find inefficient or irritating: parking problems, preregistration system, financial aid deadlines, and so on. Try to apply Phase 1, preliminary investigation, briefly identifying the problem and suggesting possible solutions. Write a short report to the school administration to help them decide whether to go ahead with Phase 2. See whether you can pose a few solutions, and find out who is in a position of authority to make possible changes.

2. *The requirements of a systems analyst* Current research in systems analysis and design suggests that a systems analyst should demonstrate a wide range of characteristics. Collect several ads for systems analyst positions. What personality traits appear to be in demand? Assessing the educational requirements and work experience required may help you discuss your findings.

3. *Job opportunities and projections* As mentioned earlier, computer systems analysts received top honours in a 1994 job survey by *Money* magazine. This survey compared the 100 most widely held jobs on several factors including salary, prestige, and security. What jobs are in your future? Research job opportunities and projections for computer systems analysts and other professions that you might be interested in.

CASE STUDY

ABC FINANCIAL GROUP

ABC Financial Group is a Victorian company with its head office in Melbourne. The management staff at head office co-ordinate the operation of the five metropolitan offices. The services provided to clients by these metropolitan offices include:

• selling insurance

• investment advice

• car leasing plans

The personnel at each metropolitan office are:

• manager

• typist/receptionist

• accountant (also acting as the payroll clerk)

• two or three salespersons

The system presently used at each metropolitan office is called the 'staff payroll system' (SPS). All details relating to the staff payroll are entered into the computer and the SPS prints pay cheques and maintains the branch's accounts. Staff details are stored in the personnel file on cards and, when required, are updated manually by the typist.

The current system has become unwieldly since information relating to the business is split between a computerised system and a manual card system. The software that controls the SPS is also not meeting present needs since each time tax legislation and tax brackets change, a programmer must be hired to modify the software.

One systems analyst is employed by head office and he travels regularly to each metropolitan office. He is responsible for maintaining all existing computer systems and recommending and implementing changes to the system as required. Head office is aware of the present deficiencies in their computer systems and has instructed the analyst to recommend an alternative solution.

The analyst has carried out the first four phases of the systems life cycle and has produced a solution called the 'personnel and payroll system' (PPS). This system maintains records of all personnel together with controlling an easily customisable payroll system.

The PPS solution does not require any additional hardware to be purchased; however, considerable effort will be required to ensure effective implementation occurs, since the staff at ABC Financial Group are familiar with the present system and are not particularly computer literate.

QUESTIONS

The ABC Financial Group need to make a decision on the method of implementation.

1. How do you think a direct approach to conversion would affect the business? Give reasons to support your answer.

2. What are the advantages and disadvantages to the business of a parallel approach to implementation?

3. How could the business implement a pilot approach?

4. (a) What are the advantages and disadvantages to the business of a phased approach to conversion?

   (b) How would the business implement a phased approach?

5. In your opinion, which of the four different ways of implementing the new system would be most effective? Give reasons to support your answer.

6. After consultation with the systems analyst, management at head office is considering the pilot approach to implementation. The manager of the metropolitan office selected for the pilot conversion is hesitant to change to the new system. Suggest a compromise on the type of implementation that would be agreeable to both levels of management.

7. (a) Describe how each of the staff at a metropolitan office would use the PPS.

   (b) Are there any staff who would not use the PPS?

8. Management is aware that training is an important part of the implementation of a new system so have decided to provide users with training appropriate to their job functions.

   For each staff member requiring training, state which of the following training options would be most suitable:

   • on-site training

   • part-time off-site training with on-the-job practice

   • software based training

   • outside experts providing in-house training

Programming and languages

COMPETENCIES

After you have read this chapter, you should be able to:

- understand the six steps of programming;

- describe Step 1, program specification;

- describe Step 2, program design, and the program design tools of top-down program design, pseudocode, flowcharts, and logic structures;

- explain Step 3, coding the program;

- describe Step 4, testing the program, and the tools for correcting programs;

- discuss Step 5, documenting the program;

- discuss Step 6, maintaining the program;

- describe CASE tools and object-oriented software development;

- explain the five generations of programming languages.

FROM THE USER'S POINT OF VIEW

How do you go about getting a job? You look through newspaper classified ads, check with employment services, write to prospective employers, and so on. In other words, you do some *general problem solving* to come up with a broad plan. This is similar to what you do in systems analysis and design. Once you have determined a *particular* job you would like to have, you then do some *specific problem solving*. That is what you do in programming. In this chapter, we describe programming in two parts. They are (1) the steps in the programming process and (2) some of the programming languages available.

Why should you need to know anything about programming? The answer is simple. You might need to deal with programmers in the course of your work. You may also be required to do some programming yourself in the future. A new field has emerged known as *end-user application development*. In this field, users like you create their own business application programs, without the assistance of a programmer. Thus, organisations avoid paying high software development costs. You and other end users avoid waiting months for programmers to get around to projects important to you.

In the last chapter, we described the six phases of the systems life cycle. They are preliminary investigation, systems analysis, systems design, systems development, systems implementation, and systems maintenance. Programming is part of Phase 4, systems development, as illustrated in Figure 12.1. Note that the bottom part of that illustration constitutes an outline of the six steps in programming. We follow that outline in this chapter.

PROGRAMS AND PROGRAMMING

Programming is a six-step procedure for producing a program—a list of instructions—for the computer.

What exactly *is* programming? Many people think of it as simply typing words into a computer. That may be part of it—but certainly not all of it. Programming, as we've hinted, is actually a *problem-solving procedure*.

What is a program?

To see how programming works, think about what a program is. A **program** is a list of instructions for the computer to follow to accomplish the task of processing data into information. The instructions are made up of statements used in a programming language, such as BASIC, Pascal, or C.

Application software or *application programs*, as we said in Chapter 1, are the kind of programs that do 'end-user work'. These are things such as word processing and accounting tasks. *System software*, we said, is concerned with 'background' tasks such as housekeeping chores involving computer operations. In this chapter we are concerned with application programs.

You are probably most familiar with one kind of application program—the *prewritten* or *packaged* programs. These are so-called off-the-shelf programs such as word processors, spreadsheets, and database managers. However, application programs may also be *created* or *custom-made*—either by a professional programmer or by you, the end user. In Chapter 11, we saw that the systems analyst looked into the availability of time-and-billing software for Advantage Advertising. Will off-the-shelf software do the job, or should it be custom written? This is one of the first things that needs to be decided in programming.

What is programming?

A program is a list of instructions for the computer to follow to process data. **Programming**, also known as **software development**, is a six-step procedure for creating that list of instructions. Only *one* of those steps consists of typing (keying) statements into a computer.

Figure 12.1 Where programming fits in the systems life cycle

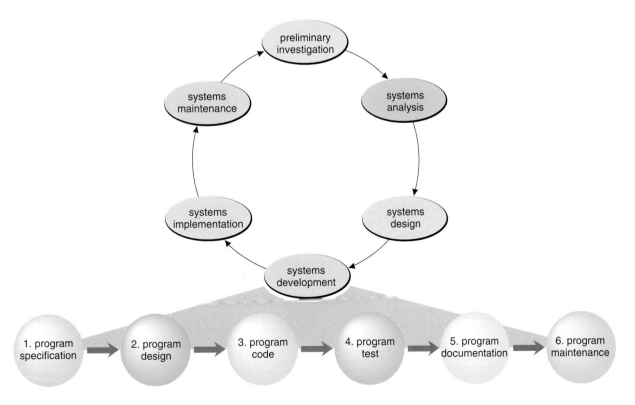

The six steps are as follows (see Figure 12.1):

1. program specification
2. program design
3. program code
4. program test
5. program documentation
6. program maintenance

STEP 1: PROGRAM SPECIFICATION

In the program specification step, the objectives, outputs, inputs, and processing requirements are determined.

Program specification is also called **program definition** or **program analysis**. It requires that the programmer—or you, the end user, if you are following this procedure—specify five tasks. They are (1) the program's objectives, (2) the desired output, (3) the input data required, (4) the processing requirements, and (5) the documentation. Let us consider these.

Determining program objectives

You solve all kinds of problems every day. A problem might be deciding how to commute to school or work or which homework or report to do first. Thus, every day you determine your *objectives*—the problems you are trying to solve. Programming is the same. You need to make a clear statement of the problem you are trying to solve (see Figure 12.2). An example would be 'I want a time-and-billing system to record the time I spend on different jobs for different clients of Advantage Advertising'.

Determining the desired output

It is best always to specify outputs before inputs. That is, you need to list what you want to *get out* of the computer system. Then you should determine what will *go into* it. The best way to do this is to draw a

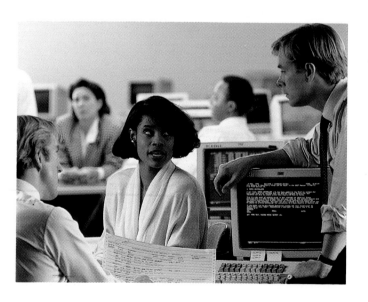

Figure 12.2 Problem definition: make a clear statement of the problem

Figure 12.3 End user's sketch of desired output

picture. You—the end user, not the programmer—should sketch or write how you want the output to look when it's done. It might be printed out or displayed on the monitor.

For example, if you want a time-and-billing report, you might write or draw something like Figure 12.3. Another form of output from the program might be bills to clients.

Determining the input data

Once you know the output you want, you can determine the input data and the source of this data. For example, for a time-and-billing report, you can specify that one source of data to be processed should be time cards. These are usually logs or statements of hours worked submitted on paper forms. The log shown in Figure 12.4 is an example of the kind of input data used in Advantage Advertising's manual system. Note that 24-hour time is used. For example, instead of writing '5:45 pm', people would write '1745'.

Determining the processing requirements

Here you define the processing tasks that must happen for input data to be processed into output. For Advantage, one of the tasks for the program will be to add the hours worked for different jobs for different clients.

Figure 12.4 Example of statement of hours worked—manual system. Hours are expressed in 24-hour time

225

Documenting the program's specifications

As in the systems life cycle, ongoing documentation is essential. Record program objectives, desired outputs, needed inputs, and required processing. This leads to the next step, program design.

STEP 2: PROGRAM DESIGN

In the program design step, a solution is created using programming techniques such as top-down program design, pseudocode, flowcharts, and logic structures.

After program specification, you then take the **program design** step. Here you plan a solution, preferably using **structured programming techniques**. These techniques consist of the following: (1) top-down program design, (2) pseudocode, (3) flowcharts, and (4) logic structures.

Top-down program design

First you determine the outputs and inputs of the computer program you will create. Then you can use **top-down program design** to identify the program's processing steps. Such steps are called **program modules** (or just **modules**). Each module is made up of logically related program statements.

An example of a top-down program design for a time-and-billing report is shown in Figure 12.5. Each of the boxes shown is a module. Under the rules of top-down design, each module should have a single function. The program must pass in sequence from one module to the next until all modules have been processed by the computer. Three of the boxes—'obtain input', 'compute hours for billing', and 'produce output'—correspond to the three principal computer system operations. These operations are *input, process*, and *output*.

Pseudocode

Pseudocode (pronounced 'soo-doh-code') is an outline of the logic of the program you will write. It is like doing a summary of the program

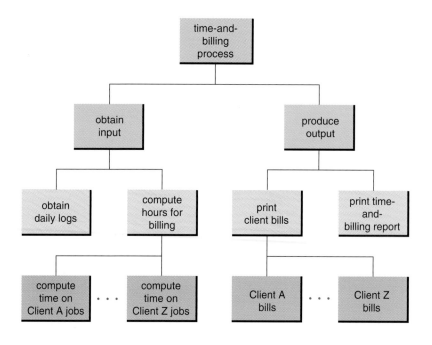

Figure 12.5 Example of top-down program design

Compute time for Client A
Set total regular hours and total overtime hours to zero.
Get time in and time out for a job.
If worked past 1700 hours, then compute overtime hours.
Compute regular hours.
Add regular hours to total regular hours.
Add overtime hours to total overtime hours.
If there are more jobs for that client, go back and compute for that job as well.

Figure 12.6 Example of pseudocode

before it is written. Figure 12.6 shows the pseudocode you might write for one module in the time-and-billing program. This shows the reasoning behind determining hours, including overtime hours, worked for different jobs for one client, Client A. Again, note this expresses the *logic* of what you want the program to do.

Flowcharts

We mentioned system flowcharts in the previous chapter. Here we are concerned with **program flowcharts**. These graphically present the detailed sequence of steps needed to solve a programming problem. Figure 12.7 presents the standard flowcharting symbols and gives an example of a program flowchart. This flowchart expresses all the logic for just *one* module—'Compute time on Client A jobs'—in the top-down program design.

Perhaps you can see from this flowchart why a computer is a computer, and not just a fancy adding machine. A computer does more than arithmetic. It also *makes comparisons*—whether something is greater than or less than, equal to or not equal to.

But have we skipped something? How do we *know* which kind of twists and turns to put in a flowchart so that it will logically work? The answer is based on the use of logic structures, as we will explain.

Logic structures

How do you link the various parts of the flowchart? The best way is a combination of three **logic structures** called *sequence*, *selection*, and *loop*. Using these arrangements enables you to write so-called *structured programs*, which take much of the guesswork out of programming. Let us look at the logic structures:

• In the **sequence structure**, one program statement follows another (see Figure 12.8).

  Consider, for example, the 'compute time' flowchart (refer back to Figure 12.7). The two 'add' boxes are 'Add regular hours to total regular hours' and 'Add overtime hours to total overtime hours'. They logically follow each other. There is no question of 'yes' or 'no', of a decision suggesting other consequences.

• The **selection structure** occurs when a decision must be made. The outcome of the decision determines which of two paths to follow (see Figure 12.9). This structure is also known as an **IF-THEN-ELSE structure**, because that is how you can formulate the decision.

Figure 12.7 Flowchart symbols and example of a program flowchart for computing time worked

Flowchart symbols

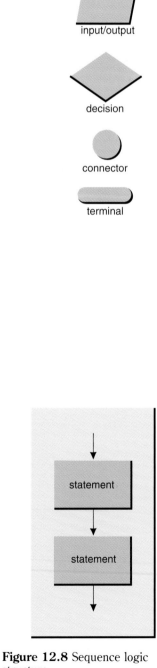

processing

input/output

decision

connector

terminal

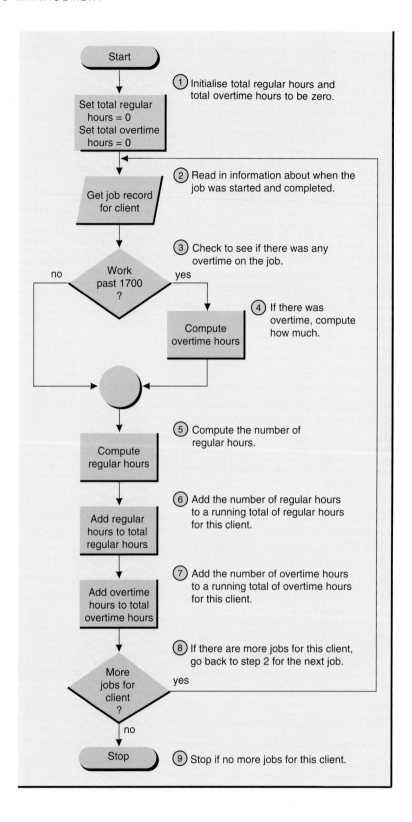

statement

statement

Figure 12.8 Sequence logic structure

Consider, for example, the selection structure in the 'compute time' flowchart, which is concerned about computing overtime hours (refer back to Figure 12.7). It might be expressed in detail as follows:

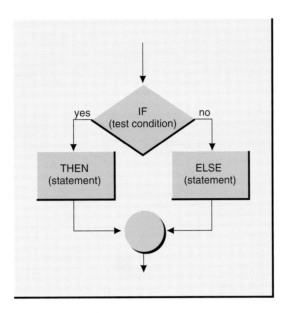

Figure 12.9 Selection (IF-THEN-ELSE) logic structure

IF hour finished for this job is later than or equal to 1700 hours (5:00 pm),
THEN overtime hours equal the number of hours past 1700 hours,
ELSE overtime hours equal zero.

• The **loop structure** describes a process that may be repeated as long as a certain condition remains true. The structure is called a 'loop' or 'iteration' because the program loops around (iterates or repeats) again and again.

The loop structure has two variations: *DO UNTIL* and *DO WHILE* (see Figure 12.10). The **DO UNTIL structure** is the most used form. An example is as follows:

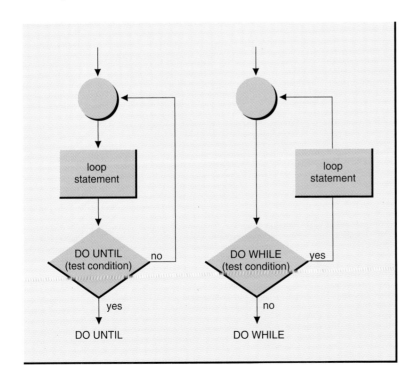

Figure 12.10 Loop logic structures: DO UNTIL and DO WHILE

DO read in job information UNTIL there are no more jobs.

An example of the **DO WHILE structure** is:

DO read in job information WHILE (that is, as long as) there are more jobs.

There is a difference between the two loop structures. You may have several statements that need to be repeated. If so, the decision when to *stop* repeating them can appear at the *beginning* of the loop (DO WHILE). Or, it can appear at the *end* of the loop (DO UNTIL). The DO UNTIL loop means that the loop statements will be executed at least once. This is because the loop statements are executed *before* you are asked whether to stop.

A summary of the structured programming techniques is presented in Figure 12.11.

The last thing to do before leaving the program design step is to document the logic of the design. This report typically includes pseudocode, flowcharts, and logic structures. Now, you are ready for the next step, program code.

STEP 3: PROGRAM CODE

'Coding' is the actual writing of the program, using a programming language.

Writing the program is called **coding**. Here you use the logic you developed in the program design step to actually write the program. That is, you write out—using pencil and paper or typing on a computer keyboard—the letters, numbers, and symbols that make up the program. An example of the handwritten code for the 'compute time' module is shown below in Figure 12.12. This is the 'program code' that instructs the computer what to do. Coding is what many people think of when they think of programming. As we've pointed out, however, it is only one of the six steps in the programming process.

The good program

What are the qualities of a good program? Above all, it should be reliable—that is, it should work under most conditions. It should catch

STRUCTURED PROGRAMMING TECHNIQUES

Technique	Description
Top-down design	Major processing steps called program modules, are identified
Pseudocode	A narrative expression of the logic of the program is written
Program flowcharts	Graphic representation of the steps needed to solve the programming problem is drawn
Logic structures	Three arrangements are used in program flowcharts to write structured programs

Figure 12.11 Summary of structured programming techniques

```
begin
total_regular :=0;
total_overtime: =0;
while not eof(input_file)do

      begin
      readln (input_file, hour_in, minute_in, hour_out, minute_out):
      if (hour_out >= 17) then
          overtime := (hour_out - 17) + (minute_out/60)
      else
          overtime := p;
      regular := (hour_out - hour_in) +(minute_out - minute_in)/60) - overtime;

      total_regular := total_regular + regular;
      total_overtime := total_overtime - overtime;
      end;
end.
```

Figure 12.12 Example of handwritten code for computing the time worked

obvious and common input errors. It should also be well documented and understandable by programmers other than the person who wrote it. After all, someone may need to make changes in the program in the future. The best way to code effective programs is to write so-called *structured programs*, using the logic structures described in Step 2.

Which language?
An important decision is the selection of the programming language. There are hundreds of programming languages, but for micro-computers the most popular have been BASIC, Pascal, and C. We describe programming languages later in this chapter. First you must determine the program's logic. Then you can write (code) it in whatever language you choose that is appropriate and available on your computer. A Pascal program for the 'compute time' module is illustrated in Figure 12.13. The next step is testing, or debugging, the program.

STEP 4: PROGRAM TEST

'Debugging' is testing a program and correcting syntax and logic errors.

Debugging is a programmer's word for testing and then *eliminating* errors ('getting the bugs out'). It means running the program on a computer and then fixing the parts that do not work (see Figure 12.14). Programming errors are of two types: *syntax errors* and *logic errors*.

Syntax errors
A **syntax error** is a violation of the rules of the programming language. For example, in the programming language called Pascal, the instruction 'write In' is wrong. It is supposed to be 'writeln'. That is an example of a syntax error.

Logic errors
A **logic error** occurs when the programmer uses an incorrect calculation or leaves out a programming procedure. For example, a

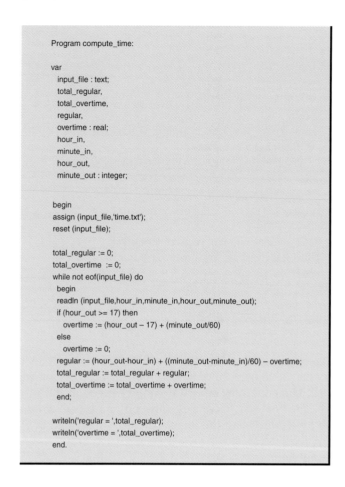

```
Program compute_time:

var
   input_file : text;
   total_regular,
   total_overtime,
   regular,
   overtime : real;
   hour_in,
   minute_in,
   hour_out,
   minute_out : integer;


begin
assign (input_file,'time.txt');
reset (input_file);

total_regular := 0;
total_overtime  := 0;
while not eof(input_file) do
  begin
  readln (input_file,hour_in,minute_in,hour_out,minute_out);
  if (hour_out >= 17) then
     overtime := (hour_out – 17) + (minute_out/60)
  else
     overtime := 0;
  regular := (hour_out-hour_in) + ((minute_out-minute_in)/60) – overtime;
  total_regular := total_regular + regular;
  total_overtime := total_overtime + overtime;
  end;

writeln('regular = ',total_regular);
writeln('overtime = ',total_overtime);
end.
```

Figure 12.13 The 'compute time' program written in Pascal

payroll program that did not compute overtime hours would have a logic error.

The testing process
Several methods have been devised for finding and removing both types of errors, as follows:

Desk checking In **desk checking**, a programmer sitting at a desk checks (proofreads) a printout of the program. The programmer goes through the listing line by line looking for syntax and logic errors.

Figure 12.14 Debugging: testing and eliminating program errors using sample data

Manual testing with sample data Both correct and incorrect data is run through the program—manually, not with a computer—to test for correct processing results.

Attempt at translation The program is run through a computer, using a translator program. The translator attempts to translate the written program from the programming language (such as Pascal) into the machine language. Before the program will run, it must be free of syntax errors. Such errors will be identified by the translating program.

Testing sample data on the computer After all syntax errors have been corrected, the program is tested for logic errors. Sample data is used to test the correct execution of each program statement.

Testing by a select group of potential users This is sometimes called beta testing. It is usually the final step in testing a program. Potential users try out the program and provide feedback.

STEP 5: PROGRAM DOCUMENTATION

'Documenting' means writing a description of the purpose and process of the program.

Documentation consists of written descriptions and procedures about a program and how to use it. It is not something done just at the end of the programming process. Documentation is carried on throughout all the programming steps. This documentation is typically within the program itself and in printed documents. In this step, all the prior documentation is reviewed and finalised. Documentation is important for people who may be involved with the program in the future (see Figure 12.15). These people may include the following:

Figure 12.15 Documentation: describe the program so that others can understand it

Users Users need to know how to use the software. Some organisations may offer training courses to guide users through the program. However, other organisations may expect users to be able to learn a package just from the written documentation. Two examples of this sort of documentation are the manuals that accompany the software and the help option within most microcomputer applications.

Operators Documentation must be provided for computer operators. If the program sends them error messages, for instance, they need to know what to do about them.

Programmers As time passes, even the creator of the original program may not remember much about it. Other programmers wishing to update and modify it—that is, perform program maintenance—may find themselves frustrated without adequate documentation. This kind of documentation should include text and program flowcharts, program listings, and sample output. It might also include system flowcharts to show how the particular program relates to other programs within an information system.

STEP 6: PROGRAM MAINTENANCE

Programmers update software to correct errors, improve usability, standardise, and adjust to organisational changes.

Figure 12.16 Maintenance: ensure that the programs continue to operate efficiently and effectively

The final step is **program maintenance**. As much as 75 percent of the total lifetime cost for an application program is for maintenance (see Figure 12.16). This activity is so commonplace that a special job title, maintenance programmer, exists.

The purpose of program maintenance is to ensure that current programs are operating error free, efficiently, and effectively. Activities in this area fall into two categories: operations and changing needs.

Operations

Operations concerns locating and correcting operational errors, making programs easier to use, and standardising software using structured programming techniques. For properly designed programs these activities should be minimal.

Changing needs

The second category is unavoidable. All organisations change over time, and their programs must change with them. Programs need to be adjusted for a variety of reasons, including new tax laws, new information needs, and new company policies.

This completes the six steps of the programming process (see Figure 12.17).

IMPROVING EFFICIENCY AND PRODUCTIVITY

CASE tools automate the development process. Object-oriented software development changes the approach.

You hear about efficiency and productivity everywhere. They are particularly important for software development. Two resources that promise to help are *CASE tools* and *object-oriented software development*.

CASE tools

Professional programmers are constantly looking for ways to make their work easier, faster, and more reliable. One tool we mentioned in the last chapter, CASE, is meeting this need. **CASE (computer-aided software engineering) tools** provide some automation and assistance in program design, coding, and testing (see Figure 12.18).

PROGRAMMING STEPS

Step	Primary activity
1. Program specification	Determine program objectives, desired output, required input, processing requirements
2. Program design	Use structured programming techniques
3. Program code	Select: programming language; write the program
4. Program test	Perform desk check and manual checks; attempt translation; test using sample data; beta test with potential users
5. Program documentation	Write procedure for users, operators, programmers
6. Program maintenance	Adjust for errors, inefficient or ineffective operations, non-standard code, and changes over time

Figure 12.17 Summary of six steps in programming

Object-oriented software development

Traditional systems development is a careful, step-by-step approach focusing on the procedures needed to complete a certain objective. **Object-oriented software development** is a new approach. It focuses less on the tasks and more on defining the relationships between previously defined procedures or objects. **Object-oriented programming (OOP)** is a process by which a program is organised into objects. Each object contains both the data and processing operations necessary to perform a task. Let's explain what this means.

In the past, programs were developed as giant entities, from the first line of code to the last. This has been compared to building a car

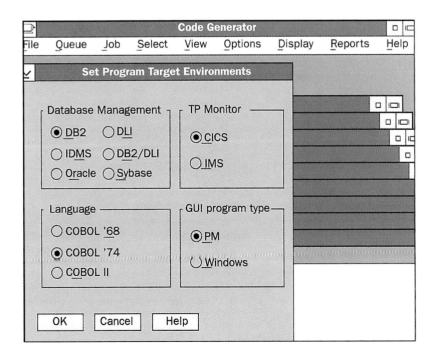

Figure 12.18 CASE tools: Knowledge-Ware's Code Generator

from scratch. Object-oriented programming is like building a car from prefabricated parts—carburettor, generator, bumpers, and so on. Object-oriented programs use *modules* called 'objects'. Objects are reusable, self-contained components. Programs built with these objects assume that certain functions are the same. For example, many programs, from spreadsheets to database managers, have an instruction that will sort lists of names in alphabetical order. A programmer might use this module or object for alphabetising in many other programs. There is no need to invent this activity anew every time.

Some expect that object-oriented software development will improve productivity and efficiency tenfold. However, this will depend upon how many available objects are clearly defined, programmed, documented, and saved in libraries for later use. C + + is one of the most widely used object-oriented programming languages.

FIVE GENERATIONS OF PROGRAMMING LANGUAGES

Languages are described as occurring in 'generations', from machine languages to natural languages.

Computer professionals talk about **levels** or **generations of programming languages**, ranging from 'low' to 'high'. Programming languages are called *lower level* when they are closer to the language the computer itself uses. The computer understands the 0s and 1s that make up bits and bytes. Programming languages are called *higher level* when they are closer to the language humans use—that is, for English speakers, more like English.

There are five generations of programming languages. These are (1) machine languages, (2) assembly languages, (3) procedural languages, (4) problem-oriented languages, and (5) natural languages.

Machine languages: the first generation

We mentioned earlier that a byte is made up of *bits*, consisting of 1s and 0s. These 1s and 0s may correspond to electricity being on or off in the computer. They may also correspond to a magnetic charge being present or absent on storage media such as disk or tape. From this two-state system have been built coding schemes that allow us to construct letters, numbers, punctuation marks, and other special characters. Examples of these coding schemes, as we saw, are ASCII and EBCDIC.

Data represented in 1s and 0s is said to be written in **machine language**. To see how hard this is to understand, imagine if you had to code this:

111100100111001111010010000100000111000000101011

Machine languages also vary according to make of computer—another characteristic that makes them hard to work with.

Assembly languages: the second generation

Assembly languages have a clear advantage over the 1s and 0s of machine language because they use abbreviations or mnemonics. These are easier for human beings to remember. The machine language code we gave above could be expressed in assembly language as

ADD 210(8,13),02B(4,7)

This is still pretty obscure, of course, and so assembly language is also considered low level.

Assembly languages also vary from computer to computer. With the third generation, we advance to high-level languages, many of which are considered **portable**. That is, they can be run on more than one kind of computer—they are 'portable' from one machine to another.

High-level procedural languages: the third generation

People are able to understand languages that are more like their own (e.g. English) than machine languages or assembly languages. These more English-like programming languages are called 'high-level' languages. However, most people still require some training in order to use higher-level languages. This is particularly true of procedural languages.

Procedural languages are programming languages with names like BASIC, Pascal, C, COBOL, and FORTRAN. They are called 'procedural' because they are designed to express the logic—the procedures—that can solve general problems. Procedural languages, then, are intended to solve *general* problems. COBOL, for instance, is used in all kinds of business applications, such as payroll and inventory control. It is fourth-generation languages, discussed next, that are intended to solve *specific* problems.

For a procedural language to work on a computer, it must be translated into machine language so that the computer understands it. Depending on the language, this translation is performed by either a *compiler* or an *interpreter*.

- A **compiler** converts the programmer's procedural language program, called the *source code*, into a machine language code, called the *object code*. This object code can then be saved and run later. Examples of procedural languages using compilers are the standard version of Pascal, COBOL, and FORTRAN.

- An **interpreter** converts the procedural language one statement at a time into machine code just before it is to be executed. No object code is saved. An example of a procedural language using an interpreter is the standard version of BASIC.

What is the difference between using a compiler and using an interpreter? When a program is run, the compiler requires two steps. The first step is to convert the entire program's source code to object code. The second step is to run the object code. The interpreter, in contrast, converts and runs the program one line at a time. The advantage of a compiler language is that once the object code has been obtained, the program executes faster. The advantage of an interpreter language is that programs are easier to develop.

The principal procedural languages with which you may come in contact are as follows:

BASIC Short for *Beginner's All-purpose Symbolic Instruction Code*, **BASIC** is a popular microcomputer language. Widely used on microcomputers and easy to learn, it is suited to both beginning and experienced programmers. It is also interactive—user and computer communicate with each other directly during the writing and running of programs.

Another version created by the Microsoft Corporation is Visual BASIC, which has been hailed as a programming breakthrough. Visual

BASIC makes it easier for novice programmers, as well as professionals, to develop customised applications for Windows. The new language is expected to become quite popular for corporate, in-house development.

Pascal Another language that is widely used on microcomputers and easy to learn is **Pascal**. It is named after Blaise Pascal, a seventeenth-century French mathematician. Pascal has become quite popular in computer science educational programs. One advantage is that it encourages programmers to follow structured coding procedures. It also works well for graphics. We showed an example of Pascal earlier (refer back to Figure 12.13).

C/C++ **C** is a general-purpose language that also works well with microcomputers. It is useful for writing operating systems, spreadsheet programs, database programs, and some scientific applications. Programs are portable: they can be run without change on a variety of computers. **C++** is a version of C that incorporates object-oriented technologies. It is popular with some software developers and promises to increase programmer productivity.

COBOL **COBOL**—which stands for *CO*mmon *B*usiness-*O*riented *L*anguage—is one of the most frequently used programming languages in business. Though harder to learn than BASIC, its logic is easier for a person who is not a trained programmer to understand. Writing a COBOL program is sort of like writing the outline for a term paper. The program is divided into four divisions. The divisions in turn are divided into sections, which are divided into paragraphs, then into statements.

FORTRAN Short for *FOR*mula *TRAN*slation, **FORTRAN** is a widely used scientific and mathematical language. It is very useful for processing complex formulas. Thus, many scientific and engineering programs have been written in this language.

Ada **Ada** is named after Augusta Ada, the English Countess of Lovelace who is regarded as the first programmer. Ada was developed under the sponsorship of the US Department of Defense. Originally designed for weapons systems, it has commercial uses as well. Because of its structured design, modules (sections) of a large program can be written, compiled, and tested separately—before the entire program is put together.

Problem-oriented languages: the fourth generation
Third-generation languages are valuable, but they require training in programming. Problem-oriented languages, also known as very high-level languages, require little special training on the part of the user.

Unlike general-purpose languages, **problem-oriented languages** are designed to solve specific problems. Some of these fourth-generation languages are used for very specific applications. For example, IFPS (interactive financial planning system) is used to develop financial models. Many consider Lotus 1-2-3 and dBASE to be flexible fourth-generation languages. This group also includes query languages and application generators:

Query languages **Query languages** enable non-programmers to use certain easily understood commands to search and generate reports from a database. An example is the commands used on an airline reservations system by clerks needing flight information.

Application generators An **application generator** contains a number of modules—logically related program statements—that have been preprogrammed to accomplish various tasks. An example would be a module that calculates overtime pay. The programmer can simply state which task is needed for a particular application. The application generator creates the program code by selecting the appropriate modules.

Natural languages: the fifth generation

Natural languages are still being developed. They are designed to give people a more human ('natural') connection with computers. The languages are human languages: English, French, Japanese, or whatever. Researchers also hope that natural languages will enable a computer to *learn*—to 'remember' information, as people do, and to improve upon it. Clearly, this area is extremely challenging.

The five generations of programming languages are summarised in Figure 12.19.

A LOOK AT THE FUTURE

Object-oriented techniques, visual development environments, and evolving programming languages lead the way.

Ten years ago, a computer program of a few thousand lines was considered long. Today a word processing program may contain 50 000 lines. Programs needed to run modern aircraft, medical equipment, or financial institutions can run to millions of lines. Thus, in the future, programming will become only more important, not less. Not long ago, *one* software error (bug) plunged American Telephone & Telegraph's long-distance telephone network into chaos for nine hours. During this time, AT&T was able to put through only about half of all long-distance calls attempted. Severely affected were airline reservations systems, among other businesses.

PROGRAMMING GENERATIONS

Generation	Name	Sample statement
First	Machine	10010001
Second	Assembly	ADD 210(8, 13), 02B(4, 7)
Third	Procedural	Overtime: 0
Fourth	Problem	FIND NAME 'JONES'
Fifth	Natural	IF patient is dizzy, THEN check temperature and blood pressure

Figure 12.19 Summary of five programming generations

Professional programmers are constantly looking for development tools to make their work easier, faster, and more reliable. These tools are just beginning to use object-oriented techniques, visual development environments, and evolving programming languages. Borland International is a leader in this area with its Application Frameworks, C++. Another leader is Microsoft with its continuing development of Microsoft Visual BASIC. Both of these software development companies are paving the way for future application development tools.

REVIEW QUESTIONS

True/false

1. A program is a list of instructions for the computer to follow to accomplish the task of processing data into information.

2. All documentation is performed in the last step in the programming.

3. CASE stands for computer association of scientific engineers.

4. A translator converts a programming language into machine language.

5. Assembly is in the first generation of programming languages.

Multiple choice

1. Another name for application software is:
   (a) application programs
   (b) system software
   (c) programming languages
   (d) package software
   (e) custom-made programs

2. The structured programming technique that graphically presents the detailed steps needed to solve the problem is called:
   (a) top-down design
   (b) pseudocode
   (c) flowcharts
   (d) logic structures
   (e) object-oriented programming

3. The last thing to do before leaving the program design step is to:
   (a) determine outputs
   (b) document
   (c) test
   (d) select programming language
   (e) code

4. The last step in programming is:
   (a) design
   (b) analysis
   (c) test
   (d) maintenance
   (e) coding

5. A translator that converts procedural languages one statement at a time into machine code before it is to be executed is:
   (a) BASIC
   (b) interpreter
   (c) Pascal
   (d) query language
   (e) compiler

Fill in the blank

1. In program specification, you should specify _____ before inputs.

2. The logic structure _____ is used when a decision must be made.

3. _____ is another name for testing the program.

4. Unlike traditional software development, object-oriented development focuses on defining the _____ between procedures or objects.

5. _____ is the most frequently used language in business programming.

Open ended

1. Describe the six steps involved in programming.

2. Identify and give an example for each of the three logic structures.

3. List and discuss the five generations of programming languages.

4. Explain the difference between a compiler and an interpreter.

5. Discuss the principal advantage(s) of natural languages if researchers are successful in developing them.

DISCUSSION QUESTIONS

1. *Pencil-and-paper programming* Suppose you are the manager of a clothing store. Using just pencil and paper, see if you can devise the steps in a program that will do the following:

   (a) Pay a sales bonus of 1 percent of total sales to salespeople who sell $50 000 worth of clothes.

   (b) Pay a sales bonus of 5 percent of total sales to salespeople who sell $250 000 worth of clothes.

   (c) Pay a sales bonus of 10 percent of total sales to salespeople who sell $500 000 worth of clothes.

2. *Programming the beginning of your day* Flowcharts can be used to graphically present the sequence of steps involved in almost any activity. Different shapes and symbols are used to represent different kinds of activities: processing, input and output of data, decision-making, and starting and stopping. The lines and arrows

connecting the shapes show the sequence of steps used to complete the activity. Create a flowchart that describes what you do each morning to get ready for the day.

3. *More on object-oriented programming* Buying prewritten software allows you to do a predetermined task, such as run a spreadsheet. But unless the manufacturer already thought of a particular task, you can't do it with that software unless you know how to modify it—that is, do programming. Object-oriented programming, we said, is like building a car from prefabricated parts rather than from scratch. The attraction of object-oriented programming is that it can make programming easy for ordinary users.

This is your chance to investigate ways to make programming fun for you. Pick one of the following subjects and use the library or other resources to look into it in detail:

(a) HyperCard, available as a standard feature on many Apple Macintoshes, uses a concept of computerised 'index cards', each of which stores information. You arrange the cards into 'stacks' according to whatever method of grouping you choose. HyperCard is not only modular but also highly visual.

(b) Visual BASIC, designed to work with Microsoft's Windows, has many modular elements. The user can construct the components of a Windows application by manipulating a variety of visual elements that were preassembled by Microsoft programmers.

(c) An IBM product under development called Constellation is supposed to provide blocks of software that users can mix and match as they choose.

CASE STUDY

SMART SOFTWARE

Smart Software is a software house that develops custom written applications to meet clients' needs. Its main area of expertise is developing Windows-based application software.

Mary Birch, a systems analyst employed by Smart Software, has been given the task of managing the development of a solution for the Perfect Personnel Employment Agency.

• Perfect Personnel is a growing small business that matches the skills of job seekers with requirements of prospective employers. Due to the ever increasing number of their clients, the management of Perfect Personnel realise that their existing paper-based method of recording has become far too time-consuming and inefficient. Consequently, they have approached Smart Software requesting a solution to their problem.

QUESTIONS

1. Mary has completed the first three phases of the systems life cycle: preliminary investigation, systems analysis and systems design. A significant part of the fourth phase (systems development) involves software development or programming. List the six steps that she must now work through when developing the software for this problem.

2. From the program specification step:
   (a) describe the program's objectives
   (b) describe the form the output may take
   (c) list the input data which will be required
   (d) describe some of the processing requirements of this problem

3. List four techniques Mary may use in the program design step.

4. Mary has given Belinda the task of coding the program for Perfect Personnel. What qualities must Belinda's program have if it is to be considered a good program?

5. At what step in the software development process are:
   (a) syntax errors introduced
   (b) logic errors introduced?

6. List four techniques that Belinda can use to test for logic errors.

7. Describe the different types of documentation which Smart Software will need to produce.

8. Most of the programs developed by Smart Software are written in the language Visual Basic. Why is this language particularly suited to the work that Smart Software undertakes?

Workplace issues: ergonomics, ethics, security, and the environment

COMPETENCIES

After you have read this chapter, you should be able to:

- describe ergonomics and how it helps avoid physical and mental risks;

- describe the four ethical issues: privacy, accuracy, property, and access;

- discuss the ethical issues raised by the presence of large databases and electronic networks;

- list the major laws on privacy;

- explain the effects of computer crimes, including the spreading of computer viruses;

- describe other hazards to the computer;

- discuss security measures that may be taken;

- discuss what the computer industry is doing to help protect the environment;

- discuss what you can do to help protect the environment.

FROM THE WORKER'S POINT OF VIEW

The tools and products of the information age do not exist in a world by themselves. As we said in Chapter 1, a computer system consists not only of software, hardware, data, and procedures but also of *people*. Because of people, computer systems may be used for both good and bad purposes. In this chapter we examine what some of the people issues are.

There are more than 200 million microcomputers in use today. Millions of workers use these machines every day for hours at a time. What are the consequences of the widespread presence of this technology? We consider some of the effects below.

ERGONOMICS

Ergonomics helps computer users take steps to avoid physical and mental health risks and to increase productivity.

Even though the cost of computers has decreased significantly, they are still expensive. Why have them, then, unless they can make workers more effective? Ironically, however, there are certain ways in which computers may actually make people *less* productive. Many of these problems will most likely affect workers in data entry-intensive positions, such as clerks and word processor operators. However, they may also happen to anyone whose job involves heavy use of the computer. As a result, there has been great interest in a field known as ergonomics.

Ergonomics (pronounced 'er-guh-*nom*-ix') is defined as the study of human factors related to computers. It is concerned with fitting the job to the worker rather than forcing the worker to contort to fit the job. As computer use has increased, so has interest in ergonomics. People are devising ways that computers can be designed and used to increase productivity and avoid health risks.

Physical health matters

Sitting in front of a screen in awkward positions for long periods may lead to physical problems. These can include eyestrain, headaches, and back pain. Users can alleviate these by taking frequent rest breaks and by using well-designed computer furniture. Some recommendations by ergonomic experts for the ideal setup for a microcomputer are illustrated in Figure 13.1.

The physical health matters related to computers that have received the most attention recently are the following:

Avoiding eyestrain and headache Our eyes were made for most efficient seeing at a distance. However, monitors require using the eyes at closer range for a long time, which can create eyestrain, headaches, and double vision.

To make the computer easier on the eyes, take a 15-minute break every hour or two. Avoid computer screens that flicker. Keep computer screens away from windows and other sources of bright light to minimise reflected glare on the screen. Special antiglare screen coatings and 'glare shields' are also available. Make sure the screen is three to four times brighter than room light. Keep everything you're focusing on at about the same distance. For example, the computer screen, keyboard, and a document holder containing your work might be positioned about 50 centimetres away. Clean the screen of dust from time to time.

Avoiding back and neck pain Many people work at monitors and keyboards that are in improper positions. The result can be pains in the back and neck.

To avoid such problems, make sure equipment is adjustable. You should be able to adjust your chair for height and angle, and the

Figure 13.1 Recommendations for the ideal microcomputer work environment

245

chair should have good back support. The table on which the monitor stands should also be adjustable, and the monitor itself should be of the tilt-and-swivel kind. The monitor should be at eye level or slightly below eye level. Keyboards should be detachable. Document holders should be adjustable.

Avoiding effects of electromagnetic fields Like many household appliances, monitors generate invisible electromagnetic field (EMF) emissions, which can pass through the human body. Some observers think that there could be a connection between these EMF emissions and possible miscarriages (and even some cancers). A study by the US government's National Institute of Occupational Safety and Health found no statistical relationship between monitors and miscarriages. Even so, several companies have introduced low-emission monitors. They state that no health or safety problems exist with older monitors; rather, they are merely responding to market demands.

One recommendation is that computer users should follow a policy of 'prudent avoidance' in reducing their exposure to EMF emissions. They should try to sit about 60 centimetres or more from the computer screen and 90 centimetres from neighbouring terminals. The strongest fields are emitted from the sides and backs of terminals. Pregnant women should be particularly cautious and are encouraged to consult with their physician.

Avoiding repetitive strain injury Data-entry operators may make as many as 23 000 keystrokes a day. Some of these workers and other heavy keyboard users have fallen victim to a disorder known as repetitive strain injury.

Repetitive strain injury (RSI)—also called **repetitive motion injury** and **cumulative trauma disorders**—is the name given to a number of injuries. These result from fast, repetitive work that can cause neck, wrist, hand and arm pain. In 1993, RSI accounted for over 60 percent of all workplace illnesses in private industry, compared with only 20 percent in 1981. Some RSI sufferers are slaughterhouse, textile, and automobile workers, who have long been susceptible to the disorder. However, the large increase was mainly caused by the addition of so many more computer users in the intervening years. One particular RSI, **carpal tunnel syndrome**, found among heavy computer users, consists of damage to nerves and tendons in the hands. Some victims report the pain is so intense that they cannot open doors or shake hands and require corrective surgery.

Before the computer, typists would stop to change paper or make corrections, thus giving themselves short but frequent rest periods. Ergonomically correct keyboards have recently been developed (see Figure 13.2). Because RSI is caused by repetition and a fast work pace, avoidance means finding ways to take frequent short rest breaks. Experts also advise getting plenty of sleep and exercise, losing weight, sitting up straight, and learning stress-management techniques.

Mental health matters

Computer technology offers not only ways of improving productivity but also some irritants that may be counterproductive.

Avoiding noise Computing can be quite noisy. Voice input and output can be distracting for other workers. Working next to an impact printer

Figure 13.2 Ergonomic keyboard: Select-Ease keyboard from Lexmark International

for several hours can leave one with ringing ears. Also, users may develop headaches and tension from continual exposure to the high-frequency, barely audible squeal produced by computer monitors and cooling fans inside the system unit. This is particularly true for women, who hear high-frequency sounds better than men do. They may be affected by the noise even when they are not conscious of hearing it.

Acoustical tile and sound-muffling covers are available for reducing the noise from co-workers and impact printers. However, there appears to be no immediate solution for abating the noise from monitors.

Avoiding stress from excessive monitoring Research shows that workers whose performance is monitored electronically suffer more health problems than do those watched by human supervisors. For instance, a computer may monitor the number of keystrokes a data-entry clerk completes in a day. It might tally the time a customer-service person takes to handle a call. The company might then decide to shorten the time allowed and to continue monitoring the employees electronically. By so doing, it may force a pace leading to physical, RSI-type problems and mental health difficulties. One study found that electronically monitored employees reported more boredom, higher tension, extreme anxiety, depression, anger, and severe fatigue.

Recently it has been shown that electronic monitoring actually is not necessary. For instance, both Federal Express and Bell Canada replaced electronic monitoring with occasional monitoring by human managers. They found that employee productivity stayed up and even increased.

A new word—'technostress'—has been proposed to describe the stress associated with computer use that is harmful to people. Technostress is the tension that arises when we have to unnaturally adapt to computers rather than having computers adapt to us.

Design with people in mind

Electronic products from microwave ovens to VCRs to microcomputers offer the promise of more efficiency and speed. Often, however, the products are so overloaded with features that users cannot figure them out. Because a microprocessor chip handles not just one operation but several, manufacturers feel obliged to pile on the 'bells and whistles'. Thus, many home and office products, while being fancy technology platforms, are difficult for humans to use.

A recent trend among manufacturers is to deliberately reduce the features offered, rather than to constantly do all that is possible. In appliances, this restraint is shown among certain types of high-end audio equipment, which come with fewer buttons and lights. In computers, there are similar trends. Surveys show that consumers want 'plug and play' equipment—machines that they can simply turn on and quickly start working. Thus, computers are being made easier to use, with more menus, windows, and use of icons and pictures.

Similar attempts at designing computers for ease in human use are found in other areas. For example, psychologists have found that workers regard expert systems—the complex programs that emulate human experts—much as they would human expertise. To be trusted by humans, the programs must contain procedures that are very close to the logic processes used by experts. That is, they must appear to think like humans in order to be acceptable.

ETHICS

Every computer user should be aware of ethical matters, including how databases and online networks are used and the major privacy laws.

What do you suppose controls how computers can be used? You probably think first of laws. Of course that is right, but technology is moving so fast that it is very difficult for our legal system to keep up. The essential element that controls how computers are used today is ethics.

Ethics, as you may know, are standards of moral conduct. Computer ethics are guidelines for the morally acceptable use of computers in our society. There are four primary computer ethics issues:

- **Privacy** concerns the collection and use of data about individuals.

- **Accuracy** relates to the responsibility of those who collect data to ensure that the data is correct.

- **Property** relates to who owns data and rights to software.

- **Access** relates to the responsibility of those who have data to control who is able to use that data.

We are all entitled to ethical treatment. This includes the right to keep personal information, such as credit ratings and medical histories, from getting into the wrong hands. Many people worry that this right is severely threatened. Let us see what some of the concerns are.

Use of large databases

Large organisations are constantly compiling information about us. For instance, our tax file numbers are now used routinely as key fields in databases for organising our employment, credit, and tax records. Shouldn't we be concerned that cross-referenced information might be used for the wrong purposes?

Every day, data is gathered about us and stored in large databases. For example, for billing purposes, telephone companies compile lists of the calls we make, the numbers called, and so on. A special telephone directory (called a reverse directory) lists telephone numbers followed by subscriber names. Using it, governmental authorities and others could easily get the names, addresses, and other details about the persons we call. Credit card companies keep similar records. Supermarket scanners in grocery checkout counters record what we buy, when we buy it, how much we buy, and the price (see Figure 13.3). Publishers of magazines, newspapers, and mail-order catalogues have our names, addresses, phone numbers, and what we order.

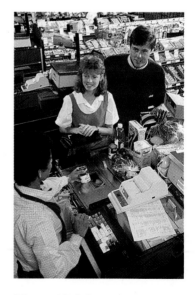

Figure 13.3 Large organisations are constantly compiling information about us, such as the kinds of products we buy

A vast industry of data gatherers or 'information resellers' now exists that collects such personal data. They then sell it to direct marketers, fund-raisers, and others. Even government agencies contribute; in the United States, some state motor vehicle departments sell the car registration data they collect. Database companies have been able to collect names, addresses, and other information on about 80 percent of American households. The average person is on 100 mailing lists and 50 databases, according to some privacy experts.

In such ways, our personal preferences and habits become marketable commodities. This raises two areas of concern:

Spreading information without personal consent How would you feel if your name and your taste in movies were made available nationwide? For a while, Blockbuster, a large American video rental company, considered doing just this. What if a great deal of information about your shopping habits—collected about you without your consent—was made available to any microcomputer user who wanted it? Before dropping the project, Lotus Development Corporation and Equifax Inc. planned to market disks containing information on 120 million American consumers. (Lotus claimed it was providing only small businesses with the same information currently available to larger organisations.) Finally, how would you feel if your employer were using your *medical* records to make decisions about placement, promotion, and firing? A University of Illinois survey found that half the Fortune 500 companies were using employee medical records for that purpose.

Spreading inaccurate information How *accurate* is the information being circulated? Mistakes that creep into one computer file may find their way into other computer files. For example, credit records may be in error. Moreover, even if you correct an error in one file, the correction may not be made in other files. Indeed, erroneous information may stay in computer files for years. It's important to know, therefore, that you have some recourse. In the United States, the law allows you to gain access to those records about you that are held by credit bureaus. Under the Freedom of Information Act (described below), you are also entitled to look at your records held by government agencies. (Portions may be deleted for national security reasons.)

Use of electronic networks
Suppose you use your company's electronic mail system to send a co-worker an unflattering message about your supervisor. Later you find the boss has been spying on your exchange. Or suppose you are a subscriber to an online electronic bulletin board. You discover that the company that owns the bulletin board screens all your messages and rejects those it deems inappropriate. Both these cases have actually happened.

The first instance, of firms eavesdropping on employees, has inspired attempts at federal legislation. One US survey revealed that over 20 percent of businesses search employees' electronic mail and computer files. Currently this is legal. One proposed law would not prohibit electronic monitoring but would require employers to provide prior written notice. They would also have to alert employees during the monitoring with some sort of audible or visual signal. The second instance, in which online information services restrict libellous, obscene, or otherwise offensive material, exists with most commercial services. In one case in America, the Prodigy Information Service terminated the accounts of eight members who had been using the electronic mail system to protest Prodigy's rate hikes.

Prodigy executives argued that the US Constitution does not give members of someone's private network the right to express their views without restrictions. Opponents say that the United States is becoming a nation linked by electronic mail. Therefore, there has to be fundamental protection for users against other people reading or censoring their messages.

Laws relating to privacy in Australia

The 'common law' countries such as England and Australia have never recognised a tort (or wrong) of privacy. Other torts, however, such as defamation or trespass, may assist in the preservation of a person's privacy. Trespass to land, for example, is designed to discourage an unwelcome visitor from remaining on another person's property and may then offer incidental protection to the privacy of the land owner. This can be contrasted with the US legal system, where the law does recognise an action for the 'invasion of privacy'. This legal acceptance of a right to privacy coupled with the rise of computer systems in the United States has resulted in significant legislative initiatives. These include the *Fair Credit Reporting Act 1970*, the *Freedom of Information Act 1970*, the *Privacy Act 1974* and the *Computer Fraud and Abuse Act 1986*.

Australian governments, both state and federal, have generally been influenced by the US experience. Major pieces of legislation in this area include the **Privacy Act 1988** (Commonwealth) and the **Credit Reporting Act 1978** (Victoria), which are discussed below:

- *Privacy Act 1988* (Commonwealth): The aims of the *Privacy Act 1988* can be summarised as follows:

  (1) that personal information gathered and recorded by federal government departments or agencies be protected;

  (2) that tax file numbers are used and collected for matters relating to taxation only;

  (3) that personal credit information of individuals is managed correctly and that personal privacy is not infringed.

  The federal government is required to have its departments and agencies comply with 'Information Privacy Principles', which include the security and storage of personal information, the accuracy of records, how personal information may be used and disclosed to third parties, and individuals having access to their own personal records. There is a Privacy Commissioner who has the power to inspect an agency's records and, if necessary, to require them to alter the way they handle and collate information, so as to abide by the Information Privacy Principles.

- *Credit Reporting Act 1978* (Victoria): Usually, before a financial institution will lend money to a potential borrower, it will check that borrower's credit rating. The resulting credit report may detail information about whether any court judgments have been made against the borrower, or whether he or she has been declared bankrupt.

The aims of the *Credit Reporting Act 1978* can be summarised as follows:

(1) to place control over what is included in credit reports;

(2) to give a borrower who has been refused a loan the means of challenging the data that resulted in the refusal;

(3) to allow errors in the credit report to be rectified.

Besides the two pieces of legislation outlined above, the *Freedom of Information Act 1982* and legislation relating to intellectual property—for example, the *Copyright Act 1968*—also regulate this area of the law.

- *Freedom of Information Act:* Generally this Act allows people access to information held by the Victorian government. There are exceptions, however, to this general rule. For example, documents defined as Cabinet documents, documents affecting personal privacy and documents relating to trade secrets may be considered exempt and therefore not obtainable under the Act.

- *Copyright Act 1968:* Under section 31 of this Act it is an infringement of copyright to reproduce a literary work in a material form or to make an adaptation of that work without the permission of the author.

1. *No secret databases:* There must be no record-keeping systems containing personal data whose very existence is kept secret.

2. *Right of individual access:* Individuals must be able to find out what information about them is in a record and how it is used.

3. *Right of consent:* Information about individuals obtained for one purpose cannot be used for other purposes without their consent.

4. *Right to correct:* Individuals must be able to correct or amend records of identifiable information about them.

5. *Assurance of reliability and proper use:* Organisations creating, maintaining, using, or disseminating records of identifiable personal data must make sure the data is reliable for its intended use. They must take precautions to prevent such data from being misused.

Figure 13.4 Principles of the Code of Fair Information Practice

Under section 10 of the Act a 'literary work' is defined to include 'a computer program or compilation of computer programs'. Thus, if a person develops a computer program that is original or novel in nature it may be afforded the protection of copyright, which means that it may not be reproduced or copied without the permission of the author or creator of the original program.

SECURITY

Threats to computer security are computer crimes, including viruses, electronic break-ins, and natural and other hazards. Security measures consist of encryption, restricting access, anticipating disasters, and making backup copies.

We are all concerned with having a safe and secure environment to live in. We are careful to lock our car doors and our homes. We are careful about where we walk at night and who we talk to. This is physical security. What about computer security? Does it matter if someone gains access to personal information about you? What if someone learns your credit card number or your cheque account number? What if a mistake is made and your credit history shows a number of large unpaid loans? What if all your school records are lost? These are just a few of the reasons to be concerned about computer security.

Threats to computer security
Keeping information private depends on keeping computer systems safe from criminals, natural hazards, and other threats.

A **computer crime** is an illegal action in which the perpetrator uses special knowledge of computer technology. Computer criminals are of four types:

Employees The largest category of computer criminals consists of those with the easiest access to computers—namely, employees (see Figure 13.5). Sometimes the employee is simply trying to steal something from the employer—equipment, software, electronic funds, proprietary information, or computer time. Sometimes the employee may be acting out of resentment and is trying to 'get back' at the company.

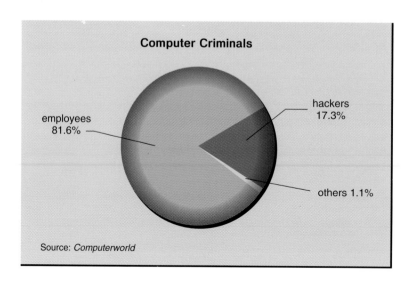

Figure 13.5 The experts reply: whom do you consider to be a threat against your network?

Outside users Not only employees but also some suppliers or clients may have access to a company's computer system. Examples are bank customers who use an automatic teller machine. Like employees, these authorised users may obtain confidential passwords or find other ways of committing computer crimes.

'Hackers' and 'crackers' Some people think of these two groups as being the same, but they are not. **Hackers** are people who gain unauthorised access to a computer system for the fun and challenge of it. **Crackers** do the same thing but for malicious purposes. They may intend to steal technical information or to introduce what they call a 'bomb'—a destructive computer program—into the system.

Organised crime Organised crime has discovered that computers can be used just like legitimate business people use them, but for illegal purposes. For example, they are useful for keeping track of stolen goods or illegal gambling debts. In addition, counterfeiters and forgers use microcomputers and printers to produce sophisticated-looking documents, such as cheques and driver's licences.

Computer crime can take various forms, as follows:

Damage Disgruntled employees sometimes attempt to destroy computers, programs, or files. For example, in a crime known as the **Trojan horse program** instructions can be written to destroy or modify software or data.

In recent years, computer viruses have gained wide notoriety. **Viruses** are programs that 'migrate' through networks and operating systems and attach themselves to different programs and databases (see Figure 13.6). Creating and knowingly spreading a virus is a US federal offence punishable under the *Computer Abuse Amendments Act* of 1994.

A variant on the virus is the **worm**. This destructive program fills a computer system with self-replicating information, clogging the system

Figure 13.6 How a computer virus can spread

```
1  PROGRAM MAIN
     REAL X, A, B, WIDTH, *AREA, F
     INTEGER I, N
     F(X) = SQRT ( ABS(4 - X **2) )
     PRINT *, 'VIRUS'
     D *, A, B
     T *, 'YOUR COMPUTER IS DEAD'
     D *, N
     WIDTH = (B-A)/N
     X = A
     AREA = 0
     DO 20 I = 1, N
       AREA = AREA + WIDTH * F (X + WIDTH/2)
       X = X + WIDTH
     CONTINUE
     PRINT *, ' SUPER HACKER '
     END
```

(1) A virus begins when a 'cracker' or programmer writes a program that attaches itself to an operating system, another program, or piece of data.

(2) The virus travels via floppy disk or downloading from networks or bulletin boards anywhere that the operating system, program, or data travels.

(3) The virus is set off. A non-destructive virus may simply print a message ('Surprise!'). A destructive virus may erase data, destroy programs, and even (through repeated reading and writing to one location) wear out a hard disk. The virus may be set off either by a time limit or by a sequence of operations by the user.

253

so that its operations are slowed or stopped. The most infamous is known as the Internet Worm. In 1988, it travelled across North America, stopping thousands of computers along its way.

Viruses typically find their way into microcomputers through copied floppy disks or programs downloaded from electronic bulletin boards. Because viruses can be so serious—certain 'disk-killer' viruses can destroy all the information on one's system—computer users are advised to exercise care in accepting new programs and data from other sources. Detection programs called *virus checkers* are available to alert users when certain kinds of viruses enter the system. Unfortunately, new viruses are being developed all the time, and not all viruses can be detected. There are recommended procedures to reduce the risk of catching a computer virus and to minimise its potential damage (see Figure 13.7).

Theft Theft can take many forms—of hardware, of software, of data, of computer time. Thieves steal equipment, of course, but there are also 'white-collar crimes'. Thieves steal data in the form of confidential information such as preferred client lists. They also use (steal) their company's computer time to run another business.

Unauthorised copying—a form of theft—of programs for personal gain is called **software piracy**. According to the *Copyright Act* (1968), it is legal for a program owner to make backup copies of that program. *It's important to note that none of these copies may be resold or given away. This may come as a surprise to students who copy software from a friend, but that's the law. It is illegal, not to mention unethical.*

Pirated software accounts for 40 per cent of software used in the United States. The problem of pirated software is even more serious overseas in such countries as Italy (82 per cent) and Thailand (92 per

VIRUS PROTECTION

Step	Action
1.	Make backup copies of your data on a frequent basis
2.	Protect data on your floppy disks by using write-protect tabs
3.	Turn off your microcomputer when you're not using it
4.	Don't use master disk to install software programs. Make a working copy and store the master
5.	Avoid downloading computer games from electronic bulletin boards
6.	Limit your use of 'shareware' programs and check for viruses before running
7.	Do not loan out your utility or other software programs
8.	Run a virus protection program frequently
9.	Update your virus protection program regularly

Figure 13.7 How to prevent computer viruses and minimise damage

cent). Penalties for violating this law are payment of monetary damages to the developer of the program and even prison terms.

Manipulation Finding entry into someone's computer network and leaving a prankster's message may seem like fun, which is why hackers do it. It is still against the law. Moreover, even if the manipulation seems harmless, it may cause a great deal of anxiety and wasted time among network users.

There are plenty of other hazards to computer systems and data besides criminals. They include the following:

Natural hazards Natural forces include fires, floods, wind, hurricanes, tornadoes, and earthquakes. Even home computer users should store backup disks of programs and data in safe locations in case of fire or storm damage.

Civil strife and terrorism Wars, riots, and other forms of political unrest are real risks in some parts of the world. Even developed countries, however, must be mindful that acts of sabotage are possible.

Technological failures Hardware and software don't always do what they are supposed to do. For instance, too little electricity, caused by a brownout or blackout, may cause the loss of data in primary storage. Too much electricity, as when lightning or other electrical disturbance affects a power line, may cause a **voltage surge**, or **spike**. This excess of electricity may destroy chips or other electronic components of a computer.

Most microcomputer users buy a **surge protector**, a device that separates the computer from the power source of the wall outlet. When a voltage surge occurs, it activates a circuit breaker in the surge protector, protecting the computer system.

Another technological catastrophe is when a hard-disk drive suddenly 'crashes' or fails, perhaps because it has been bumped inadvertently. If the user has forgotten to make backup copies of data on the hard disk, data may be lost.

Human errors Human mistakes are inevitable. Data-entry errors are probably the most commonplace. Programmer errors also occur frequently. Some mistakes may result from faulty design, as when a software manufacturer makes a deletion command closely resembling another command. Some errors may be the result of sloppy procedures. One such example occurs when office workers keep important correspondence under file names that no one else in the office knows.

Measures to protect computer security

Security is concerned with protecting information, hardware, and software. They must be protected from unauthorised use as well as from damage from intrusions, sabotage, and natural disasters (see Figure 13.8). Considering the numerous ways in which computer systems and data can be compromised, we can see why security is a growing field. Some of the principal aspects are as follows:

Figure 13.8 Disasters—both natural and artificial—can play havoc with computers

Encrypting messages Whenever information is sent over a network, the possibility of unauthorised access exists. The longer the distance the message has to travel, the higher the security risk. For example, an e-mail message on a LAN meets a limited number of users operating in controlled environments such as offices. An e-mail message travelling across the country on the National Information Highway affords greater opportunities for the message to be intercepted.

Businesses have been **encrypting**, or coding, messages for years. They have become so good at it that some law enforcement agencies are unable to 'wire-tap' messages from suspected criminals. Some federal agencies have suggested that a standard encryption procedure be used so that law enforcement agencies can monitor suspected criminal communications. The US government is encouraging businesses that use the National Information Highway to use a special encryption program. This program is available on a processor chip called the Clipper chip and is also known as the Key Escrow chip.

Restricting access Security experts are constantly devising ways to protect computer systems from access by unauthorised persons. Sometimes security is a matter of putting guards on company computer rooms and checking the identification of everyone admitted. Oftentimes it is a matter of being careful about assigning passwords to people and of changing them when people leave a company. *Passwords*, you'll remember, are secret words or numbers that must be keyed into a computer system to gain access. In some 'dial-back' computer systems, the user telephones the computer, punches in the correct password, and hangs up. The computer then calls back at a certain preauthorised number.

Some security systems use **biometrics**, the science of measuring individual body characteristics. This may consist of using machines that can recognise one's fingerprints, signature, voice, or even photograph.

Anticipating disasters Companies (and even individuals) that do not make preparations for disasters are not acting wisely. **Physical security** is concerned with protecting hardware from possible human and natural disasters. **Data security** is concerned with protecting software and data from unauthorised tampering or damage. Most large organisations have a **disaster recovery plan** describing ways to continue operating until normal computer operations can be restored.

Hardware can be kept behind locked doors, but often employees find this restriction a hindrance, so security is lax. Fire and water (including the water from ceiling sprinkler systems) can do great damage to equipment. Many companies therefore will form a co-operative arrangement to share equipment with other companies in the event of catastrophe. Special emergency facilities may be created called **hot sites** if they are fully equipped computer centres. They are called **cold sites** if they are empty shells in which hardware must be installed.

Backing up data Equipment can always be replaced. A company's *data*, however, may be irreplaceable. Most companies have ways of trying to keep software and data from being tampered with in the first place. They include careful screening of job applicants, guarding passwords, and auditing data and programs from time to time. The safest procedure, however, is to make frequent backups of data and to store them in remote locations.

Security for microcomputers

If you own a microcomputer system, there are several procedures to follow to keep it safe:

Avoid extreme conditions Don't expose the computer to extreme conditions. Direct sun, rain from an open window, extreme temperatures, cigarette smoke, and spilled drinks or food are harmful to microcomputers. Clean your equipment regularly. Use a surge protector to protect against voltage surges.

Guard the computer Put a cable lock on the computer. If you subscribe or belong to an online information service, do not leave passwords nearby in a place accessible by others. Etch your driver's licence number or tax file number into your equipment. That way it can be identified in the event it is recovered after theft.

Guard programs and data Store disks properly, preferably in a locked container. Make backup copies of all your important files and programs. Store copies of your files in a different—and safe—location from the site of your computer.

See Figure 13.9 for a summary of the different measures to protect computer security.

THE ENVIRONMENT

Computer industry responds to the Energy Star program with the Green PC. You can help by conserving, recycling, and educating.

What do you suppose is the greatest user of electricity in the workplace? Microcomputers are. They account for 5 per cent of the electricity used. If current trends continue, this will increase to 10 per cent by the year 2000. Increased power production translates to increased air pollution, depletion of non-renewable resources, and other environmental hazards.

The US Environmental Protection Agency (EPA) has created the **Energy Star** program to discourage waste in the microcomputer

COMPUTER SECURITY

Measure	Description
Encrypting	Coding all messages sent over a network
Restricting	Limiting access to authorised persons using such measures as passwords, dialback systems and biometrics
Anticipating	Preparing for disasters by ensuring physical security and data security through a disaster recovery plan
Backing up	Routinely copying data and storing at a remote location
Securing	Protecting microcomputer by avoiding extreme conditions, guarding the computer programs, and data

Figure 13.9 Measures to protect computer security

257

industry. Along with over 50 manufacturers, the EPA has established a goal of reducing power requirements for system units, monitors, and printers. The industry has responded with the concept of the **Green PC** (see Figure 13.10).

The Green PC

The basic elements of the Green PC are the following:

System unit Using existing technology from portable computers, the system unit: (1) uses an energy-saving microprocessor that requires less power, (2) employs microprocessor and hard-disk drives that shift to an energy-saving or sleep mode when not in operation, (3) replaces the conventional supply unit with an adapter that requires less electricity, and (4) eliminates the cooling fan.

Display Displays have been made more energy efficient by using: (1) flat panels that require much less energy than the traditional monitors, (2) special power-down monitors that automatically reduce their power consumption when not in use, and (3) screen-saver software that clears the display whenever it is not in use.

Manufacturing Computer manufacturers such as Intel, Apple, Compac, and others are using less harmful chemicals in production. Particular attention is given to **chlorofluorocarbons (CFCs)** in solvents and cleaning agents. (CFCs can travel into the atmosphere and are suspected by some in the scientific community to deplete the earth's ozone layer.) Toxic nickel and other heavy metals are being eliminated or reduced in the manufacturing processes.

Of course, not all of these technologies and manufacturing processes are used for all microcomputers. But, more and more of them are.

Personal responsibility

There are some things that you, as a computer user, can do to help protect the environment. Some of these include the following:

Conserve The EPA estimates that 30 to 40 percent of computer users leave their machines running days, nights, and weekends. After working for the day, turn off all computers and other energy-consuming devices. The EPA also estimates that 80 percent of the time a monitor is on, no one is looking at it. Use screen-saver programs that blank the computer screen after 3 to 5 minutes of inactivity.

low-power microprocessor

sleep modes for microprocessor and hard disk drive

flat panel display

power-down monitor

screen-saver software

low-power supply unit

no cooling fan

Figure 13.10 The Green PC

Recycle Businesses use an enormous amount of paper each year—a pile 78 240 kilometres high. Much of that, as well as the paper we throw out at home, can be recycled. Other recyclable items include computer boxes, packaging material, printer cartridges, and floppy disks.

Educate Be aware and learn more about ecological dangers of all types. Make your concerns known to manufacturers and retail agencies. Support ecologically sound products.

A LOOK AT THE FUTURE

New legislation will be needed to define access to government files and to regulate government interference in free speech in the new electronic world.

Technology often has a way of outracing existing social and political institutions. For instance, citizens have a right to request government records under the *Freedom of Information Act* 1982. But even in its most recent amendment, in 1986, the act does not mention 'computer' or define the word 'record'. Can the government therefore legally deny, as one agency did, a legitimate request for data on corporate compliance with occupational safety and health laws? *Access laws* lag behind even as the government collects more information than ever.

In addition, there has been a rise in computer-related crimes. These include bank and credit-card fraud, viruses, and electronic break-ins of government and private computer systems. Law-enforcement agencies continue to crack down on these computer operators. Yet they may also be jeopardising the rights of computer users who are not breaking the law. Such users may be suffering illegal searches and violation of constitutional guarantees of free speech.

REVIEW QUESTIONS

True/false

1. Most people who use computers are mid-level managers.

2. Electromagnetic field EMF emissions can travel through a person's body.

3. Our legal system is the essential element used to control computers today.

4. Over 20 percent of businesses search through employees' electronic messages and computer files.

5. A Trojan horse is a virus that keeps replicating itself until the computer system's operations are slowed or stopped.

Multiple choice

1. The study of human factors related to computers is called:
   (a) data analysis
   (b) human system performance
   (c) ergonomics
   (d) expert analysis
   (e) personal design

2. A repetitive strain injury that causes damage to nerves and tendons in hands is called:
   (a) RSI
   (b) carpal tunnel syndrome
   (c) EMF
   (d) hacker
   (e) virus

3. The ethical issue that deals with the responsibility to control the availability of data is:
   (a) privacy
   (b) accuracy
   (c) property
   (d) ownership
   (e) access

4. The largest category of computer criminals is:
   (a) students
   (b) hackers
   (c) outside users
   (d) employees
   (e) database managers

5. The computer industry's response to the Energy Star program is the:
   (a) Green PC
   (b) multimedia PC
   (c) flat-panel display
   (d) Privacy Act
   (e) network encryption standard

Fill in the blank

1. The new word _____ is used to describe harmful stress associated with computer use.

2. Computer _____ are guidelines for the morally acceptable use of computers in our society.

3. A common security measure for business is _____ or coding messages.

4. People who gain unauthorised access to a computer system for fun and challenge are called _____.

5. _____ _____ is the unauthorised copying of programs for personal gain.

Open ended

1. What kind of activities can you perform to avoid computer-related eyestrain, headaches, and back and neck pain?

2. Describe some mental health problems associated with frequent computer use.

3. What are four types of computer criminals?

4. What are computer ethics? What are the four major issues?

5. How are computers a threat to the environment? Discuss three things you can do to protect the environment.

DISCUSSION QUESTIONS AND PROJECTS

1. *Your national identification number* One characteristic of many dictatorships is that all citizens are made to carry 'papers'. These are a kind of internal passport, each with its own number. They enable the government to keep track of—and regulate—one's travel, employment, and so on. In the United States, the founding fathers were deeply concerned about the government's having tyranny over its citizens. Thus, internal papers have never been required in that country, nor in Australia.

   Unfortunately, the US social security number, or SSN, has been stretched to cover purposes for which it was never intended. It has become a national identification number that, once given out, never goes away. It can be a person's student ID, tax number, military ID, medical insurance number, criminal file number, and credit number. Every time the number is scrawled on a credit or job application or other form, it becomes available to thousands of unknown people. It will be available to anyone with access to a legal database.

   Discuss with classmates or write an essay on your worst scenario of what could happen to you because of the easy availability of your social security number.

2. *Computer crime* Whether by damage, theft, or manipulation, computer crime is a serious problem. It affects us all. Perhaps you have been a direct victim of a computer crime without even knowing it. Perhaps you are being victimised right now. Certainly all of us are indirect victims. Computer crime, like many other types of crimes, causes higher prices and increased insurance costs.

   Go to the library and prepare a report on one computer crime. Discuss the following:

   (a) The nature of the crime. Identify whether the form of the crime was damage, theft, manipulation, or something else.

   (b) The crime itself. Describe the criminals, the victims, and the situation.

   (c) The effect of the crime. Report how the criminals were caught (if they were caught).

   (d) The impact of the crime. Consider whether you were a direct or indirect victim and the costs to you.

   (e) Protection against the crime. Suggest how the crime could have been prevented and how you can protect yourself from this type of crime.

CASE STUDY

WONDERFUL WIDGETS

Wonderful Widgets is a small company that designs, manufactures, markets and sells small plastic toys for children. Computers are used in two major areas:

- The design office, where two designers (Peter and Sarah) use PCs and CAD (computer-aided design) software to create and modify designs for the toys.

- The reception area, where two office workers (Penny and Julie) use PCs and word processing software to produce all correspondence. Julie also uses an accounting package, which maintains all the financial records of the business.

This business began trading one year ago and all computer hardware was purchased at that time. The four staff who use computers each have their own IBM-compatible systems. There is a high speed impact printer located next to Sarah's workstation. Although the software used has been upgraded each time new versions are released, the hardware is essentially in its original configuration. The company has been using an e-mail system that enables interdepartmental communication as well as allowing staff to access the computer system from home.

The owner of Wonderful Widgets has been approached by the personnel officer about the working conditions at the company. Several staff members have at various times complained about the circumstances under which they work. A list of the concerns of staff is detailed in the report below. The report was expanded to include privacy and security issues.

Wonderful Widgets

TO: Manager

FROM: Personnel officer

Confidential report on workplace issues

1. The four staff who frequently use computers, have been complaining about the poor ergonomic standards in their work place, in particular the non-ergonomic chairs.

2. The software used in the business originally ran quickly and responded promptly to all user requests. However, since the software in use has been upgraded, both the designers and the office workers are finding that their applications now run too slowly. Even though the current software is capable of more advanced functions than the original versions, their speed of operation is causing quite a degree of frustration.

3. Since Julie uses her computer for both word processing tasks and accounting, she often spends a large part of her working day at her computer. Recently, Julie has been taking a number of days off through illness. She has been complaining of sore eyes and pains in her back.

4. Julie's doctor has indicated that she may be risking RSI if her work environment is not modified.

(continued)

5. Sarah is experiencing hearing problems.

6. Several of the staff are concerned that they have been approached by a life insurance agent who appears to have personal details of all the staff at Wonderful Widgets.

7. Peter is concerned that his designs are appearing elsewhere and thinks that somehow his work is being copied.

QUESTIONS

1. (a) Explain the term ergonomics.

   (b) Why would the manager of Wonderful Widgets be wise to address the problems associated with poor ergonomics?

2. Suggest a possible cause for each of Julie's ailments together with alterations to her working environment to alleviate these problems.

3. Suggest two possible remedies for the problems associated with the software.

4. (a) What do the letters RSI stand for?

   (b) What causes RSI?

   (c) List four different strategies that can be employed to reduce the risk of RSI for Julie.

5. (a) Suggest two possible reasons for Sarah's hearing problems.

   (b) Suggest one way that Sarah's problems may be alleviated.

6. The company maintains a database of all their staff, which includes personal details as well as information on the number of sick days taken, past illnesses and departmental assessments for promotion possibilities.

   (a) Suggest two possible ways that the information contained in the database might have reached the insurance agent.

   (b) What two negative outcomes are possible because of the database information being available to outsiders?

7. What safeguards should Wonderful Widgets take to guard against the problems associated with the use of electronic networks?

8. What are three possible ways that Peter's designs may be getting stolen?

9. (a) Are the company's computers at threat from a virus attack?

   (b) How could their computers become infected?

10. The company is considering introducing a number of security measures.

    (a) Who should have restricted access to the designers' files?

    (b) What is the safest way to protect the company's data from accidental loss or damage?

Your future: using information technology

COMPETENCIES

After you have read this chapter, you should be able to:

- explain why it's important to have an individual strategy in order to be a 'winner' in the information age;

- describe how technology is changing the nature of competition;

- discuss three ways people may react to new technology;

- describe how you can use your computer competence to stay current and to take charge of your career.

FROM THE USER'S POINT OF VIEW

Throughout this book, we have emphasised practical subjects that are useful to you now or will be very soon. Accordingly, this final chapter is not about the far future of, say, 10 years from now. Rather, it is about the near future—about developments whose outlines we can already see. It is about how organisations adapt to technological change. It is also about what you as an individual can do to keep your computer competency up to date.

Are the times changing any faster now than they ever have? It's hard to say. People who were alive when radios, cars, and aeroplanes were being introduced certainly lived through some dramatic changes. Has technology made our own times even more dynamic? Whatever the answer, it is clear we live in a fast-paced age. The challenge for you as an individual is to devise ways to stay current.

CHANGING TIMES

To be a winner in the information revolution, you need an *individual* strategy.

Most businesses have become aware that they must adapt to changing technology or be left behind. Many organisations are now making formal plans to keep track of technology and implement it in their competitive strategies. For example, banks have found that automated teller machines (ATMs) are vital to retail banking (see Figure 14.1). Not only do they require fewer human tellers, but they can also be made available 24 hours a day. More and more banks are also trying to go electronic, doing away with paper transactions wherever possible. Thus, ATM cards can now be used in certain places to buy petrol or groceries. Many banks are also trying to popularise home banking, so that customers can use microcomputers for certain financial tasks. In

Figure 14.1 Automatic teller machines are examples of technology used in business strategy

addition, banks are exploring the use of some very sophisticated application programs. These programs will accept and analyse cursive writing (the handwriting on cheques) directly as input.

Clearly, such changes do away with some jobs—those of many bank tellers and cashiers, for example. However, they create opportunities for other people. New technology requires people who are truly capable of working with it. These are not the people who think every piece of equipment is so simple they can just turn it on and use it. Nor are they those who think each new machine is a potential disaster. In other words, new technology needs people who are not afraid to learn it and are able to manage it. The real issue, then, is not·how to make technology better. Rather, it is how to integrate the technology with people.

You are in a very favourable position compared with many other people in industry today. After reading the previous thirteen chapters, you have learned more than just the basics of hardware, software, and connectivity. You have learned the most *current* technology. You are therefore able to use these tools to your advantage—to be a winner.

How do you become and stay a winner? In brief, the answer is: you must form your own individual strategy for dealing with change. First let us look at how businesses are handling technological change. Then let's look at how people are reacting to these changes. Finally, we will offer a few suggestions that will enable you to keep up with—and profit by—the information revolution.

TECHNOLOGY AND ORGANISATIONS

Technology changes the nature of competition by introducing new products, new enterprises, and new relationships among customers and suppliers.

Technology can introduce new ways businesses compete with each other. Some of the principal changes are as follows.

Figure 14.2 The Sabre reservations system used by American Airlines

New products

Technology creates products that operate faster, are priced cheaper, are often of better quality, or are wholly new. Indeed, new products can be custom tailored to a particular customer's needs. For example, in the United States financial services company Merrill Lynch took advantage of technology to launch a cash management account. This account combines information on a person's cheque, savings, credit card, and securities accounts into a single monthly statement. It automatically sets aside 'idle' funds into interest-bearing money market funds. The result is that customers can get a complete picture of their financial condition at one time. However, even if they don't pay much attention to their statements, their surplus funds are invested automatically.

New enterprises

Information technology can build entire new businesses. An example is the availability of facsimile (fax) machine business. Now chains of quick-print and photocopying shops offer fax services. You can send a fax message to, or receive one from, nearly anywhere in a number of countries.

A company may use its extra information systems capability to develop new services for customers outside the area it serves directly. For example, American Airlines has a reservations system called Sabre that lists the flight schedules of every major airline in the world. Travel agents with online access to Sabre pay American a fee for every reservation made on Sabre for other airlines (see Figure 14.2).

New customer and supplier relationships

Businesses that make their information systems easily available may make their customers less likely to take their business elsewhere. For instance, Federal Express, a US overnight package delivery service, does everything possible to make its customers dependent on it. Upon request, customers receive airbills with their name, address, and account number preprinted on them, making shipping and billing easier. Package numbers are scanned into the company's information system, so that they can be tracked from pickup point to destination (see Figure 14.3). Thus, apprehensive customers can be informed very quickly of the exact location of their package as it travels toward its destination.

Figure 14.3 Federal Express couriers scan bar codes on every package, transferring customer and delivery data to a worldwide network that can be closely monitored by customer service agents

Figure 14.4 The cynic: 'These gadgets are overrated'

TECHNOLOGY AND PEOPLE

People may be cynical, naïve, or frustrated by technology.

Clearly, recent technological changes, and those sure to come in the near future, will produce some upheavals in the years ahead. How should we be prepared for them?

People have different coping styles when it comes to technology. It has been suggested, for instance, that people react to the notion of microcomputers in business in three ways. These ways are *cynicism*, *naïveté*, and *frustration*.

Cynicism

The cynic feels that, for a manager at least, the idea of using a microcomputer is overrated (see Figure 14.4). Learning and using it take too much time, time that could be delegated to someone else. Doing spreadsheets and word processing, according to the cynic, are tasks that managers should understand. However, their real job is to develop plans and set goals for the people being supervised.

Cynics may express their doubts openly, especially if they are top managers. Or they may only pretend to be interested in microcomputers, when actually they are not interested at all.

Naïveté

Naïve people may be unfamiliar with computers. Thus, they may think computers are magic boxes capable of solving all kinds of problems that they really can't handle (see Figure 14.5). In contrast, some naïve persons are actually quite familiar with computers. However, such people underestimate the difficulty of changing computer systems or of generating information.

Figure 14.5 The naïve: 'Let the computer make the decision'

Figure 14.6 The frustrated: 'This stuff doesn't make sense half the time'

Frustration

The frustrated person may already be quite busy and may hate having to take time to learn about microcomputers. Such a person feels imposed on at having to learn to keep up. Often he or she is too impatient to try to understand the manuals explaining what hardware and software are supposed to do. The result, therefore, is continual frustration (see Figure 14.6). Some people are frustrated because they try to do too much. Or they're frustrated because they find manuals difficult to understand. Oftentimes, they feel stupid, when actually the manuals are at fault.

Cynicism, naïveté, and frustration are not just confined to microcomputers, of course. They apply to all new technology. Do you see yourself reacting in any of these ways? They are actually commonplace responses—part of just being human. Knowing which, if any, of these reactions characterise you or those around you may be helpful. It can help you survive and react in positive ways in organisational life.

HOW YOU CAN BE A WINNER

Individuals need to stay current, develop specialties, and be alert to organisational changes and opportunities for innovation.

So far we have described how progressive organisations are using technology in the information age. Now let's concentrate on you as an individual. How can you stay ahead? Here are some ideas.

Stay current

Whatever their particular line of work, successful professionals keep up both with their own fields and with the times. We don't mean you should try to become a computer expert and read a lot of technical magazines. Rather, you should concentrate on your intended profession and learn how computer technology is being used within it.

Every field has trade journals, whether the field is interior design, personnel management, advertising, or whatever. Most such journals regularly present articles about the uses of computers. Once you have entered the workforce, it's important that you also belong to a trade or industry association and go to its meetings. Many associations sponsor seminars and conferences that describe the latest information and techniques. Another way to stay current is by participating electronically with interest groups on the Internet.

Maintain your computer competence

Actually, you should try to stay *ahead* of the technology. Books, journals, and trade associations are the best source of information about new technology that applies to your intended field (see Figure 14.7). The general business press—*Business Week, Fortune, Inc., The Wall Street Journal, The Financial Review* and the business section of your local newspaper—also carries computer-related articles.

However, if you wish, you can subscribe to a magazine that covers microcomputers and information more specifically. Examples are *Australian Personal Computer, PC World*, and *MacWorld*. You may also find it useful to look at newspapers and magazines that cover the computer industry as a whole. An example of such a periodical is *PC Weekly*.

Figure 14.7 Some books covering computers

Develop professional contacts

Besides being members of professional associations, successful people make it a point to maintain contact with others in their field. They stay in touch by telephone and letter and go to lunch with others in their line of work. Doing this lets them learn what other people are doing in their jobs. It tells them what other firms are doing and what tasks are being automated. Developing professional contacts can keep you abreast not only of new information but also of new job possibilities (see Figure 14.8). It also offers social benefits. An example of a professional organisation found in many areas is the local association of estate agents.

Develop specialties

Develop specific as well as general skills. You will want to be well-rounded within your field, but certainly not a 'jack of all trades, master of none'. After you have entered your profession, master a trade or two *within* the profession. At the same time, don't become identified with a specific technological skill that might very well become obsolete.

The best advice is to specialise to some extent. However, don't make your specialty so tied to technology that you'll be in trouble if the technology shifts. For example, if your career is in marketing or graphics design, it makes sense to learn about desktop publishing (see Figure 14.9). That way you can learn to make high-quality, inexpensive graphics layouts. It would not make as much sense for you to become an expert on, say, the various types of monitors used to display the graphics layouts, because such monitors are continually changing.

Figure 14.8 Professional organisations and contacts help you keep up in your field

269

Figure 14.9 Desktop publishing: a good specialty to develop for certain careers

Expect to take classes during your working life to keep up with developments in your field. Some professions require more keeping up than others—a computer specialist, for example, compared with a human resources manager. Whatever the training required, always look for ways to adapt and improve your skills to become more productive and marketable. There may be times when you are tempted to start all over again and learn completely new skills. However, a better course of action is to use emerging technology to improve your present base of skills. This way you can build on your current strong points and then branch out to other fields from a position of strength.

Be alert for organisational change

Every organisation has formal lines of communication, for example supervisor to middle manager to top manager. However, there is also the grapevine—informal lines of communication (see Figure 14.10). Some service departments will serve many layers of management and be abreast of the news on all levels. For instance, the art director for advertising may be aware of several aspects of a company-wide marketing campaign. Secretaries and administrative assistants know what is going on in more than one area.

Being part of the office grapevine can alert you to important changes—for instance, new job openings—that can benefit you. However, you always have to assess the validity of what you hear on the grapevine. Moreover, it's not advisable to be a contributor to 'office

Figure 14.10 Informal communication can alert you to important organisational changes

gossip'. Behind-the-back criticisms of other people have a way of getting back to the person criticised.

Be especially alert for new trends within the organisation—about future hiring, layoffs, automation, mergers with other companies, and the like. Be alert for areas receiving the greatest attention from top management. One tip-off is to see what kind of outside consultants are being brought in. Independent consultants are usually invited in because a company believes it needs advice in an area with which it has insufficient experience.

Look for innovative opportunities

You may understand your job better than anyone—even if you've only been there a few months. Look for ways to make it more efficient. How can present procedures be automated? How can new technology make your tasks easier? Discuss your ideas with your supervisor, the training director, or the head of the information systems department. Or discuss them with someone else who can see that you get the recognition you deserve. (Co-workers may or may not be receptive and may or may not try to take credit themselves.)

A good approach is to present your ideas in terms of *saving money* rather than 'improving information' (see Figure 14.11). Managers are generally more impressed with ideas that can save dollars than with ideas that seem like potential breakthroughs in the quality of decisions.

In general, it's best to concentrate on the business and organisational problems that need solving. Then look for a technological way of solving them. That is, avoid becoming too enthusiastic about a particular technology and then trying to make it fit the work situation.

A LOOK AT THE FUTURE: THE REST OF YOUR LIFE

Being computer competent means taking positive control.

This is not the end; it is the beginning. Being a skilled computer end user—being computer competent—is not a matter of thinking 'Some day I'll ...' ('Some day I'll have to learn all about that.') It is a matter of living in the present and keeping an eye on the future. It is also a matter of having the discipline to keep up with the prevailing

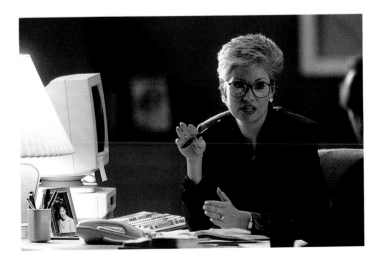

Figure 14.11 Present your ideas as saving money rather than 'improving information'

technology. It is not a matter of focusing on vague 'what-ifs'. It is a matter of concentrating on your goals and learning how the computer can help you achieve them. Being an end user, in short, is not about trying to avoid failure. Rather, it is about always moving toward success—about taking control over the exciting new tools available to you.

REVIEW QUESTIONS

True/false

1. Most businesses are making formal plans to track and to implement technology into their competitive strategies.

2. Businesses never allow customers access to their information systems.

3. In all fields, successful professionals have to be experts in their own field as well as in computer technology.

4. *Australian Personal Computer*, *PC World*, and *MacWorld* are magazines that specifically cover microcomputers and information.

5. The office grapevine can be a good source to alert you to organisational changes.

Multiple choice

1. The real issue with new technology is:
   (a) how to make it better
   (b) which printer is better
   (c) how to control it
   (d) how to integrate it with people
   (e) managing its impact on government

2. By giving their customers access to their package tracking information system, Federal Express is developing new:
   (a) global computer facilities
   (b) customer and supplier relationships
   (c) airline reservation procedures
   (d) serious security problems
   (e) governmental delivery systems

3. The type of person who underestimates the difficulty of changing computer systems or of generating information is:
   (a) a cynic
   (b) frustrated
   (c) naïve
   (d) a loser
   (e) a winner

4. By staying in touch with others in your field, you are:
   (a) developing professional contacts
   (b) staying current
   (c) developing specialties
   (d) maintaining computer competence
   (e) being alert to organisational changes

5. A good approach to presenting your innovative ideas is to present them:
   (a) in terms of improving decision making
   (b) to co-workers
   (c) in terms of improving information
   (d) to the union chief
   (e) in terms of saving money

Fill in the blank

1. ATM cards, home banking, and programs to analyse cursive writing are examples of how some banks are looking to use technology in their competitive _____ .

2. The person who thinks that microcomputers are overrated can be classified as a _____ .

3. Reading trade journals about the use of technology is a good way to stay_____ .

4. _____ is another name for the informal lines of communication within an organisation.

5. Being computer competent means taking _____ control.

Open ended

1. How do you become and stay a winner in the information age?

2. Give an example of how technology can change the nature of competition.

3. What are the three responses or attitudes that people are apt to have when confronted by new technology?

4. Name six strategies individuals should follow in order to be successful in the information age.

5. What periodicals might you read in order to keep current on changes in microcomputer technology?

DISCUSSION QUESTIONS AND PROJECTS

1. *Being careful about technology predictions* Technology forecasts have a way of often being so wide of the mark that in looking back we may wonder how the experts could have erred so badly. For instance, nuclear-powered aeroplanes, household robots, and widespread use of electric cars have never realised the rosy promises of the forecasters.

   Editor Herb Brody in *Technology Review* suggests some guidelines for reducing erroneous predictions. Among them are the following. (1) Be wary of forecasts based on information from vested interests, such as technology developers needing financing, who may in turn exert undue influence on market-forecasting firms, the news media, and investors. (2) Expect existing technologies to keep on improving and don't expect people to abandon what they have for something only somewhat better. (3) Expect truly revolutionary technologies to take 10 to 25 years to enter widespread use.

Given these guidelines, describe what kind of future uses and popularity you would expect for the following: neural-network computers; pen-based computers; shirt-pocket telephones; hyper-media; computer-generated virtual realities; flat-panel display TVs to hang on living-room walls.

2. *Looking to your future* What do you want to do with your career? Perhaps you already know, or perhaps you are still deciding. Are you interested in interior design, personnel management, advertising, computers, or some other field? For almost every area, there exist trade journals that print articles about the industry.

Go to the library and locate a trade journal in your area of interest. Browse through a recent issue, noting computer-related articles as well as other articles of interest. Prepare a short report. Discuss these topics:

(a) Your area of interest. Describe the area and why you are interested in this area.

(b) The computer-related and other interesting articles. Identify the topics and issues addressed in each article.

(c) Your future. Consider what your future plans will be, what courses you will take, how you will gain experience in the area, and how you will keep up-to-date on technical changes.

CASE STUDY

RARE BOOK SERVICES

Rare Book Services has three retail outlets that sell rare books to the public. The three stores were all taken over by Karen Batman. As part of the takeover agreement each outlet is managed by the previous owner. Managers have responsibility for the day-to-day running of their stores, including the purchase and sale of all books. Karen has installed computers at each store and has set up an 'Access' database that uses a point-of-sale bar-coding system. Purchases and sales of books are recorded in individual databases at each store. Each night the database at each store is backed up to a central database.

Customers can access the central database to find out the availability of rare books at the three stores. Prior to the takeover, customers wishing to find a particular book at another store had to rely on the knowledge of the owner of the store. All stock movements were recorded on cards that were kept locked in the office at each store.

QUESTIONS

1. Karen is concerned that individual managers are coping with the introduction of computers in different ways. Describe the three coping styles that the managers may have adopted.

2. Prior to the takeover all stores used a manual system to record all book purchases and sales. Describe the changes that have occurred for each of the following:

   (a) The retrieval of information on rare books at the other stores. Has the new retrieval system any flaws? If so, describe them.

   (b) The input of sales information into the system.

   (c) The back-up procedures.

3. One of the managers has suggested that the new computerised system has not added anything of value to the business. In response, Karen has decided to do a cost-benefit analysis and to collect survey information.

   (a) What do you think a cost-benefit analysis would look at? Why would this be useful?

   (b) Who should Karen survey? What sort of information is she seeking?

4. Karen is interested in new ways that she could expand her business using new technologies. Suggest at least one way that Rare Book Services could expand.

The Internet Guide: how to surf the net

Want to communicate with a friend across town, in another state, or even in another country? Perhaps you would like to send a drawing, a photo, or just a letter. Looking for travel or entertainment information? Perhaps you're researching a term paper or exploring different career paths. Where do you start? For these and other information-related activities, try the Internet. It is the 20th-century information resource designed for all of us to use.

The Internet is like a giant highway that connects you to millions of other people and organisations. Unlike typical highways that move people and things from one location to another, the Internet moves your *ideas* and *information*. Rather than moving through geographic space, you move through **cyberspace**—the space of electronic movement of ideas and information. In this guide, we describe the Internet, how you can get onto it, and how you can use it.

THE INTERNET

The Internet is a giant computer network. Four applications: electronic mail, discussion groups, run programs, and transfer files. Two utilities: Gopher and World Wide Web.

The Internet is a giant worldwide network. It connects computer systems located throughout the world that are willing to share their resources. The Internet has created a co-operative society that forms a virtual community stretching from one end of the globe to the other (see Figure 1).

The Internet's origin can be traced back to 1969, when the United States government funded a major research project on computer networking. A national computer network called **ARPANET (Advanced Research Project Agency Network)** was developed. It was used by government and military agencies to communicate and share computer resources with researchers working on national security projects.

276

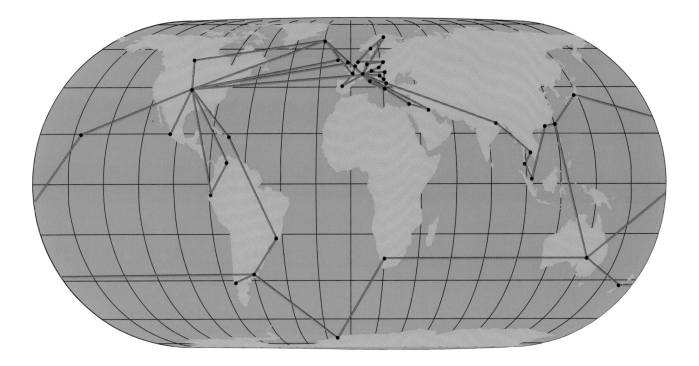

Figure 1 Internet connections around the world

From these military and research beginnings, the Internet has evolved as a tool for all of us to use in our daily lives. In 1995 over 4 million computers in 156 countries were connected to the Internet with over 30 million users. By the year 2000, 100 million computers in every country in the world are expected to be connected to over a billion users (see Figure 2).

To access the Internet, you connect to one of the computer systems already on it. After you connect to one system, you can easily connect to another. You move electronically from one computer system to another, from one site to another, and often from one country to another—all within seconds. What makes the Internet so remarkable is the incredible speed and efficiency with which these connections are

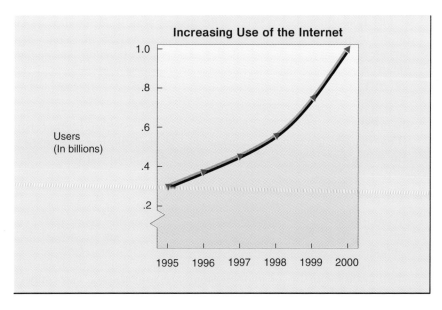

Figure 2 Internet use—past, present and future

made. Once you are on the Internet it seems like you are on a single giant computer that branches all over the world.

Internet applications

What can you do on the Internet? There are any number of uses for the Internet. The four most common are sending and receiving electronic mail (e-mail), participating in public discussions, running programs on a remote computer, and transferring files.

Electronic mail Sending and receiving e-mail is the most popular Internet service. If you know their addresses and have access to the Internet, you can send to and receive e-mail from your friends and family located almost anywhere in the world.

Discussion groups You can join and listen to discussions and debates on a wide variety of special-interest topics. There are thousands of special-interest groups, ranging from physical fitness to job hunting.

Run programs You can even run selected programs from other computers. These programs range from games like DOOM to educational programs from NASA.

Transfer files You can copy or transfer files from one computer to another. There are thousands of free programs and games available on the Internet.

Internet utilities

How do you surf the Net? The Internet provides access to a tremendous amount of information. How to find the information that you really need, however, can be challenging. Fortunately, there are several Internet utilities or programs designed to help you to navigate, or surf, the Internet. The two most widely used are gopher and World Wide Web (WWW).

Gopher Many computers on the Internet run gopher programs to provide a menu or list of their available resources. For example, many college and university libraries provide access to their card catalogues.

WWW Like gophers, WWW helps users search for and retrieve information from a specific computer system. WWW goes one step further by using a more graphical interface and providing information about resources available from other computer systems on the Internet. Additionally, direct links to those computers are provided.

Where should you begin to learn more about how to use and to surf the Internet? First, you should gain access to or get onto the Internet. Then, explore the applications and use the available Internet utilities. The following sections of this guide will help you do just that.

ACCESS

Providers give access to the Internet. Internet connections are either direct, SLIP and PPP, or dial-up. Protocols are rules for exchanging information between computers.

The Internet and the telephone system are similar—you can connect to the Internet much like you connect a phone to the telephone system.

Once you are on the Internet, your computer becomes an extension of what seems like a giant computer—a computer that branches all over the world.

Providers

The most common way to access the Internet is through a **provider** or **host computer**. The providers are already connected to the Internet and provide a path or connection for individuals to access the Internet. There are two widely used providers.

College and universities One source is through colleges and universities. Many provide free access to the Internet through their local area networks. You may be able to access the Internet through your school or through other local colleges and universities. Check with the computer services department at your school as well as other nearby schools.

Service providers A widely used source for access is through online commercial service providers, discussed in Chapter 8. They provide access to the Internet and numerous other electronic services for a fee. The best-known service providers are America Online, CompuServe, Prodigy, Microsoft Network, and AT&T Interchange (see Figure 3).

Connections

To gain access to the Internet, you must have a connection. This connection can be made either directly to the Internet or indirectly through a provider. There are three types of connections:

Direct or dedicated To have access to all the functions on the Internet, you need a direct or dedicated link. This requires a special high-speed communication line that is either owned or leased. Individuals rarely have direct connections because they are quite expensive. However, many organisations such as colleges, universities, service providers, and corporations do have direct links.

Figure 3 Microsoft Network

The primary advantages of a direct link are complete access to Internet functions, ease of connection for individual users, and fast response and retrieval of information. The primary disadvantage is cost.

SLIP and PPP Using a high-speed modem and standard telephone lines, you can connect to a provider that has a direct connection to the Internet. This type of connection requires special software such as **SLIP (serial line internet protocol)** or **PPP (point to point protocol)**. Using this type of connection, you computer becomes part of a client/server network. The provider or host computer is the server providing access to the Internet. Your computer is the client. Using special client software, your computer is able to communicate with server software running on the provider's computer and on other Internet computers.

This type of connection is widely used by end users to connect to the Internet. It provides a high level of service at a lower cost than a direct or dedicated connection. Of course, it is somewhat slower and may not be as convenient.

Dial-up Another way to access the Internet using a high-speed modem and standard telephone lines is called a **dial-up** or **terminal connection**. Using this type of connection, your computer becomes a part of a terminal network. Unlike a SLIP or PPP connection, your computer's operations are very limited. It operates as a terminal that simply displays the communication that occurs between the provider and the other computers on the Internet. Compared with a SLIP or PPP connection, dial-up is less expensive but not as fast or as convenient.

For a summary of the costs and typical users of the three types of connections, see Figure 4.

TCP/IP

When information is sent over the Internet, it usually travels through numerous interconnected networks. Before a message is sent, it is broken down into small parts called **packets**. Each packet is then sent separately over the Internet, possibly travelling different routes to one common destination. At the receiving end, the packets are reassembled into the correct order. Protocols control how the messages are broken down, sent, and reassembled. They govern how and when computers talk to one another. The standard protocol for the Internet is called **TCP/IP (transmission control protocol/internet protocol)**.

USERS AND CONNECTION COSTS

Connection	User	Costs
Direct/dedicated	Medium to large company	$4000 to $15 000 per year
SUP/PPP	Individual or small company	$250 to $750 per year plus hourly charges
Dial-up	Individual	$0 to $250 per year

Figure 4 Typical user and connection costs

E-MAIL

An e-mail message has three basic elements. Internet addresses use the domain name system. E-mail etiquette is called netiquette.

E-mail is a way of sending an electronic letter or message between individuals or computers. It is like an answering machine in that you can receive messages even when you are not at home. Unlike an answering machine, e-mail can contain text, graphics, and images as well as sound. E-mail can also be used to communicate with more than one person at a time, to conveniently schedule meetings, to keep current on important events, and much more.

Sending and receiving e-mail is by far the most common Internet activity. You can communicate with anyone in the world who has an Internet address or e-mail account with a system connected to the Internet. E-mail programs such as Pine, Elm, and Eudora automate the process of creating, sending, reading, and receiving messages.

Suppose that you have a friend, Chris James, who is going to an out-of-state school. You and Chris have been calling back and forth at least once a week for the past month. Unfortunately, your telephone bill has skyrocketed. Fortunately, you both have Internet e-mail accounts through your schools. To save money, you and Chris agree to communicate via the Internet instead of the telephone. After exchanging e-mail addresses, you are ready to send your first Internet e-mail message to Chris.

Basic elements

A typical e-mail message has three basic elements: header, message, and signature (see Figure 5). The header appears first and typically includes the following information:

To line   The e-mail address for the person that is to receive the letter.

Figure 5 Basic elements of an e-mail message

Figure 6 Parts of an Internet address

From line The address of the person sending the e-mail follows the To line.

Subject line A one-line description of the message is used to present the topic of the message. Subject lines typically are displayed when a person checks his or her mailbox.

Attachment line Many e-mail programs allow you to attach files such as documents and worksheets. If a message has an attachment, the file name appears on the attachment line.

The letter or message comes next. It is typically short and to the point. Finally, the signature line provides additional information about the sender. Typically, this information includes the sender's name, address, and telephone number. This information is automatically 'stamped' onto all e-mail sent out.

Addresses

One of the most important elements of an e-mail message is the address of the person who is to receive the letter. The Internet uses an addressing method known as the **domain name system (DNS)** to assign names and numbers to people and computers. This system divides an address into three parts (see Figure 6).

Internet addresses typically are read backwards. The last part of the address is the **domain code**, which identifies the geographical description or organisational identification. For example, *edu* in Figure 6 indicates an address at an educational and research institution (see Figure 7).

ORGANISATIONAL IDENTIFICATIONS

Domain	Identification
com	Commercial organisations
edu	Educational and research institutions
gov	Nov-military government agencies
mil	Military agencies
net	Major network support centres
org	Other organisations

Figure 7 Commonly used Internet organisational identifications

Separated from the domain code by a dot (.) is the **domain name**. It is a reference to the particular organisation. In this case, *cmc* represents Claremont McKenna College. Separated from the domain name by an 'at' (@) symbol, the **user name** identifies a unique person or computer at the listed domain. The address shown in Figure 6 is for Chris James (cjames) at Claremont McKenna College (cmc), which is an education and research institution (edu).

Netiquette

Netiquette refers to the etiquette you should observe when using e-mail. Remember that you are communicating with people, not computers—these people have the same feelings and sensibilities that you do (see Figure 8).

DISCUSSION GROUPS

Mailing lists send e-mail to all members. Newsgroups use the Usenet. Lurk before you contribute.

You can also use e-mail to communicate with people you do not know but with whom you wish to share ideas and interests. You can participate in discussions and debates that range from general topics like current events and films to specialised forums like computer troubleshooting and Star Trek.

Mailing lists

Mailing lists are one type of discussion group available on the Internet. Members of a mailing list communicate by sending messages to a **list address**. Each message is then copied and sent via e-mail to every member of the mailing list.

There are thousands of different mailing lists. To participate in one, you must first subscribe by sending an e-mail request to the mailing list **subscription address** (see Figure 9). Once you are a member of a list, you can expect to receive e-mail from others on the list. You may find the number of messages to be overwhelming. If you want to cancel a mailing list, send an e-mail request to 'unsubscribe' to the subscription address.

NETIQUETTE

1. Don't send abusive, threatening, or bigoted messages. You could be held criminally liable for what you write

2. DO NOT TYPE YOUR MESSAGES IN ALL UPPERCASE CHARACTERS! This is called shouting and is perceived as very harsh. Use a normal combination of upper and lowercase characters. Sometimes all lower-case is perceived as too informal or timid

3. Keep line length to 60 characters or less so your messages can be comfortably displayed on most monitors

4. Before sending a message, carefully check the spelling, punctuation, and grammar. Also think twice about the content of your message. Once it is sent, you can't get it back

Figure 8 E-mail etiquette

MAILING LISTS

Mailing List	Subscription address	Description
Harleys	harleys-request@think.age.on.ca	For people who love motorcycles
Info-Aids	info-aids@rainbow.uucp	A clearinghouse for information and discussion about AIDS
Luckytown	luckytown-request@netcom.com	For fans of Bruce Springsteen
Musicals	musicals-request@world.std.com	For fans of musical theatre
Outdoor-I	outdoor-I@ulkyum	For those who love the outdoors

Figure 9 Five popular mailing lists

Newsgroups

Newsgroups are the most popular type of discussion group. Unlike mailing lists, **newsgroups** use a special network of computers called the **UseNet**. Each of these computers maintains the newsgroup listing. The newsgroups are organised into major topic areas that are further subdivided into hierarchies.

This hierarchy system is similar to the Domain Name System. For example, the newsgroup specialising in motion picture discussions is categorised under the major topic REC (for 'recreational'), then the subtopic ARTS, and then the further subdivision CINEMA (see Figure 10).

Contributions to a particular newsgroup are sent to one of the computers on the UseNet. This computer saves the messages on its system and periodically shares all its recent messages with the other computers on the UseNet. Unlike mailing lists, a copy of each message is not sent to each member of a list. Rather, interested individuals check contributions to a particular newsgroup, reading only those of interest.

There are thousands of newsgroups covering a wide variety of topic areas (see Figure 11).

Lurking

Before you submit a contribution to a discussion group, it is recommended that you observe or read the communications from others. This is called **lurking** (see Figure 12).

By lurking, you can learn about the culture of a discussion group. For example, you can observe the level and style of the discussions. You may decide that a particular discussion group is not what you were looking for—in which case, unsubscribe. If the discussions are appropriate and you wish to participate, try to fit into the prevailing culture. Remember that your contributions will likely be read by hundreds of people.

Figure 10 Newsgroup hierarchy

NEWSGROUPS

Newsgroup	Description
clari.biz.finance	Financial news
misc.fitness	Discussion about physical fitness
misc.jobs.offered	Online job hunting
rec.travel	Discussion for those who love to travel
soc.women	Discussions of women's issues

Figure 11 Five popular newsgroups

TELNET AND FTP

Telnet runs programs on remote computers. FTP transfers files.

Telnet

Many computers on the Internet will allow you to connect to them and to run selected programs on them. **Telnet** is the Internet service that allows you to dial another computer (host) on the Internet and log on to that computer as if you were a terminal in the next room. There are hundreds of computers on the Internet that you can connect to. Some allow limited free access and others charge fees for their use.

The NASA SPACElink computer, located in Huntsville, Alabama, allows free public access. The Internet address for this computer is spacelink.msfc.nasa.gov. This Telnet link was originally designed for science teachers and is now available to the general public through the Internet. With it you can learn about NASA's history, read about exploration plans, view animated clips, and participate in a variety of other space-related activities (see Figure 13).

DISCUSSION GROUP TERMS

Term	Description
Lurking	Reading news but not joining in to contribute
FAQ	Frequently asked question
Flaming	Insulting, a putting-down, or attacking
RFD	Request for discussion
Saint	Someone who aids new users by answering questions
Thread	A sequence of ongoing messages on the same subject
Wizard	Someone who has comprehensive knowledge about a subject

Figure 12 Selected discussion group terms

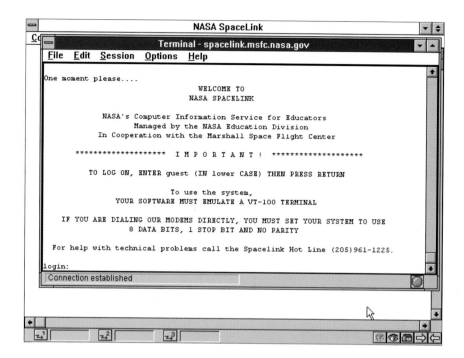

Figure 13 NASA SPACElink

Medline is an example of a fee-based Telnet link. Medline is the National Library of Medicine database. This database is not universally available to the public. It is a commercial database that charges for its services and controls its Telnet access. Medline contains millions of articles from more than 4000 medical journals. It is an excellent medical research tool. Many university and public libraries license Medline, so you may have access to it without incurring special fees.

FTP

FTP (file transfer protocol) is an Internet service for transferring files. Many computers on the Internet allow you to copy files to your computer. This is called **downloading**. Using FTP you can also copy files from your computer to another computer on the Internet. This is called **uploading**.

FTP and Telnet are not the same. Telnet allows you to run programs from remote computers but does not support copying of files. FTP allows copying of files but does not support running of programs from another computer.

Computers on the Internet that allow copying of their files are called **FTP sites**. There are more than 1500 separate FTP sites that allow access to millions of publicly available files. FTP allows access to a large number of databases, from stock market quotations to personal income census data.

With all the information that is available on the Internet, finding a particular file can be difficult. Fortunately, specialised search programs are available to help locate information on the Internet. One of the best known is called **Archie**. It is a program that automatically checks FTP sites at least once every month to see what files are publicly available. Archie notes file names, locations, and descriptions (if available). Computers on the Internet that run Archie are called **Archie servers**.

To locate information on specific topics, you can connect to an Archie server. There are more than 40 Archie servers located throughout the world. Although some of these servers are fee-based, many are free (see Figure 14).

Figure 14 Five public Archie servers

GOPHERS

Gophers provide menus for each gopher site. Veronica provides custom menus for many gopher sites. WAIS looks into documents.

Looking for information on the Internet is called 'surfing the net'. It can be quite enjoyable when you have the time. But it can be pretty frustrating if you need some specific information in a timely manner.

There are millions of public files available on host computers all around the world. How can you find what you're looking for? How can you effectively surf the net? A good way is to use Internet search tools. One widely used tool is called *gopher*.

Menus

Gopher is a software application that provides menu-based search and retrieval functions for a particular computer site. It was originally developed at the University of Minnesota in 1991. Internet **gopher sites** are computers that provide menus describing their available resources and direct links to the resources. Essentially, these menus are a 'table of contents' for organising and locating information. In addition, these sites typically handle transferring of files (FTP) and connecting to other computers (Telnet) (see Figure 15).

Public gophers

There are thousands of gophers on the Internet that provide free access. These free gopher sites are called **public gophers** (see Figure 16).

To search for information, you would likely begin at one of the public gophers, search its available resources, and then move to another gopher site and continue this process. Gophers are used to search for a wide variety of different types of information. They can find e-mail addresses, locate mailing lists and newsgroups, and research specific topics.

Veronica

Veronica is typically one of the options available from a gopher menu. It is a software application that makes searching for information with gophers much more efficient. Veronica periodically checks with a large number of gopher sites and maintains a list of the menus at each site.

Figure 15 Gopher menu

Figure 16 Five public gopher sites

Upon request, Veronica will search this list for a specific word or topic. It will then display a custom-menu listing each gopher menu that contains the word or topic. The user can then select from the Veronica menu to connect directly to the topic area (see Figure 17).

WAIS

Another search tool, **WAIS (wide area information server)** (pronounced 'wayz'), extends the search capabilities of gopher and Veronica. Veronica creates its list of available resources by investigating menu options from various gopher sites. WAIS goes one step further by examining individual documents and maintaining an extensive list of key words and phrases. A WAIS search on a topic is more thorough and provides more specific references. There are

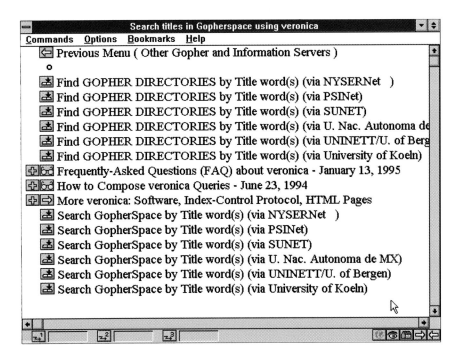

Figure 17 Veronica menu

Location	Internet address	Log in
California	quake.think.com	wais
California	swais.cwis.uci.edu	swais
North Carolina	sunsite.unc.edu	swais
Massachusetts	nnsc.nsf.net	swais
Finland	info.funet.fi	wais

Figure 18 Five WAIS sites

hundreds of WAIS sites available. Each site generally maintains information on a single subject (see Figure 18).

WORLD WIDE WEB

WWW uses hypertext to jump from document to document and from computer to computer. Browsers are software programs to access the WWW.

One of the newest Internet search tools is **World Wide Web**, also known as **WWW, W3**, and the **Web**. It was introduced in 1992 at CERN, the Center for European Nuclear Research in Geneva, Switzerland. Like gopher, WWW provides a search and retrieval system that conveniently handles transferring of files (FTP) and connecting to other computers on the Internet (Telnet). But WWW takes gopher one step further by using hypertext.

Hypertext

A **hypertext** document contains more than information. It also contains references and links to other documents that contain related information. These documents may be located on a nearby computer system or one located halfway around the world. These references are similar to traditional footnotes or bibliographies.

The references appear as highlighted text in the hypertext document. To access the references material, all you do is click on the highlighted text. A link is automatically made to the computer containing the material, and the referenced material appears.

These linked information sources are called **pages**. Any one page may contain many hypertext links to related information—text files, graphic images, movies, audio, or video clips. WWW allows you to jump from one page to another in a non-sequential manner (see Figure 19).

Browsers

The WWW is typically accessed by using special software known as **browsers**. This software connects to remote computers, opens and transfers files, displays text and images, and provides in one tool an uncomplicated interface to the Internet and WWW documents. Three well-known browsers are Lynx, Mosaic, and Netscape (see Figure 20).

See Figure 21 for a summary of Internet search tools.

A LOOK AT THE FUTURE

The Internet is making the world smaller, providing a foundation for the NIH, and creating global villages in cyberspace.

Is the world getting smaller? It is in the sense that we can share ideas and resources with people halfway around the world just as though they were in the next room. Many have compared the Internet to a superhighway of information and ideas for the 20th century.

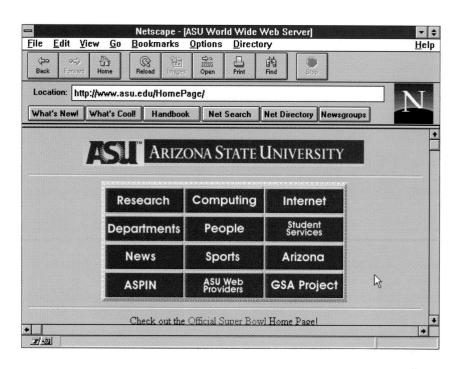

Figure 19 WWW page with hypertext links

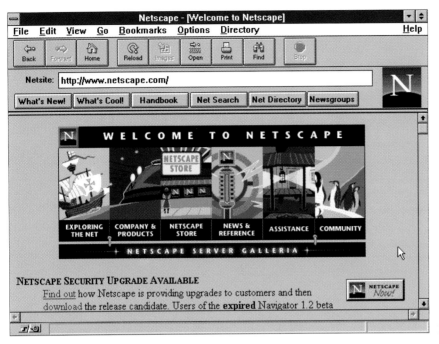

Figure 20 Netscape

INTERNET SEARCH TOOLS

Tool	Description
Gopher	Provides a menu of available information resources from a particular computer
Veronica	Lists available information resources at several computer sites by searching each site's gopher menu
WAIS	Searches individual documents available at several computer sites for specific key words and phrases
WWW	Uses hypertext to link information resources on different computers

Figure 21 Four Internet search tools

The Internet is the foundation for a large project called the **National Information Highway (NIH)**, also known as the **National Information Infrastructure (NII)** and as the **information superhighway**. These popular phrases are used to describe the future of communication networks and computers. Legislation proposed and championed by US Vice President Gore has laid the foundation for this billion-dollar project. Because of this legislation, Congress is now encouraging private investment, competition, and two-way universal access for the NIH.

We are just at the forefront of this rapidly evolving area. Sociologists suggest that the most significant advances will develop from the so-called global village. Unlike a normal village where members are located near one another, the global village is not constrained by geographic space. It is constrained only by cyberspace, or communication links with computers. Members will likely develop close relationships without ever seeing one another. In fact, they may live in different parts of the world with widely varying cultures and backgrounds.

What is the future of the Internet and the information superhighway? No one knows for certain, but the clear consensus is that they will provide a wide-open highway from your home and future office to the rest of the world.

ACKNOWLEDGMENTS

West Stock, Zephyr Picture #991106: 1.1, 1.8, 1.10, 4.1, 8.1 (*inserts*)
Courtesy of Gateway 2000: 1.3
Courtesy of IBM Corporation: 1.4, 1.6, 1.9 (*left*), 3.11, 4.2 (*left*), 5.11, 6.10, 6.15, 7.17, 11.13, 12.14
Courtesy of Motorola and Cummingham Communication: 1.5
Courtesy of Cray Research, Inc.: 1.7
Courtesy of Apple Computer, Inc.: 1.9 (*right*), 1.14, 4.2 (*right*), 4.10, 5.10, 6.5, 7.1
Courtesy of Microsoft Corporation: 1.11 (*insert*), 2.5, 2.15, 3.5, 3.6, 6.3, 6.4, 8.3
Courtesy of Dell Creative Services: 1.12, 5.1
Fredrik D. Bodin: 1.13, 3.8
Courtesy of BASF: 1.16
Courtesy of QMS, Inc.: 1.17
Courtesy of Hayes Microcomputer Products: 1.18
Courtesy of Bank of America: 1.19, 14.1
Courtesy of Aldus Corporation: 2.11
Courtesy of The Software Toolworks: 3.10
Courtesy of AimTech Corporation and Brodeur & Partners: 3.13
TSW/Andrew Sachs: 3.15
Courtesy of Trinzic Corporation: 3.16
Courtesy of SRI International: 3.18
Courtesy of Sun Microsystems, Inc.: 4.11
Courtesy of Intel: 5.7, 8.10
Courtesy of Xircom: 5.14
Mark Richards/Photo Edit: 6.1
Courtesy of Epson America, Inc.: 6.6, 6.20
Courtesy of Ford Motor Company: 6.7
Courtesy of H.E.I.: 6.8
Courtesy of Caterpillar Inc.: 6.9

Courtesy of Hewlett-Packard: 6.11, 6.17, 6.21, 6.22 (*insert*), 6.26
Courtesy of Lanier Worldwide, Inc.: 6.12
Courtesy of NCR: 6.13, 6.14
Courtesy of Toshiba America: 6.18
Courtesy of Tektronix, Inc.: 6.23
Courtesy of CalComp: 6.25
Courtesy of Bose Corporation: 6.27
Courtesy of Seagate Technologies: 7.7
Courtesy of SyQuest Technology, Inc.: 7.8
Courtesy of Stac Electronics: 7.11
Scott R. Goodwin, Inc.: 7.19
Richard Laird/FPG International: 8.2
Spencer Grant/Stock Boston: 9.12
Courtesy of Bob Waldrop: 10.2
TSW/Chuck Keeler: 10.3
Copyright Canadian Airlines International: 10.8
Copyright TSW: 10.10
AT&T Archives: 10.12
Copyright Darrell Peterson and West Stock: 11.2, 11.11
Courtesy of Honeywell, Inc.: 11.10
Copyright © TSW/Tim Brown: 11.12, 12.2, 12.16
Courtesy of Patton & Patton: 12.6
Copyright © 1991 Matthew Borkoski/West Stock: 12.13
Courtesy of KnowledgeWare, Inc.: 12.18
Courtesy of Lexmark International, Inc.: 13.2
Stacy Pickerell/Tony Stone Images: 13.3
AFP/Bettmann: 13.8
Courtesy of American Airlines: 14.2
Courtesy of Federal Express: 14.3
Copyright 1990 Bill Delzell: 14.4, 14.5, 14.6, 14.7
Courtesy of The Interface Group, Inc.: 14.8
Copyright TSW, Bruce Ayres: 14.11

INDEX

Visual Summaries
to accompany

Information
Processing and
Management

Second Edition

Mark Scott

John Holland

Timothy J. O'Leary

Linda I. O'Leary

VISUAL SUMMARY

1

You and Computer Competency

PEOPLE AND PROCEDURES	SOFTWARE

People

People are competent end users working to increase their productivity. **End users** use microcomputers and prewritten programs (such as word processing and spreadsheet programs) to solve information-related or decision-making problems.

Procedures

Procedures are manuals and guidelines that instruct end users on how to use the software and hardware.

Software is another name for **programs**—instructions that tell the computer how to process data. Two kinds are application and system software.

Application Software

Application software performs useful functions.

APPLICATION SOFTWARE

BASIC TOOLS	POWER TOOLS
Word processors	Personal information managers
Spreadsheet programs	Groupware
Database managers	Project managers
Graphics programs	Desktop publishing
Communications programs	Multimedia
Integrated programs	Artificial intelligence

System Software

System software is "background" software that helps a computer manage its internal resources. An example is the **operating system.** Popular microcomputer operating systems:

SYSTEM SOFTWARE

OPERATING SYSTEM	DESCRIPTION
DOS	Today's standard operating system for IBM and IBM-compatible microcomputers
Windows	Environment that extends capability of DOS
Windows 95	New operating system that does not require DOS
Windows NT	Operating system for very powerful microcomputers
OS/2 Warp	Developed for very powerful microcomputers
Macintosh operating system	Standard operating system for Apple's Macintosh computers
Unix	Runs on many powerful microcomputers

2

TYPES OF COMPUTERS	
TYPE	**DESCRIPTION**
Microcomputers	Desktop and portable computers, widely used and number increasing fast
Minicomputers	Medium-sized, also known as midrange, used by medium-sized organisations and departments within larger organisations
Mainframes	Large computers for large organisations
Supercomputers	High-capacity machines for specialised uses like research

Increasing Use of Microcomputers

Microcomputers (In millions)

Source: Intel Corporation

HARDWARE

Input Devices

Input devices take data and put it into a form the computer can process. Especially important is the **keyboard**, a typewriter-like keyboard with specialised keys.

The System Unit

The **system unit** consists of electronic circuitry with two parts:

- **The central processing unit (CPU)**—controls and manipulates data to produce information
- **Memory (primary storage)**—temporarily holds data, program instructions, and processed data

Secondary Storage

Secondary storage stores data and programs. Three storage "media":

- **Floppy disk**—removable flexible 3½-inch or 5¼-inch plastic disks
- **Hard disk**—non-removable, enclosed disk drive
- **Optical disc**—removable, **CD-ROM** best known

Output Devices

Output devices output processed information from CPU. Two important output devices:

- **Monitor**—TV screen-like device to display results
- **Printer**—device that prints out images on paper

Communications Devices

These send and receive data and programs from one computer to another. A device that connects a microcomputer to a telephone is a **modem.**

DATA AND CONNECTIVITY

Data

Data describes something and is typically stored electronically in a file. A **file** is a collection of characters organised as a single unit. Common types of files:

- **Document:** letters, research papers, memos
- **Worksheet:** budget analyses, sales projections
- **Database:** structured and organised data

Connectivity

Connectivity is a concept describing the ability of end users to tap into resources well beyond their desktops. Two important aspects of connectivity are:

- **Computer networks**—microcomputers can be linked to other microcomputers, minicomputers, or mainframes to share data and resources.
- **National Information Highway (NIH)**—also known as the **National Information Infrastructure (NII)** or **information superhighway**—is a term used to describe the future of communication networks and computers. **Internet** is the foundation for the NIH.

* Should read 'Application Software: Basic Tools'.

Applications Software: **Power Tools***

Application software does "useful work." The five basic tools or types of general-purpose applications programs are used by many people for different kinds of tasks.

WORD PROCESSING	SPREADSHEETS	DATABASE MANAGERS

WORD PROCESSING

A **word processor** creates, edits, saves, and prints **documents.** Especially useful for deleting, inserting, and replacing. Principal features:

Word Wrap and Enter Key

Word wrap automatically moves insertion point to new line. **Enter key** enters new paragraph or blank line.

Search and Replace

Search command allows users to quickly find a character, word, or phrase in a document. **Replace** command allows users to automatically replace with other text.

Other Features

- Aligning, bolding, underlining, and italicising.
- Inserting table of contents, footnotes, end notes, page numbers, and bulleted lists.
- **Spelling** and **grammar checking.**
- Providing **thesaurus, mail-merge** capabilities, **drawing programs, clip-art,** and **word-art.**

Examples of Packages

Ami Pro, Word, and WordPerfect

SPREADSHEETS

A **spreadsheet** presents and analyses data. A **worksheet area** is bounded by **column** and **row headings.** A **cell** is the intersection of column and row. The position of a cell is called **cell address.** The **cell pointer (cell selector)** indicates where data is to be entered. Principal features:

Format

Labels (column and row headings) and **values** (numbers in cells) can be displayed in different ways.

Formulas and Functions

Formulas are instructions for calculations. **Functions** are built-in formulas.

Recalculation

Recalculation is automatic recomputation.

Analysis Tools

Built-in tools for **what-if, goal-seeking, solving,** and **scenario** analyses.

Other Features

- Graphing data on spreadsheet.
- 3-D spreadsheets.
- Linking worksheet files.

Examples of Packages

Excel, Lotus 1-2-3, Quattro Pro

DATABASE MANAGERS

A **database manager** (or **database management system, DBMS**) is used to structure a database. A database is a collection of related data. **Relational databases** are organised as fields, records, and tables for easy retrieval of selected items. Principal features:

Locate and Display

A database query used to locate information that can be displayed on the screen for viewing or updating.

Sort

Users can sort through records and rearrange them in different ways.

Calculate and Format

Maths formulas may be used to manipulate data. Data may be printed out in different report formats.

Other Features

- Customised data-entry forms.
- Professional-looking reports.
- Program control languages, like SQL (Structured Query Language).

Examples of Packages

Access, Approach, dBASE, Paradox

COMMON FEATURES

FEATURE	DESCRIPTION	FEATURE	DESCRIPTION
Version and Release	Indicates major and minor changes in software	Dialogue Box	Used to specify additional command options
Insertion Point	Shows where data can be entered	Scroll Bars	Used to display additional information
Menu	Presents commands availabe for selection	WYSIWYG	"What You See Is What You Get"
Shortcut Keys	Special-purpose keys for frequently used commands	Edit	Changes entered information
Help	Presents explanations of various commands	Cut, Copy and Paste	Deletes, moves, or copies information
Tool Bar	Presents graphic objects for commands	Undo	Restores work prior to last command

GRAPHICS	COMMUNICATIONS	PACKAGES AND SUITES

Graphics programs display results of data manipulation for easier analysis, presentation, and illustration. Three types of graphics programs are analytical, presentation, and drawing programs.

Analytical Graphics

Analytical graphics programs put data in a form easier to analyse (e.g. bar charts, line graphs).

Presentation Graphics

Presentation graphics help communicate results or persuade, using colour and titles.

Drawing Programs

Drawing programs help professional illustrators create attractive, sophisticated artwork for publications.

Examples of Packages

Most analytical graphics come as part of spreadsheet programs. Examples of presentation graphics: Freelance, Harvard Graphics, Persuasion, PowerPoint. Examples of drawing programs: Adobe Illustrator, Aldus Freehand, Micrografx Designer.

Communications software enables users to connect with and share resources with others. Communications programs permit *connectivity*—they allow microcomputers to connect with other information resources.

Data Banks

Large computerised databases (e.g. electronic encyclopaedias) are available.

Message Exchanges

Electronic bulletin boards and **electronic mail services** are available.

Financial Services

Users may look up stock quotations and airline reservations, order discount merchandise, and do home banking.

Share Resources

Laser printers, hard disks, and other expensive hardware can be shared on networks.

Examples of Packages

Crosstalk, ProComm, Smartcom

Integrated Packages

An **integrated package** is an all-in-one software program. It includes word processor, spreadsheets, database manager, graphics, and communications. Some features:

- Common structure for easy data exchange between applications.
- Less expensive than software suite.
- Each application not as powerful as "stand-alone" application.

Examples of Packages

Lotus Works and Microsoft Works

Software Suites

A **software suite** is a collection of individual windows applications packages sold together. Some features:

- Windows (discussed in detail in next chapter) allows sharing of data between completely different applications programs.
- Less expensive than buying each individual software package.

Examples of Packages

Lotus SmartSuite and Microsoft Office

5

Applications Software: Power Tools

Applications

Some recent important microcomputer applications are personal information managers, groupware, project management software, desktop publishing, multimedia and artificial intelligence—robotics, knowledge-based and expert systems, and artificial reality.

| PERSONAL INFORMATION MANAGERS | GROUPWARE | PROJECT MANAGEMENT |

Personal information managers (PIMs) help keep you organised and maximise your personal productivity. They generally include electronic calendars, to-do lists, address books, and notepads.

Some PIMs are able to schedule group meetings with busy people.

Groupware, also known as collaborative technology, allows groups of workers to schedule and hold meetings, communicate, collaborate on ideas, and share documents, knowledge, and information.

Lotus Notes, the most widely used groupware software, shares a database consisting of documents. The documents can contain text, graphics, images, and videos. Users create documents using forms and view summaries of the database.

Examples of Packages

Lotus Notes, Microsoft's Workgroup for Windows

Project management software allows you to plan, schedule, and control the people, resources, and costs of a project.

Two important tools found in project management software are:

Gantt Charts

A **Gantt chart** uses bars and lines to indicate the time scale of a series of tasks so you can see whether the tasks are being completed on schedule.

PERT Charts

A **PERT chart** shows not only the timing of a project but also the relationships among its tasks.

Examples of Packages

Harvard Project Manager, Microsoft Project for Windows, Project Scheduler, SuperProject, Time Line

Examples of Packages

Computer Associates International Inc.'s UpToDate, Franklin Quest Co.'s Ascend, Lotus Organiser

TOP-SELLING CD-ROMS

RANK	TITLE	PUBLISHER
1	Myst	Broderbund
2	Dark Forces	Lucas Arts
3	Doom II: Hell on Earth	ID/GT
4	NASCAR Racing	Virgin
5	NBA Live '95	Electronic Arts

Source: G. Meir Inc., May 1995

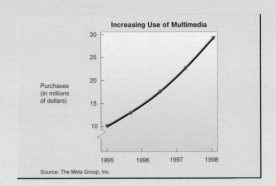

Increasing Use of Multimedia

Purchases (In millions of dollars)

Source: The Meta Group, Inc.

DESKTOP PUBLISHING	MULTIMEDIA	ARTIFICIAL INTELLIGENCE

Desktop publishing is the process of using a microcomputer, laser printer, and necessary software to mix text and graphics and create publications of almost professional quality. Once a document is composed on the monitor screen, it is transmitted by a **page description language,** which describes the shape and position of letters and graphics, to a printer for printing out.

Examples of Packages

First Publisher, PageMaker, Quark Express, Ventura Publisher.

Multimedia or **hypermedia** combines and controls information in a variety of forms including: text, graphics, animation, video, music, and voice. Two key components of multimedia applications are multimedia PCs and hypermedia databases:

Multimedia PCs

Multimedia PCs are powerful microcomputers with large disk drives, sound boards, speakers, and CD-ROM drives. Multimedia PCs used for creating presentations require additional hardware such as: microphones, video cameras, scanners, and floptical disks. **Authoring software** is also required to create and link the different types of inputs.

Hypermedia Databases

Hypermedia databases store and link all kinds of data. The data is stored in **cards** and **stacks** and allows users to navigate this information in creative and useful ways through buttons.

Artificial intelligence is a research field to develop computer systems simulating human thought processes and actions. Three areas include:

Robotics

Robotics is a research field to develop machines that can be reprogrammed to do more than one task. Some types are industrial robots, perception systems, and mobile robots.

Knowledge-Based (Expert) Systems

These are computer programs that duplicate the knowledge humans have for performing specialised tasks. They are unlike conventional programs in that they provide advice, use a knowledge base, fire rules, and process according to user interaction. **Fuzzy logic** is used to allow human-like input.

Virtual Reality

Also known as **artificial reality** or **virtual environments,** this consists of interactive sensory equipment to simulate alternative realities to the physical world.

7

Systems Software

Applications

System software does "background work" (like helping the computer do internal tasks). Five different kinds of operating systems are: DOS, Microsoft Windows, OS/2, Macintosh, and Unix. Three basic variations of Microsoft Windows: Windows, Windows 95, and Windows NT.

SYSTEM SOFTWARE PROGRAMS

PROGRAM	FUNCTION
Bookstrap loader	Reads operating system from disk and loads into mem
Diagnostic routines	Tests parts of system to ensure computer is running properly.
Basic input-output	Transmits characters from the keyboard to a monitor o disk.
Operating system	Helps manage computer resources. Most important typ are DOS, Microsoft Windows, OS/2, Macintosh, and Ur

WINDOWS	WINDOWS 95	WINDOWS NT

Windows is not an operating system. It is a program that runs with DOS as the operating system. Windows extends the capability of DOS. Compared to DOS:

Advantages

- **Multitasking** is possible (several applications sharing multiprocessor that switches between applications).
- **Graphical user interface (GUI)** is provided. Commands can be executed by manipulating graphic symbols called **icons.**
- More memory can be accessed.
- Share data between applications.

Disadvantages

- System requirements are much greater than DOS.
- Unrecoverable errors were a problem with earlier versions of Windows.

Windows 95 is an operating system. It does not require DOS. Windows 95 is an advanced operating system for powerful microcomputers. Compared to Windows:

Advantages

Like Windows, it supports multitasking, graphical user interface, more memory access, and data sharing. Additionally:

- **Microprocessing** capability allows multiple applications to run independently and at the same time.
- Flexibility to run with wider variety of powerful computers and microprocessors.
- Internet utilities to connect to an online service.
- Plug and Play support to simplify new hardware installation.

Disadvantages

- System requirements are much greater than Windows.
- Few applications written specifically for Windows 95.

Windows NT is an operating system that offers an advanced alternative to Windows and Windows 95. It is designed for very powerful microcomputers and networks. Compared to Windows 95:

Advantages

Like Windows 95, it supports multitasking, graphical user interface, more memory access, data sharing, multiprocessing, and flexibility. Additionally:

- **Multiuser** capability allows more than one user to operate at the same time.
- Easy to install and use networking capabilities.

Disadvantages

- System requirements much greater than for Windows 95.
- Plug and Play is not supported.

DOS is the most widely used operating system for IBM and IBM-compatible computers. There are six versions of MS-DOS. All are "backward compatible"—applications programs can run on newer versions of DOS.

VERSION	FEATURES
1.0	Original operating system for IBM PC and compatibles. Supported only floppy-disk drives.
2.0	Developed for IBM XT microcomputer. First version to support hard-disk drives.
3.0	Appeared about the same time as IBM AT microcomputer. Starting with 3.2 release, supported networking and 3½-inch disk drives.
4.0	Included pull-down menus and other sophisticated modifications.
5.0	Allowed access to more memory and task switching.
6.0	Include disk compression, advanced memory and file management and virus protection.

OS/2	MACINTOSH OPERATING SYSTEMS	UNIX

OS/2 is an operating system initially developed jointly by IBM and Microsoft. Compared to Windows NT:

Advantages

LIke Windows NT, it supports multitasking, graphical user interface, more memory access, data sharing, flexibility, and multiprocessing.

- Systems requirements are slightly less.

Disadvantages

Like Windows NT, it does not support Plug and Play and system requirements much greater than Windows 95. Additionally:

- Networking capabilities are not as advanced.
- Multiuser capability not supported.

Several operating systems have been designed for Apple's **Macintosh.** New versions have been developed as new versions of the Macintosh have been developed.

Advantages

- Easy to learn and to use.
- Offers a high standard for graphics processing.
- Can do multitasking—running of multiple programs at the same time.
- Can share data with other applications programs.

Disadvantages

- Some corporate buyers do not view Macintosh as a serious business machine.
- Does not support multiprocessing
- Programs written for DOS will not run on a Macintosh unless specialty hardware and software have been installed.

Unix, originally developed for minicomputers, is able to run on more powerful models of microcomputers. Unix is available in a number of different versions, many of which are not compatible.

Advantages

- Allows multitasking—running of multiple programs.
- Allows multiprocessing—running multiple programs independently and at the same time.
- Allows multiple users to share computer simultaneously.
- History of sharing files over electronic networks with different equipment.

Disadvantages

- Few business application programs are presently available.
- No one Unix standard exists; there are several versions (principal ones: Unix System V, Berkeley 4.2 Unix, SunOS).
- Commands are often long and complex, making it difficult for some users to learn and to use.

9

The Processing Unit

The central processing unit (CPU) and memory are two major parts of a microcomputer system unit.

PROCESSING SPEEDS

UNIT	SPEED
Millisecond	thousandth of a second
Microsecond	millionth of a second
Nanosecond	billionth of a second
Picosecond	trillionth of a second

THE CPU AND MEMORY

Central Processing Unit

The central processing unit (CPU) is the **processor,** the part of the computer that runs the program. The CPU has two parts:

- The **control unit** directs electronic signals between memory and the ALU, and between the CPU and input/output devices.
- The **arithmetic-logic unit (ALU)** performs *arithmetic* (maths) operations and *logical* (comparison) operations.

Memory

Memory (**primary** or **internal storage**) holds data, instructions for processing data (the program), and information (processed data). The contents are held in memory only temporarily. Capacity varies with different computers.

- Additional storage units (in control unit and ALU) called **registers** help make processing more efficient.
- Characters of data or instructions are stored in memory locations called **addresses.**

THE BINARY SYSTEM

Data and instructions are represented electronically with a two-state **binary system** of numbers (0 and 1).

Measure of Capacity

- **Bit** (*bi*nary dig*it*)—0 or 1, corresponding to electricity being *on* or *off*.
- **Byte**—eight bits. Each byte represents one character. The primary storage capacity of a computer is measured in bytes.

MEMORY CAPACITY

UNIT	CAPACITY
Kilobyte	one thousand bytes
Megabyte	one million bytes
Gigabyte	one billion bytes
Terabyte	one trillion bytes

Binary Coding Schemes

Two popular schemes for representing bytes are:

- **ASCII**—used in microcomputers.
- **EBCDIC**—used in larger computers.

Parity Bit

A **parity bit** is an extra bit added to a byte for error detection purposes.

SYSTEM UNIT

COMPONENT	FUNCTION
System board	Holds the various other system components
Microprocessor	Contains the CPU on a single chip
Memory	Holds programs and instructions
System clock	Controls the speed of computer operations
Expansion slots and boards	Increases memory and other system capabilities
Bus lines	Connects various internal system components
Ports	Connects outside devices to system unit

System Board

The **system board** contains the CPU and primary storage on **chips** (also called **silicon chips, semiconductors, integrated circuits**).

MICROPROCESSORS

MICROPROCESSOR	TYPICAL APPLICATIONS	USERS
Intel 80486	DOS, Windows, basic tools, personal information management	Single user, office staff, home user, home office user
Pentium	Windows 95, OS/2 Warp, groupware, desktop publishing, project management	All of the above, networked users, workgroups
Pentium Pro	Windows NT, Unix, multimedia, artificial intelligence, network communications, large database applications	All of the above, specialists
Motorola 68040	Macintosh operating system, basic tools, personal information management, desktop publishing	Single user, home user, home office user
PowerPC	Unix, groupware, project management, artificial intelligence, network communications, large database applications	All of the above, networked

Microprocessor Chips

The **microprocessor chip** contains the CPU. Capacities are expressed in word sizes. A **word** is the number of bits accessed at one time by the microprocessor. Two types are **CISC** and **RISC**.

Memory Chips

- **RAM chips** temporarily hold data and instructions. Four types of memory are: **conventional, upper, extended,** and **expanded.**
- **ROM chips (firmware)** have programs built into them for operating important system devices.

System Clock

System clock controls the speed of computer operations. It is measured in **megahertz (MHz).**

Expansion Slots and Boards

Expansion (or **plug-in**) **boards** can increase memory, connect to networks, and increase portable computer's expansion capabilities.

Bus Lines

A **bus line** (or **bus**) is a data roadway. Three bus standards: **ISA, MCA,** and **EISA.** Local buses support video demands for graphical user interfaces. Two local bus standards: **PCI** and **VL-bus.**

Ports

Ports connect outside devices to the system unit. Parallel ports are used to connect to nearby devices that send lots of data. Serial ports are widely used for devices that send data one bit at a time.

11

Input and Output

Input devices translate symbols that people understand into symbols the computer can process. Two kinds of input are keyboard and direct entry.

INPUT

Keyboard entry may be categorised as keyboards and terminals.

Keyboards

In keyboard entry, data is typed. A keyboard consists of:

- **Typewriter keys,** for regular letters, numbers, etc., and **Enter** key to enter commands.
- **Function keys** (*F1, F2,* etc.), for special tasks.
- **Numeric keys,** for typing in numbers.
- **Special-purpose keys** (e.g. *Del* for Delete) and **cursor control (directional arrow) keys** (to move cursor).

Terminals

A **terminal** is an input/output device with keyboard, monitor, and communications link. Terminals are of three types:

- **Dumb**—sends and receives only; does no processing.
- **Smart**—allows some editing of data.
- **Intelligent**—has processing and primary and secondary storage and software for processing data.

Direct-entry devices may be categorised as pointing, scanning, or voice-input devices.

Pointing Devices

- **Mouse**—directs cursor on screen.
- **Touch screen**—touching your finger to the screen selects actions.
- **Light pen**—recognises a spot on the screen as input.
- **Digitiser**—converts image to digital data. A **digitising tablet** converts images using a stylus.
- **Pen-based computing**—computer with stylus to write on display screen.

Scanning Devices

- **Image scanner (bit-mapping device)**—converts an image to digital code.
- **Facsimile transmission (fax) machine**—converts images to electronic signals for sending over telephone lines. **Dedicated fax machines** are specialised devices. **Fax boards** may be inserted in microcomputers to send and receive images.

- **Bar-code reader**—scans zebra-striped **bar codes** on products to reveal their prices.
- Character and mark recognition devices include: **magnetic-ink character recognition (MICR)**, used by banks to read magnetised-ink numbers on cheques, which are sorted by a **reader/sorter** machine; **optical-character recognition (OCR)**, used to read special preprinted characters (e.g. on utility bills); **optical-mark recognition (OMR)**, which senses pencil marks (e.g. on College Board tests).

Voice-Input Devices

Voice-input devices convert a person's spoken words to digital code. Combined with appropriate software, these devices are part of the **voice recognition system** that allows users to operate microcomputers using voice commands.

- **Continous speech recognition systems** control operations and issue commands for application packages.
- **Discrete-word recognition systems** convert and store dictation in a word processing file.

Output devices translate machine output to output that people can understand. Output devices include monitors, printers, plotters, and voice-output.

Microcomputer Printers

dot-matrix 30%

laser 33%

thermal 3%

ink-jet 34%

Source: BIS Strategic Decisions   1996

MONITORS

STANDARD	PIXELS	COLOURS
CGA	320 × 200	4
EGA	640 × 350	16
VGA	640 × 200	I16
	320 × 200	256
Super VGA	800 × 600	256
	1024 × 768	256
XGA	1024 × 768	65536rts

Monitors

Monitor **display screens** create images by individual dots ("picture elements") called **pixels.** The three most common monitor standards are shown above.

- **Desktop monitors** typically are placed on the system unit or desk. **Interlaced monitors** create images by scanning down and skipping every other line. They can cause eye strain. **Non-interlaced monitors** avoid problems by scanning down each line.
- **Portable monitors** are less bulky and flat. **Passive-matrix monitors** require little power but images not as sharp. **Active-matrix monitors** require more power, are more expensive, produce better images.

Printers

Output from display screens is called **soft copy.** Output from a printer is called **hard copy.** Four types of printers are:

- **Dot-matrix**—forms text and graphic images with a matrix of pins.
- **Ink-jet**—sprays droplets of ink on paper; it is good for colour and provides very good quality.
- **Laser**—prints with light beam and magnetically charged toner. Lasers print high-quality text and graphics; **personal lasers** used by individual user; **shared lasers** used by many.
- **Thermal**—heat elements produce images on special heat-sensitive paper; expensive; produces very high quality art and design output.

Plotters

Plotters produce multicolour bar charts, maps, architectural drawings. Four types are:

- **Pen**—has been most popular and least expensive.
- **Ink-jet**—fastest and very good at producing solid colour output.
- **Electrostatic**—electrostatic charges create high-quality and high-volume work on specially treated paper (shown).
- **Direct imaging**—electrically charged pins create two-colour output on special heat-sensitive paper.

Voice-Output Devices

- **Voice-output devices** make sounds resembling human speech.

Secondary Storage

Primary storage in microcomputers is **volatile;** some things disappear when the power is turned off. Secondary storage is **nonvolatile;** it stores data and programs even after the power is turned off.

SECONDARY STORAGE

TYPE	ADVANTAGE	DISADVANTAGE	TYPICAL USE	COST/MEGABYT
Floppy disk	Inexpensive, direct access, removable	Low capacity, slow access	Store files for word processors and spreadsheets	$1.00
Hard disk	Fast, direct access	Limited capacity	Store programs and data	$0.40 to $0.80
CD-ROM	High capacity, direct access	Slow access	Reference material	$0.04 to $1.00
Magnetic tape	High capacity	Slow sequential data access	Backup programs and data	$0.10 to $0.40

FLOPPY DISK

Cover slides over to expose disk.

Floppy disks (disks, diskettes) are circular plastic disks. Two principal types are 3½-inch and 5¼-inch.

FLOPPY DISK CAPACITY

DESCRIPTION	BYTES
3½-inch	
Double-sided, double-density	720 KB
Double-sided, high-density	1.44 KB
Floptical	21 MB
5¼-inch	
Double-sided, double-density	360 KB
Double-sided, high-density	1.2 KB

The Disk Drive

- A floppy disk is inserted through a **drive gate** into a *disk drive,* which has an **access arm** equipped with **read-write heads** that move on the disk (**seek** operation), which is rotated to the proper position (**search** operation).
- The read-write head *reads* (obtains) data or programs from the disk and sends it to the CPU or *writes* (transfers) data from the CPU to the disk.

Parts of Floppy Disk

- Data is recorded on a disk's **tracks** (rings) and **sectors** (sections). In **soft-sectored disks**, tracks and sectors must be adapted to particular microcomputers by *formatting (initialising)*.
- A disk is protected by the **jacket** (liner), paper envelope, and **write-protect notch** (covered by tab or shutter).

HARD DISK

Hard Disk

A **hard disk** is an enclosed disk drive that contains one or more metallic disks. Enclosing the disk in a sealed container prevents material entering that causes a **head crash.** Hard disks come in three forms:

- An **internal hard disk** has one or more metallic platters sealed inside a container. Hard disks have far more capacity than a floppy disk does.
- **Hard-disk cartridges** can be removed when they are filled or transported.
- Mini- and mainframe computers use **hard-disk packs,** which are hard disks consisting of several platters in a stack.

Performance Enhancements

- **Disk caching**—anticipates data needs by reading from hard disk to memory to reduce transfer rate of needed data.
- **Data compression (decompression)**—reduces amount of space required to store data and programs.
- **Redundant arrays of inexpensive disks (RAIDs)**—expands external storage by networking hard disks and grouping them so that they may be treated as a single large-capacity hard disk.

14

CD-ROM DRIVES

TYPE	FUNCTION
Single-speed	The original drive introduced in the mid 1980s; transfer rate of 150 KB per second; data retrieval was slow; poor sound and video capabilities
Double-speed	Introduced in 1991; transfer rate of 300 KB per second; widely used standard; acceptable data retrieval and sound production; video capabilities limited; too slow for most multimedia applications
Triple-speed	Introduced in 1993; transfer rate of 450 KB per second; also not quite fast enough for full motion video
Quad-speed	Also introduced in 1993; transfer rate of 600 KB; acceptable for full-motion video
Six-speed	Recently introduced, with faster speeds expected soon

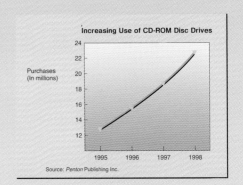

Increasing Use of CD-ROM Disc Drives

Purchases (In millions)

Source: *Penton* Publishing Inc.

OPTICAL DISCS | **MAGNETIC TAPE**

OPTICAL DISCS

DESCRIPTION	CAPACITY
CD-ROM	650 MB
CD-R	600–650 MB
Erasable	600–1000 MB

Optical Discs

An **optical disc** is a metallic disc that uses a laser beam for reading and writing. Three kinds are:

- **CD-ROM** (compact disc–read-only memory)—cannot be written on or erased by user **(read-only).**

1 book   147 books   451 books

1 book = 720 pages

1.44 MB floppy   212 MB hard disk   650 MB CD-ROM

- **CD-R** (CD-recordable) or **WORM** (write once, read many)—can be written to one time, after which it cannot be erased by users but can be read many times without deterioration.
- **Erasable optical discs**—can be written on and erased and reused.

Magnetic Tape

Magnetic tape storage is mainly used to back up (duplicate) programs and data on disks. Two forms are:

- **Magnetic Tape Streamers (backup tape cartridge units)** consist of tape cartridges used to back up microcomputer hard disks.
- **Magnetic Tape Reels,** used to back up mini- and mainframe computer storage, run on **magnetic drives (magnetic tape units).**

take-up reel

supply reel

read-write head

erase head

tape

Communications and Connectivity

Data communications systems are the electronic systems that transmit data over communications lines from one location to another.

NATIONAL INFORMATION HIGHWAY AND INTERNET	USER CONNECTION	COMMUNICATIONS CHANNELS

Internet

At the **Internet** is a worldwide computer network that is at the forefront of the **National Information Highway (NIH).**

Internet Applications

INTERNET APPLICATIONS

APPLICATION	DESCRIPTION
Electronic mail	Send and receive e-mail worldwide
Public discussion	Participate in discussions and debates using UseNet newsgroups
File transfer	Locate and copy selected files using FTP
Run programs	Allow terminal access to locate and run programs using Telnet

Utilities

Two widely known and used Internet utility programs:

- **Gophers** are programs to access computers on the Internet. **Gopher clients** request access. **Gopher servers** provide access by displaying menus.
- **Archies** are programs to help locate and copy files from **Archie servers.**

Telephones typically send and receive **analog signals.** Computers send and receive **digital signals.**

Modems and Communications Speeds

- A *modem* ("*mod*ulator *dem*odulator") converts digital to analog and vice versa. **Modulation—digital to analog. Demodulation—analog to digital.**
- Popular speeds are 2400 and 9600 bits per second.

Types of Modems

- **External modem**—outside system cabinet and connected by cable.
- **Internal modem**—plug-in circuit board inside system unit.
- **Wireless modem**—does not connect to telephone line, receives data through the air.
- **Fax modem**—unlike other modems, fax modems send and receive signals that represent graphic images.

Data may be transmitted by:

Telephone Lines

Most phone lines have consisted of copper wires called **twisted pairs**.

Coaxial Cable

Coaxial cable is high-frequency, solid core cable.

Fibre-Optic Cable

Fibre-optic cable transmits data as pulses of light through tubes of glass.

Microwave

Microwaves are high-frequency radio waves that travel in a straight line.

Satellites

Satellites act as microwave relay stations rotating above the earth.

CONNECTIVITY OPTIONS

OPTION	FUNCTION
Fax machines	Convert images to signals and send them over telephone lines to receiving fax machines
Electronic bulletin boards	Provide forums on a variety of subjects available to telephone-linked microcomputer users
Electronic mail	Systems resembling bulletin boards but are restricted in access by passwords
Voice–mail systems	Convert a voice message to digital bits and distribute to many locations over telephone lines
Shared resources	Microcomputer users may share expensive hardware, data, and information
Online services	Provide wide range of activities including teleshopping, home banking, investments, and travel reservations services

Increasing Use of LANs

LANs (In millions)

Source: Intel Corporation

DATA TRANSMISSION	NETWORK ARCHITECTURE	NETWORK TYPES

DATA TRANSMISSION

Data transmission factors:

Bandwidth

Bandwidth may be **voiceband, medium band,** or **broadband.**

Serial and Parallel Transmission

With **serial data transmission,** bits flow in a continuous stream. With **parallel data transmission,** bits flow through separate lines simultaneously.

Direction of Data Transmission

Three directions of data flow are **simplex communication**—one direction only, **half-duplex communication**—both directions but not simultaneously, and **full-duplex communication**—both directions at the same time.

Modes of Transmitting Data

Two modes are **asynchronous**—data is sent and received one byte at a time—and **synchronous**—several bytes (a block) are sent at one time.

Protocols

A **protocol** defines rules by which senders and receivers may exchange information.

NETWORK ARCHITECTURE

Network architecture describes how a computer network is configured and what strategies are used.

Configurations

Networks can be arranged or configured in several different ways. Four principal ways:

- **Star network**—small computers or peripheral devices are linked to a central unit.
- **Bus network**—each device handles its own communications.
- **Ring network**—each device is connected to two other devices, forming a ring.
- **Hierarchical network**—several computers are linked to a central host.

Strategy

Every network has a strategy for co-ordinating and sharing. The three most common are:

- With **terminal networks,** power is centralised in one large computer.
- With **peer-to-peer networks,** each node acts as both a server and a client.
- With **client/server networks,** one node co-ordinates and supplies services to all other nodes.

NETWORK TYPES

Three types of geographical networks are:

Local Area Networks

Local Area Networks (LANs) are computers and peripheral devices close together (for example, in same building). Linked by telephone, coaxial, or fibre-optic cable, LANs often take bus form. LANs may be linked to other LANs or networks by a **network gateway**.

Metropolitan Area Networks

A **metropolitan area network (MAN)** consists of citywide networks, often using cellular phones.

Wide Area Networks

Wide area networks (WANs) are countrywide and worldwide networks, often using microwave relays and satellites.

17

Files and Databases

Through communication lines, users can gain access to files and databases.

FILE ORGANIZATION

TYPE	ADVANTAGES	DISADVANTAGES
Sequential	Efficient access to all or large part of records, cost	Slow access to specific records
Direct	Fast access to specific records	Inefficient access to all or large part of records, cost
Index sequential	Faster than sequential, more efficient than direct	Not quite as efficient as sequential, not quite as fast as direct, cost

---

FILES

Understanding how files work means understanding:

Data Organisation

- **Character**—letter, number, special character.
- **Field**—set of related characters.
- **Record**—collection of related fields.
- **File**—collection of related records.
- **Database**—collection of related files.
- **Key field**—unique identifier for each record in a file.

Batch Versus Real-Time Processing

Two methods of processing:

- **Batch processing**—transactions are collected over time, then processed all at once.
- **Real-time processing**—data is processed at the same time transactions occur.

Master Versus Transaction Files

- **Master file**—complete file, current to the last update.
- **Transaction file**—temporary "holding file" used to update the master file.

Three types of file organisation:

Sequential

- **Sequential**—records are stored one after the other in ascending or descending order. This method is often used with magnetic tape.

Direct

- **Direct**—records are stored in order by a key field such as a special number. This method is often used with magnetic disk.

Index Sequential

- **Index sequential**—a compromise organisation with records stored sequentially with an index for near direct access. Used with magnetic disk storage.

DATABASE

A *database* is a collection of integrated data—logically related files and records.

The Need for Databases

Advantages of databases:

- Sharing—users may share with others.
- Security—access is restricted to authorised people.
- Fewer files—a company avoids multiple files on the same subject.
- Database integrity—changes in one file are made in other files as well.

Software for a DBMS

A **database management system (DBMS)** is the software for creating, modifying, and gaining access to the database. A DBMS consists of:

- **Data dictionary**—describes the structure of the database.
- **Query language**—language to get access to the database.

Relational databases use **tables** where rows resemble records. Related tables have a **common data element** (key field). Table entries can be easily added, deleted, and modified.

Three principal DBMS organisations are:

Hierarchical Database

In a **hierarchical database**, fields and records are structured in **nodes**, points connected like tree branches. An entry may have a **parent** node with several **child** nodes. A node may be reached by only one path.

Network Database

In a **network database**, nodes are arranged hierarchically, but a child node may have more than one parent. There are additional connections called **pointers**. A node may be reached by several paths.

Relational Database

In a **relational database,** data is stored in tables consisting of rows and columns; data items are found by means of an index.

Four types of databases are:

Individual Database

The **individual database** is a collection of integrated files useful mainly to just one person.

Company, or Shared, Database

Two types of **company (shared) database** are:

- **Common operational database**—contains data on company operations.
- **Common user database**—contains data from common operational database and from outside private databases.

Distributed Database

The **distributed database** is spread out geographically and is accessible by communications links.

Proprietary Database

A **proprietary database** is available by subscription to customers.

Databases offer increased productivity but also risks to security.

Data for Strategic Uses

Databases help users keep current and plan for the future.

Importance of Security

Two security concerns are illegal use of data and unauthorised access. **Computer viruses** are hidden instructions that "migrate" into programs and databases.

The Database Administrator

The **database administrator (DBA)** is a specialist who sets up and manages the database and determines **processing rights**—which people have access to what kind of data.

Information Systems

Technological advances in communications and database applications make available a greater *quantity* of information than was possible a few years ago. In addition, you have access to a better *quality* of information. Organisations use specialised information systems to provide accurate and timely information.

HOW INFORMATION FLOWS

Information flows up and down among managers and sideways among departments.

Functions

Most organisations have separate departments to perform five functions:

- *Accounting*—manages finances, including orders, bills, paychecks.
- *Production*—makes the product (or service).
- *Marketing*—promotes and sells the product (or service).
- *Human resources*—hires people, manages employee benefits.
- *Research*—develops new products (or services).

Management Levels

Management in many organisations has three levels:

- **Top-level managers** are concerned with long-range planning, forecasting future events.
- **Middle-level managers** are concerned with control and planning, implementing long-term goals.
- **Supervisors** are concerned with control of operational matters, monitoring day-to-day events, and supervising workers.

Information Flow

Information flows in different directions:
- For top-level managers—flow is up within the organisation and into the organisation from outside.
- For middle-level managers—flow is horizontally across and vertically within departments.
- For supervisors—flow is primarily vertical.

information from outside

strategic: future-oriented, internal and external information

tactical: historical, internal information

operational: day-to-day, internal information

Executive Support System

An **executive support system (ESS)** or **executive information system (EIS)** draws data together from an organisation's databases but is designed to be easier to use than MISs or DSSs. Information is displayed in condensed form and in bold graphics.

TYPES OF INFORMATION SYSTEMS

Transaction Processing Systems (TPS)

Record day-to-day transactions. An example is in accounting, which handles six activities: **sales order processing, accounts receivable, inventory and purchasing, accounts payable, payroll,** and **purchasing.**

Management Information Systems (MIS)

Produce predetermined **periodic, exception,** and **demand reports.** Management information systems use database management systems to integrate the databases of different departments.

Decision Support Systems (DSS)

Enable managers to get answers for unanticipated questions. A **decision support system** consists of the user, software system, data, and **decision models.** Teams formed to address large problems use **group decision support systems.**

Executive Support Systems (ESS)

Assist top-level executives. An **executive support system** is similar to an MIS and a DSS but easier to use. ESS are designed specifically for top-level decision makers.

Office Automation Systems (OAS)

Support data workers who are involved with distribution and communication of information. **Office automation systems** focus on managing documents, communicating, and scheduling.

Knowledge Work Systems (KWS)

Support knowledge workers who create information. For example, engineers involved with design and manufacturing use **CAD/CAM,** a **knowledge work system** to integrate design and manufacturing activities.

Systems Analysis and Design

Systems analysis and design is a six-phase problem-solving procedure for examining an information system and improving it. The six phases are called the **systems life cycle.**

PHASE 1: PRELIMINARY INVESTIGATION

The **preliminary investigation** determines the need for a new information system. The tasks of this phase are:

Defining the problem—The current information system is examined to determine what information is needed by whom, when, and why.

Suggesting alternative systems—Based on interviews and observations made in defining the problem, alternative information systems are identified.

Preparing a short report—To document and to communicate the findings of Phase 1, preliminary investigation, a short report is prepared and presented to management.

PHASE 2: ANALYSIS

In **systems analysis** data is collected about the present system. The tasks of this phase are:

Gathering data—Data gathered by observation, interviews, questionnaire, and looking at documents. One helpful document is the organisation chart, which shows a company's functions and levels of management.

Analysing the data—There are several tools for the analysis of data, including checklists, top-down analysis, grid charts, decision tables. See the table on the next page for more complete list and details

Documenting systems analysis—To document and to communicate the findings of Phase 2, analysis, a report is prepared for higher management.

PHASE 3: DESIGN

Systems design consists of the following three tasks:

Designing alternative systems—Alternative information systems are designed. Each alternative is evaluated for economic, technical, and operational feasibility.

Selecting the best system—Four questions considered when selecting the best system:

- Will the system fit into overall information system?
- Is the system flexible enough to be modified as needed in the future?
- Will it be secure against unauthorised use?
- Will the system's benefits exceed its costs?

Documenting system design—To document and to communicate the findings of Phase 3, design, a report is prepared for higher management.

ANALYSIS TOOLS

TOOL	DESCRIPTION
Checklist	Provides a list of questions about key issues
Top-down analysis	Divides a complex system into components, beginning at the top
Grid chart	Shows relationships between inputs and outputs
Decision table	Specifies decision rules and circumstances when specific rules are to be applied
System flowchart	Shows movement of input data, processing, and output or distribution of information
Data flow diagram	Shows data flow within an organisation or application
CASE	Automates the analysis, design, and development of information systems

PHASE 4: DEVELOPMENT   PHASE 5: IMPLEMENTATION   PHASE 6: MAINTENANCE

The **systems development** phase has three steps:

Developing software—Two ways to acquire software are:

- **Purchase**—buying off-the-shelf software to be modified if necessary.
- **Custom designed**—create programs following programming steps presented in Chapter 11.

Acquiring hardware—Acquiring hardware is very critical and involves consideration for future company growth, existing networks, communication capabilities, and training.

Testing the system—Using sample data, the new system is tested. Can take several months.

Systems implementation (conversion) is the process of changing from the old system to the new.

Types of Conversion

Four ways to convert are:

- **Direct approach**—abandoning the old and starting up the new.
- **Parallel approach**—operating the old and new side by side until the new one proves its worth.
- **Pilot approach**—trying out the new system in only one part of an organisation.
- **Phased approach**—implementing the new system gradually.

Training

A software trainer may be used to train end users on the new system.

Systems maintenance has two parts:

System audit—Once the new system is operational, the systems analyst compares it to the original design specifications. If the system does not meet these specifications, some further redesign of the system may be required.

Periodic evaluation—The new system is periodically evaluated to ensure that it is operating efficiently. If it is not, some redesign may be required.

Programming and Languages

A *program* is a list of instructions for the computer to follow to do a task. The instructions are made up of statements written in a programming language (e.g. BASIC). *Programming* is a six-step procedure for producing that list.

1. program specification → 2. program design → 3. program code → 4. program test → 5. program finalised documentation → 6. program maintenance

STEP 1: PROGRAM SPECIFICATION	STEP 2: PROGRAM DESIGN	STEP 3: PROGRAM CODE

```
begin
  total_regular :=0;
  total_overtime: =0;
  while not eof(input_file)do
    begin
      readln(input_file,hour_in,minute_in,hour_out,minute_out);
      if (hour_out >=17) then
        overtime := (hour_out - 17) + (minute_out/60)
      else
        overtime := p;
      regular := (hour_out - hour_in) + (minute_out - minute_in)/60) -

      total_regular := total_regular + regular;
      total_overtime := total_overtime - overtime;
    end;
end.
```

Program definition, also called **program analysis,** consists of specifying five tasks:

- Determining program objectives by focusing on the specific problem to be solved.
- Determining the desired output before considering the required inputs.
- Determining the input data and the source of the data.
- Determining the processing requirements to use input to produce output.
- Documenting program objectives, outputs, inputs, and processing.

In **program design,** a solution is designed using structured programming techniques. (See table below.)

Three Logic Structures

- **Sequence**—one program statement followed by another.
- **Selection** (or **IF-THEN-ELSE**)—when a decision must be made.
- **Loop**—when process is repeated as long as a condition is true. May be either **DO UNTIL** or **DO WHILE.**

Coding is writing a program. There are several important aspects of writing a program. Two are:

- Program quality—good programs are structured using logic structures.
- Language selection—a **programming language** should be chosen that is appropriate for the programming problem and the computer.

STRUCTURED PROGRAMMING TECHNIQUES

TECHNIQUE	DESCRIPTION
Top-down design	Major processing steps, called program modules, are identified
Pseudocode	A narrative expression of the logic of the program is written
Program flowcharts	Graphic representation of the steps needed to solve the programming problem is drawn
Logic structures	Three arrangements are used in program flowcharts to write structured programs

Two resources that promise to improve software development efficiency and productivity are: CASE (computer-aided software engineering) and object-oriented software development. **CASE** tools provide some automation and assistance in program design, coding, and testing. **Object-oriented software development** is a new approach that focuses less on the tasks and more on defining the relationships between previously defined procedures or objects.

Debugging consists of testing and eliminating the **syntax errors** (violation of rules of programming language) and **logic errors** (incorrect calculations or procedures). Debugging methods consist of:

- **Desk checking**—careful reading of a printout of the program.
- **Manual testing**—using sample data to test for correct processing results.
- **Attempt at translation**—running the program through a computer, using a translator program.
- **Testing sample data**—testing the program for logic errors on a computer, using sample data.
- **Testing by users**—*beta testing* by selected users is the final step.

Documentation consists of a written description of the program and the procedures for running it for users, operators, and programmers during **program maintenance**—modifying or updating of the program.

- Users need to know how to use the program and to input the data to produce correct results.
- Operators need to know how to execute the program and to recognise and correct errors.
- Programmers need to be able to explain how the program works and to maintain the program in the future.

Maintenance is the final step in the programming process. It is to ensure efficient and effective ongoing operation of the program.

Two major categories of activities in program maintenance are:

- Operation activity to locate and correct errors, improve usability, and standardise software.
- Changing needs of the organisation often require that programs be modified.

PROGRAMMING GENERATIONS

GENERATION	NAME	SAMPLE STATEMENT
First	Machine	10010001
Second	Assembly	ADD 210(8, 13),02B(4, 7)
Third	Procedural	Overtime: = 0
Fourth	Problem	FIND NAME = "JONES"
Fifth	Natural	IF patient is dizzy, THEN check temperature and blood pressure

25

Workplace Issues: Ergonomics, Ethics, Security, and the Environment

One-third of Americans use a computer at work. Thus, there are many "people issues" connected with computers.

ERGONOMICS

Users should take steps to increase productivity and avoid physical and mental health risks. **Ergonomics** is the study of human factors related to computers.

Physical Health Matters

Some computer-associated physical health matters that can be avoided:

- Eyestrain and headache: Take frequent breaks, avoid glare on monitor screen.
- Back and neck pains: Use adjustable chairs, tables, monitor stands, keyboards.
- Electromagnetic fields: May lead to miscarriages, but not proven. Sit 60 cm from screen, 90 cm from adjacent computers.
- **Repetitive strain injury (RSI):** Also known as **repetitive motion injury** and **cumulative trauma disorders,** RSIs are neck, wrist, hand, and arm injuries resulting from fast, repetitive work. **Carpal tunnel syndrome,** damage to nerves and tendons in hands, afflicts heavy keyboard users. Avoidance consists of frequent, short rest breaks.

Mental Health Matters

Irritations consist of:

- Noise from clattering printers and high-frequency squeal from monitors.
- Stress from excessive monitoring.

Design with People in Mind

Computers are being designed for easier use.

ETHICS

Computer ethics are guidelines for moral computer use. Four computer ethics issues are: privacy, accuracy, property, and access.

Use of Large Databases

Large databases are constantly compiling information about us. A vast industry of data gatherers or "information resellers" collects data about us and sells it to direct marketers and others.

Use of Electronic Networks

Some information networks have been used to eavesdrop on employees or to restrict members' messages.

Major Laws on Privacy

PRIVACY LAWS

LAW	PROTECTION
Fair Credit Reporting Act	Gives right to review and correct personal credit records; restricts sharing of personal credit histories
Freedom of Information Act	Gives right to see personal files collected by federal agencies
Privacy Act	Prohibits use of federal information for purposes other than original intent
Right to Financial Privacy Act	Limits federal authority to examine personal bank records
Computer Fraud and Abuse Act	Allows prosecution of unauthorised access to computers and databases
Electronic Communications Privacy Act	Protects privacy on public electronic-mail systems
Video Privacy Protection Act	Prevents sale of video-rental records
Computer Matching and Privacy Protection Act	Limits government's authority to match individual's data

VIRUS PROTECTION

STEP	ACTION
1	Make backup copies of your data on a frequent basis
2	Protect data on your floppy disks by using write-protect tabs
3	Turn off your microcomputer when you're not using it
4	Don't use master disk to install software programs; make a working copy and store the master
5	Avoid downloading computer games from electronic bulletin boards
6	Limit your use of "shareware" programs and check for viruses before running
7	Do not loan out your utility or other software programs
8	Run a virus protection program frequently
9	Update your virus protection program regularly

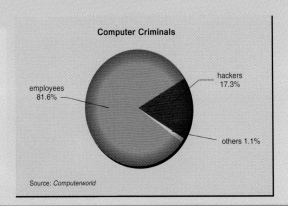

Computer Criminals

employees 81.6%

hackers 17.3%

others 1.1%

Source: *Computerworld*

SECURITY

There is a variety of sources that threaten computer security. There is also a variety of protective measures.

Threats to Computer Security

Keeping information private depends on keeping computer systems safe from:

- Computer criminals—can be employees, outside users, **hackers/crackers**, and organised-crime members.
- Computer crime—can be damage caused by computer **viruses**, theft, and manipulation, as in the unauthorised entry to a computer system for fun.
- Other hazards—include natural forces, civil strife, terrorism, technological failures, and human errors.

Measures to Protect Computer Security

Security of information, hardware, and software can be improved by:

- Restricting access through passwords and biometrics.
- Anticipating disasters by providing physical security for hardware and data security for software and data.
- Backing up data frequently and storing it in safe locations.
- Providing **security for microcomputers** by avoiding extreme conditions and guarding the computer, software, and data.

ENVIRONMENT

low-power microprocessor

sleep modes for microprocessor and hard disk drive

flat panel display

power-down monitor

screen-saver software

low-power supply unit

no cooling fan

Microcomputers are the greatest users of electricity in the workplace. The **Environmental Protection Agency (EPA)** has established the **Energy Star** program to encourage efficient use of energy by the computer industry. The industry has responded with the concept of the Green PC.

The Green PC

Basic elements of the Green PC include:

- Systems units that use energy-saving microprocessors, have sleep-mode capability, are more energy-efficient, and eliminate cooling fans.
- Display units that are more efficient by replacing CRT displays with flat panels, using special power-down monitors, and using screen-saver software.
- Manufacturing that eliminates or reduces the use of harmful chemicals such as **chlorofluorocarbons (CFCs),** nickel, and other heavy metals.

Personal Responsibility

You can help protect the environment from computer-related activities by:

- Conserving energy by turning off computer systems at the end of the workday and using screen-saver software to blank computer screens after 3 to 5 minutes of inactivity.
- Recycling paper, computer boxes, packaging materials, printer cartridges, and floppy disks.
- Educating yourself and others about ecological dangers of all types. Making sure your concerns are known by supporting ecologically sound products.

27

Your Future: Using Information Technology

Being a winner in the information revolution means devising an individual strategy for dealing with change.

TECHNOLOGY AND ORGANIZATIONS

Technology can introduce new ways for businesses to compete with each other.

New Products

Technology creates products that operate faster, are priced more cheaply, are often of better quality, or are wholly new. New products can be custom-tailored to a particular customer's needs.

New Enterprises

Technology can build entire new businesses (e.g. an airline charges travel agents for using its reservations system for making reservations on other airlines).

New Customer and Supplier Relationships

Businesses that make their information systems easily available may make their customers less likely to take their business elsewhere (e.g. overnight delivery services closely track packages and bills).

TECHNOLOGY AND PEOPLE

Three common reactions to the prospect of new technology are:

Cynicism

The cynics feel that new technology is overrated and too troublesome to learn.

Naïveté

The naïve believe that technology can solve problems it cannot.

Frustration

The frustrated are impatient and irritated about taking time to learn new technology.

Being a skilled computer end user—being computer-competent—is a matter of living in the present and keeping an eye on the future. It is a matter of concentrating on your goals and learning how the computer can help you achieve them.

Six ongoing activities that can help you be successful are as follows:

Stay Current

Stay current in your field—by reading trade journals and the general business press, by joining professional associations, and by participating in interest groups on the Internet.

Maintain Your Computer Competence

Stay current with technology—by being alert for computer-related articles in trade journals in your field, general computer magazines, and books.

Develop Professional Contacts

Develop professional contacts with others in your field.

Develop Specialties

Develop some specialties within your field, mastering a trade or two within your profession.

Be Alert for Organisational Change

Use informal lines of communication—the "grapevine"—to be alert for organisational changes.

Look for Innovative Opportunities

Improve your prospects by looking for ways to make your job more efficient—e.g. by finding ways to save money.

The Internet Guide: How to Surf the Net

The Internet is the roadway for ideas and information through **cyberspace.** It is a giant world-wide computer network.

| ACCESS | E-MAIL | DISCUSSION GROUPS |

To:	cjames@cmc.edu
From:	your Internet address
Subject:	First e-mail to Chris
Attachment:	BUDGET.XLS

Chris, this Internet stuff is really something. We should save a lot on telephone bills. I figure at least $20.00 a month. Remember the Excel spreadsheet we used this past summer to estimate our college expenses? I just revised it to reflect lower telephone expenses. It is attached in the file BUDGET.XLS.

I just talked to Joe. Unfortunately, his school does not have an Internet connection. However, he is going to subscribe to America Online so he can e-mail us. Of course, it will cost him more because he'll have to pay an online service fee. But, he figures he will still save money.

Another thing I like about this e-mail ... we don't have to schedule our calls so that we are both available at the same time. Plus we can send e-mail messages anytime we want at almost no cost.

your name, address, and telephone number

DISCUSSION GROUP TERMS

TERM	DESCRIPTION
Lurking	Reading news but not joining in to contribute
FAQ	Frequently asked question
Flaming	Insulting, a putting-down, or attacking
RFD	Request for discussion
Saint	Someone who aids new users by answering questions
Thread	A sequence of ongoing messages on the same subject
Wizard	Someone who has comprehensive knowledge about a subject

Providers

The most common access is through a **provider** or **host computer.** Three types of providers:

- **Free-Nets** are electronic towns that provide free access.
- **Colleges** and **universities** often provide free student access.
- **Online commercial service providers** provide access for a fee.

Connections

To access the Internet, you need to connect to a provider. Three types of connections:

- **Direct** or **dedicated** lines directly connect to the Internet through expensive high-speed lines.
- **SLIP** and **PPP** connections use high-speed modems. They are widely used by individuals.
- **Dial-up** connections also use high-speed modems but are not as fast or convenient as SLIP or PPP connections.

TCP/IP

TCP/IP (transmission control protocol/Internet protocol) is the standard protocol of the Internet.

Basic Elements

An e-mail message has three basic elements:

- The **header** includes To, From, Subject, and Attachment lines
- The **message** is short and to the point
- The **signature** provides additional sender information

Addresses

The Internet uses the **domain name system (DNS)** addressing system.

```
        user name              domain code
              cjames@cmc.edu
                          domain name
```

Netiquette

Netiquette is the accepted rules of etiquette when using the Internet.

Mailing Lists

Mailing lists, one type of **discussion group,** send all messages to each member of a **list address.** You can subscribe and unsubscribe to a list by sending a request to the **subscription address.**

Newsgroups

Newsgroups are the most popular. Using a special network, UseNet, discussions are organised into topic areas and hierarchies. Interested individuals copy down only those contributions of interest.

Lurking

Lurking is a commonly used discussion group term that means to observe before contributing to a discussion.

TELNET AND FTP	GOPHERS	WWW

Telnet

Telnet allows you to connect to a host computer, log on to that computer, and run programs from that computer. Your microcomputer acts as a terminal.

FTP

FTP (file transfer protocol) allows transferring or copying files from a host computer to your microcomputer **(downloading)** and transferring from your computer to a host computer **(uploading)**. **Archie servers** automatically check FTP sites monthly. **Archie public servers** are free.

PUBLIC ARCHIE SERVERS

LOCATION	INTERNET ADDRESS (LOG IN AS ARCHIE)
Maryland	archie.sura.net
Nebraska	archie. unl.edu
New York	archie.ans.net
Australia	archie.au
Japan	archie.wide.ad.jp

Menus

Gophers are programs that provide **menu**-based search and retrieval operations. These gophers run on host computers called **gopher sites** and provide access to that site's facilities.

Public Gophers

Public gophers allow free access to their facilities. Internet users seeking specific information typically begin at one public gopher and search its resources, then move to another and continue their search.

Veronica

One option on most gopher sites is **Veronica.** It is a program that searches other gopher sites, maintaining a list of the menus at these sites. Veronica can also search for a specific word or topic.

WAIS

WAIS (wide area information server) extends gopher and Veronica search capabilities. It examines individual documents located on host computers throughout the Internet. It maintains an extensive list of key words and phrases usually pertaining to a single subject.

The World Wide Web (WWW, W3, Web) is a search and retrieval system that handles FTP and Telnet operations. WWW takes gopher one step further by using hypertext.

Hypertext

Hypertext documents have highlighted text that identifies links to other **pages** of information. It allows WWW to non-sequentially jump from one page to another.

Browsers

Browsers are programs that provide an interface for the WWW. They connect, open, and transfer files as well as display text and graphs.

Three well-known browsers are Lynx, Mosaic, and Netscape.

31